IMAGES
of America

Railroads and Depots of Orange County

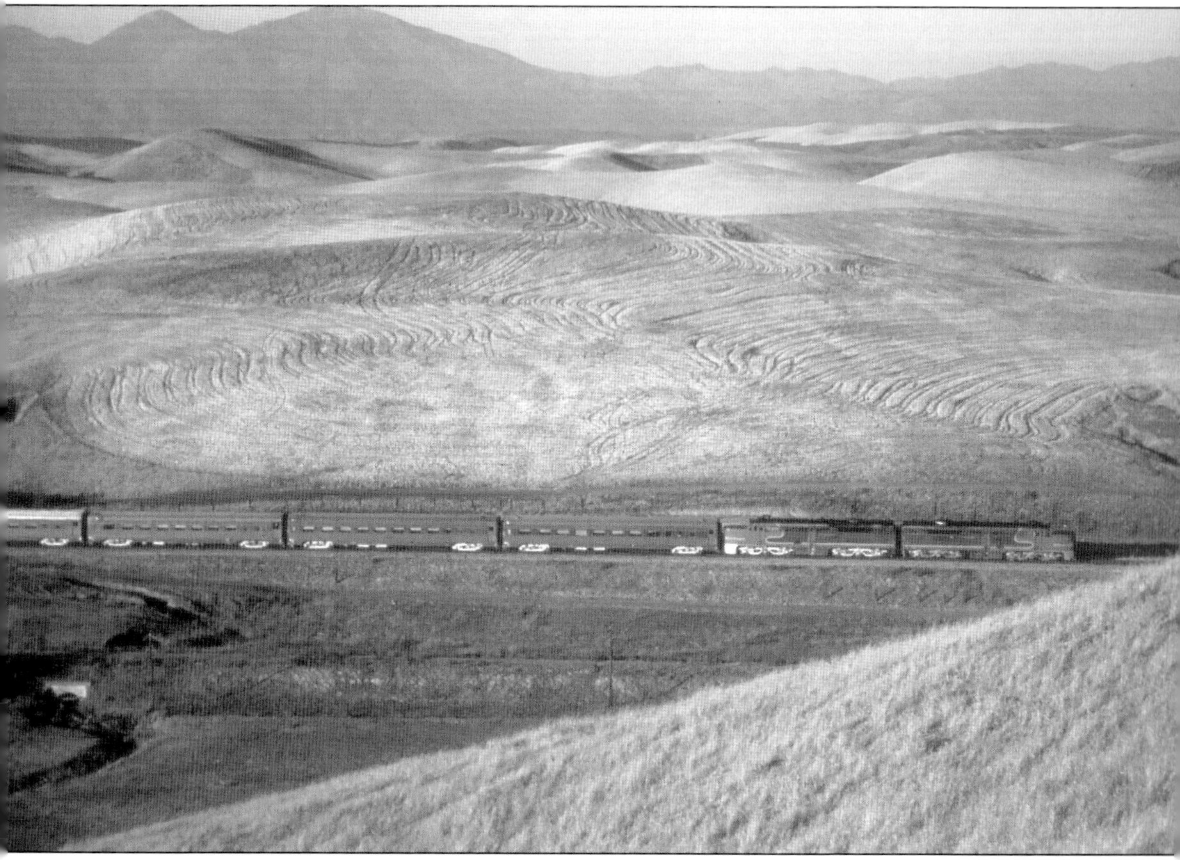

ON THE COVER: This is a scene from Orange County's recent rural past. Here a southbound San Diegan slides through the area known today as Mission Viejo. The next station stop for the southbound train will be San Juan Capistrano. During the 1950s to the early 1970s, typical motive power used by the Santa Fe centered on the use of F units. Here, however, is the pride of the American Locomotive Company (ALCO), a pair of PA-4 engines. The distant peaks belong to Saddleback. The red and silver offered a striking contrast against the golden hills of South County when this photograph was shot in June 1964. (Photograph by and courtesy of Tom Gildersleeve.)

IMAGES
of America

RAILROADS AND DEPOTS OF ORANGE COUNTY

Rob Richardson

ARCADIA
PUBLISHING

ISBN 978-0-7385-8011-1

Published by Arcadia Publishing
Charleston, South Carolina

Printed in the United States of America

Library of Congress Control Number: 2009934878

For all general information contact Arcadia Publishing at:
Telephone 843-853-2070
Fax 843-853-0044
E-mail sales@arcadiapublishing.com
For customer service and orders:
Toll-Free 1-888-313-2665

Visit us on the Internet at www.arcadiapublishing.com

Contents

Acknowledgments

This book would not be possible without the generous help that has been offered since the project began. I would especially like to thank Guy Ball of Tustin, who has helped me tremendously during this project by scanning most of the images and helping with wise counsel on how to proceed to the end product. Guy has been a longtime member of various historical groups in Orange County and willingly shares his time and expertise with others. I have had the opportunity to collaborate with him on some of his projects. Guy, thanks for all that you do to make history available to the public at large.

Various public libraries and archives opened their collections for this project. Among those I wish to thank is Lizeth Ramirez of the Orange Public Library and History Center. The Orange Public Library has done a masterful job with its new library, and the access to its material through high-speed computers is commendable. John Elliott of the Santa Ana Public Library's Santa Ana History Room and Chris Jepsen of the Orange County Archives, run by Tom Daly's Office of Clerk-Recorder, were extremely helpful to me and also gathered some images from the Fullerton Public Library. Laura McGovern of Santa Ana's Bowers Museum helped me access the Bowers extensive photograph collection; I also want to thank Peter Keller, who has led the museum to new heights. Dave Simpson and Jason Silver provided various contemporary images from the Orange County Transportation Authority (OCTA). Terry Thomas of the Garden Grove Historical Society provided great images from their collection. I would also like to thank Griselda Castillo and Casey Baughman of the Old Courthouse Museum/OC Parks for their help as well.

Finally I would like to thank Cliff Prather and Tom Gildersleeve for sharing the photograph collections of Orange County railroading from the early 1950s to the present. Both gentlemen photographed scenes that reflect the daily activities of trains during the 1950s, 1960s, and 1970s. Virtually all the elements shown in their photographs have all passed from the scene as Orange County and Orange County railroading have continued to evolve.

INTRODUCTION

The history of Orange County railroads and depots actually predates Orange County. When the first rails of the Southern Pacific Railroad arrived in Anaheim in 1875, the area was still part of Los Angeles County. The first transcontinental railroad was completed just six years earlier, and the magnetic attractiveness of California was widely advertised. As the nation's rail network grew, additional rail lines were extended from the east to Southern California, including the Atchison, Topeka, and Santa Fe Railroad (often just referred to as the Santa Fe) in 1887 and the Union Pacific in 1904. The Southern Pacific added a second transcontinental line from California via Arizona, New Mexico, and Texas. While Orange County and its rail service have steadily evolved, the 4-foot, 8.5-inch gap between rails has remained the same since the 1870s.

Not only did the railroads make Southern California accessible to new residents, it also made it possible for local farmers to reach distant markets with their crops. The combination proved irresistible for the future Orange County and, indeed, all of Southern California. And up until the end of World War II, the local economy depended heavily on local crops, including oranges, walnuts, lima beans, sugar beets, and canned food products. These crops were marketed outside of Orange County, and the development of industry in these years was also agriculture based. Oil, another natural resource, was also found in large amounts in Huntington Beach, Brea, and Olinda. In the days before pipelines, oil was shipped by railroad tank cars to the refineries. The Orange County rail network shipped local crops to distant markets.

The population of Orange County skyrocketed in the years after World War II. Soldiers who had passed through the various military bases in Orange County during the war years of the 1940s, 1950s, and 1960s were lured back to the county because of the great weather, affordable homes, and plentiful jobs. The expansion of the freeway system enabled people in the bedroom community of Orange County to commute to Los Angeles County. Since the Pacific Electric no longer offered passenger service in Orange County, there was no real public transportation. And later, the development of entire new residential areas and new commercial areas began to squeeze out the remaining orange orchards, bean fields, and eventually the industries supported by agriculture. The railroads were part of this transformation as well, as all the freight railroads began handling the shipment of building materials needed for construction of new homes and businesses.

In some ways, the railroads became victims of their own success. As real estate increased in value, agriculture became uneconomical. And eventually the increased value of land impacted residents and industries as they left Orange County for the relatively inexpensive "Inland Empire." The Irvine Ranch was a major agriculture shipper for the Santa Fe. During the last 35 years, this area was transformed into a master-planned community for residents and businesses. Some of the first businesses in and around the John Wayne Airport have been replaced with high-rise office buildings, and in the last few years, some of these properties have been replaced by high-density housing. Most of the rail shippers located within the Irvine Industrial Complex have moved to greener pastures. The cycle of change has been rapid and complete.

A similar transformation has taken place in other cities as well. At one time, there were several major industrial shippers along the Southern Pacific line in Santa Ana, including Kerr Glass, the Holly Sugar Company, Keeler Food Services, various chemical manufacturers, and plastics companies. An entire new industrial complex was built by Cadillac Fairview in southwest Santa Ana in the early 1970s, complete with a network of spur tracks and sidings. Many of these companies have relocated and have been replaced by firms that no longer ship by rail. An exception to this is the *Los Angeles Times* in Costa Mesa, which receives carloads of newsprint frequently. So one can see that the transformation of Orange County is continuing.

The Burlington Northern Santa Fe Railway (BNSF), the Union Pacific (UP), Amtrak, and Metrolink operate today's Orange County trains. BNSF and UP continue to provide local freight service for a variety of companies; however, it does appear that carload business in Orange County has continued to diminish. BNSF and UP have greatly benefited from the development of intermodal trailer and container shipping originating from the nearby ports of Los Angeles and Long Beach. The UP's mainline to the east is located north of Orange County; the BNSF transcontinental freight conveyor belt runs through north Orange County, and the daily passage of 30 or more freight trains is not unusual. The rail fans camped out at Fullerton are treated to the parade of BNSF freights powered by locomotives belonging to other rail lines, including the Kansas City Southern, CSX, and the Norfolk Southern.

All of this freight activity, coupled with expanded Metrolink and Amtrak service, has led to complete double or triple tracking on the freight line running through the county. Metrolink service has expanded dramatically, and commuter rail service is offered on weekdays and weekends. The track improvements have also included extensive signaling upgrades and the addition of several more train station locations, including the former Santa Fe station stops. Passenger service, including Amtrak, is more frequent and extensive than at any previous time in Orange County's rail history.

What does the future hold? The major rail players in Orange County—BNSF, UP, Metrolink, and Amtrak—are here to stay. The future may include high-speed rail since voters have approved a statewide bond measure to begin this project; it also appears that the new Obama administration may provide additional support for this effort. The network, as currently envisioned, would provide for high-speed trains to run between San Francisco and Los Angeles within two and a half hours. The system would also include Anaheim, and the City of Anaheim and the Orange County Transportation Authority are partners in planning and developing a terminal to serve high-speed rail from a site just east of the 57 freeway.

One

THE EARLY DAYS

The Orange County railroad story predates the beginning of Orange County. As Easterners began migrating west to seek gold, other fortunes, or a new start, the future Orange County began to take shape. The completion of the transcontinental railroad enabled growth to occur in an unprecedented fashion in the west and especially in California. The small village of Anaheim was founded in 1857 almost 20 years before the arrival of the iron horse. The Civil War interrupted developments in the 1860s and led Pres. Abraham Lincoln to sign the Pacific Railroad bill that kicked off the transcontinental railroad.

Growth would soon occur quickly as new towns were established in Tustin by Columbus Tustin in 1868, and William Spurgeon founded Santa Ana the following year. The Southern Pacific (SP) extended its line to Anaheim in 1875 and then on to Santa Ana. The Santa Fe would follow the SP into Orange County in just 12 years. Local towns were also connected in the 1880s by horse-drawn carts running from Santa Ana to Tustin and Orange. Additional street railways were opened in Anaheim, including the Anaheim Street Car (1887–1889) and the Orange, McPherson, and El Modena (1888–1889). Meanwhile the electric street railway system was rapidly evolving and led to the creation of the Pacific Electric Railway (PE). Horsecars would be sent to pasture fairly quickly because the automobile began its inexorable dominance of the roads in the early 1900s and gave the PE a run for its money, too.

While rail travel on the Santa Fe and SP made it possible to reach Los Angeles to conduct business, the trip was still long by train or by horse-drawn stages. Roads were rough, and inclement weather would make what few roads existed impassable. Soon the locals began agitating to separate the region from Los Angeles County. This move was successful in 1889, and Santa Ana was selected as the new seat of government for Orange County.

The basic Orange County railroad network was established by 1910. The SP, Santa Fe, and PE systems blanketed the county and competed head-to-head in various cities. Following the national trends, railroads began their slow retrenchment as rubber tire cars, busses, and trucks began to dominate intercity and intra-city transportation.

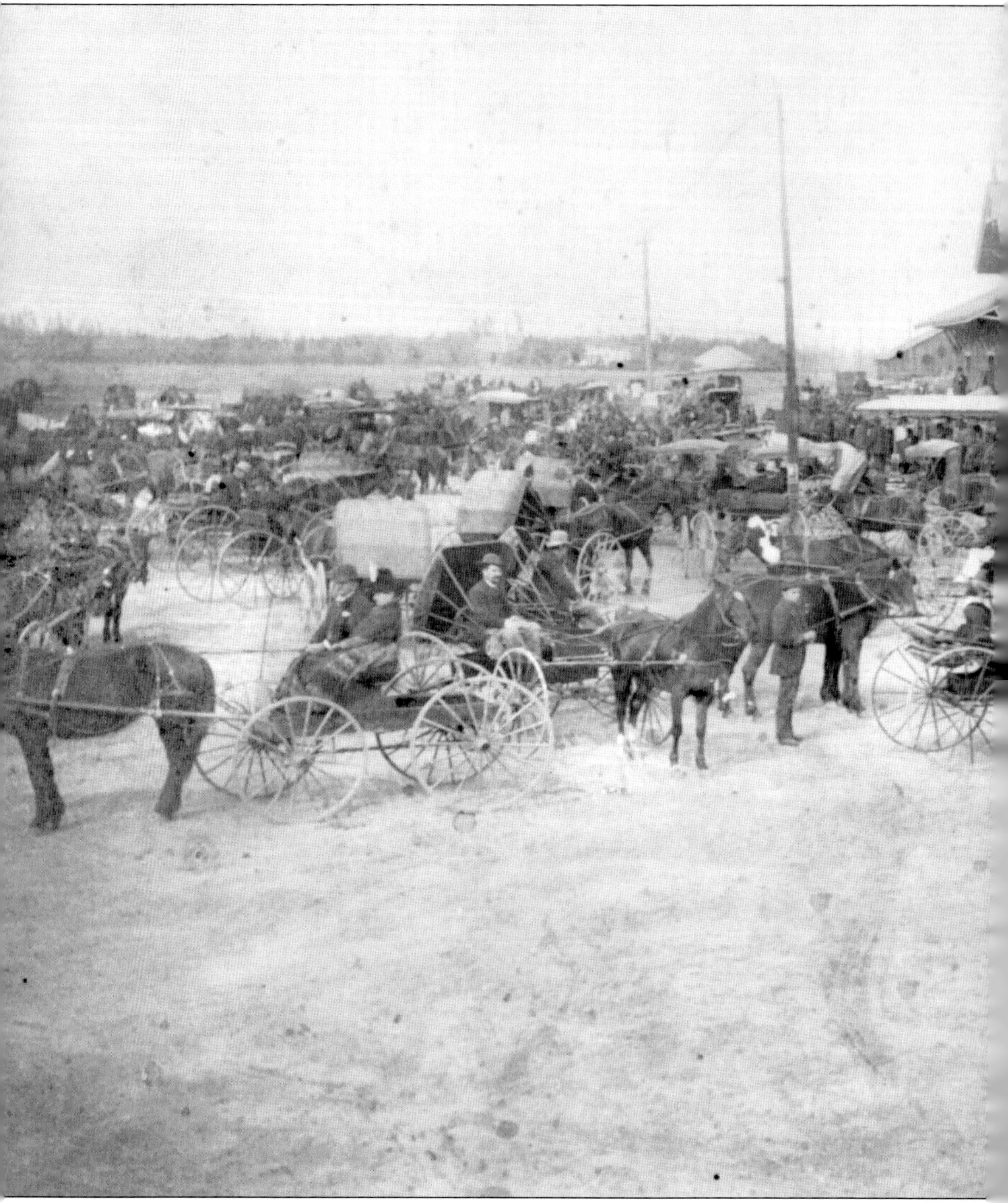

Here is a unique view of the California land boom of the late 1880s. On the right is an SP train that has arrived with hundreds of people coming for a day to visit Santa Ana and get in on the land boom while there was still time. The building in the center was SP's first Santa Ana depot,

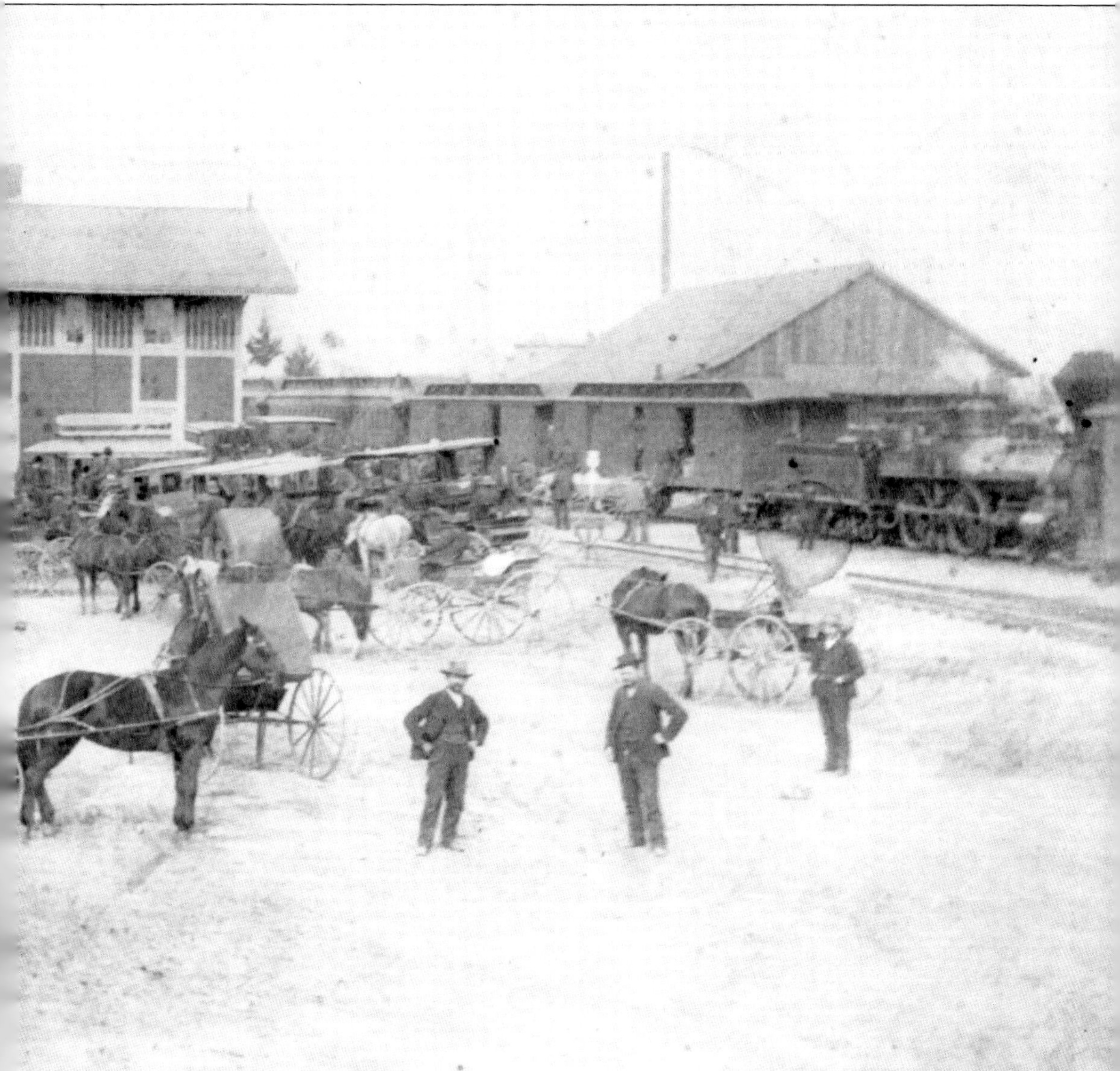

built in 1877. This view is taken from a point about one block south from today's Santa Ana Boulevard; Poinsettia Street would be on the left and appears undeveloped at this time. (Courtesy of the Orange History Center, Orange Public Library.)

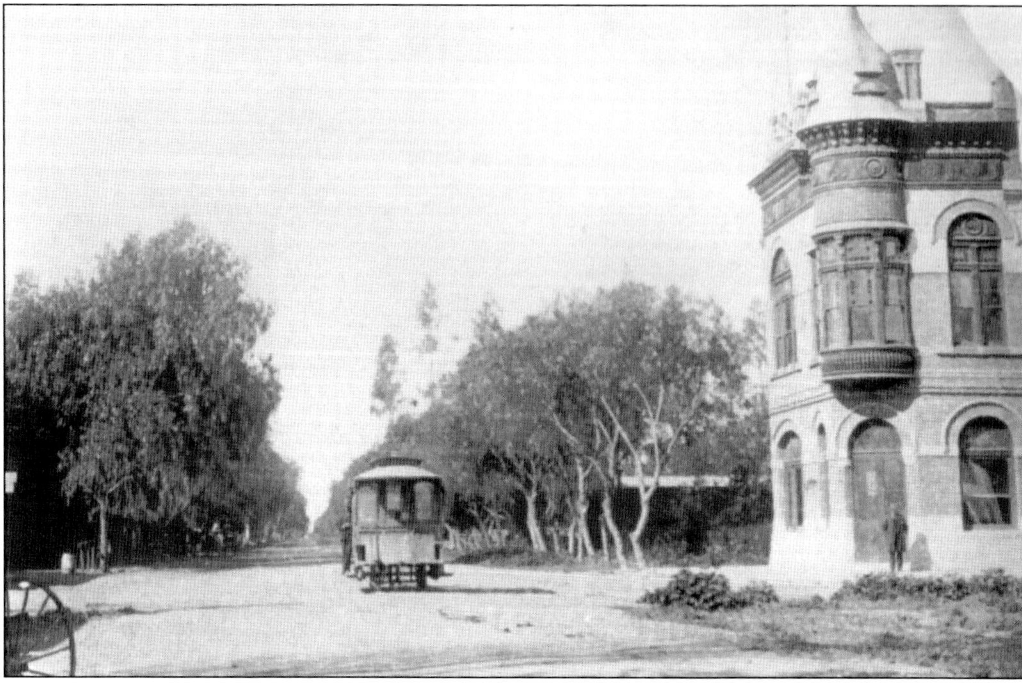

Seen here is a horse-drawn car leaving the center of bucolic Tustin around 1895. This horse-drawn cart will terminate at Fourth and Main Streets in Santa Ana. (Courtesy of the Orange County Archives.)

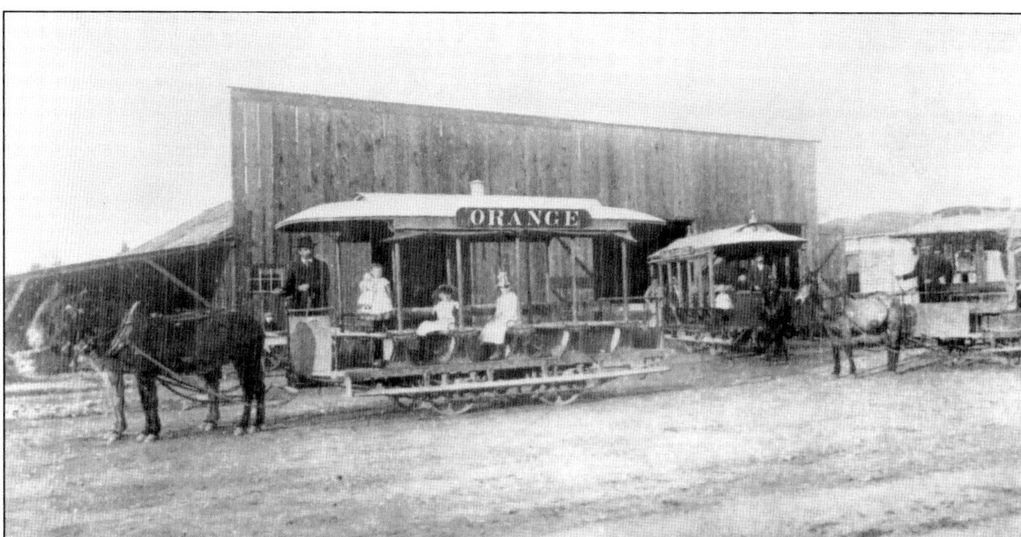

This view from the early 1890s shows the Santa Ana carbarn for horse-drawn cars. The car on the left is destined for Orange County, the next car is bound for the SP depot in Santa Ana, and the third car on the far right is bound for Tustin. Rush hour certainly looked different in those days. (Courtesy of the Orange History Center, Orange Public Library.)

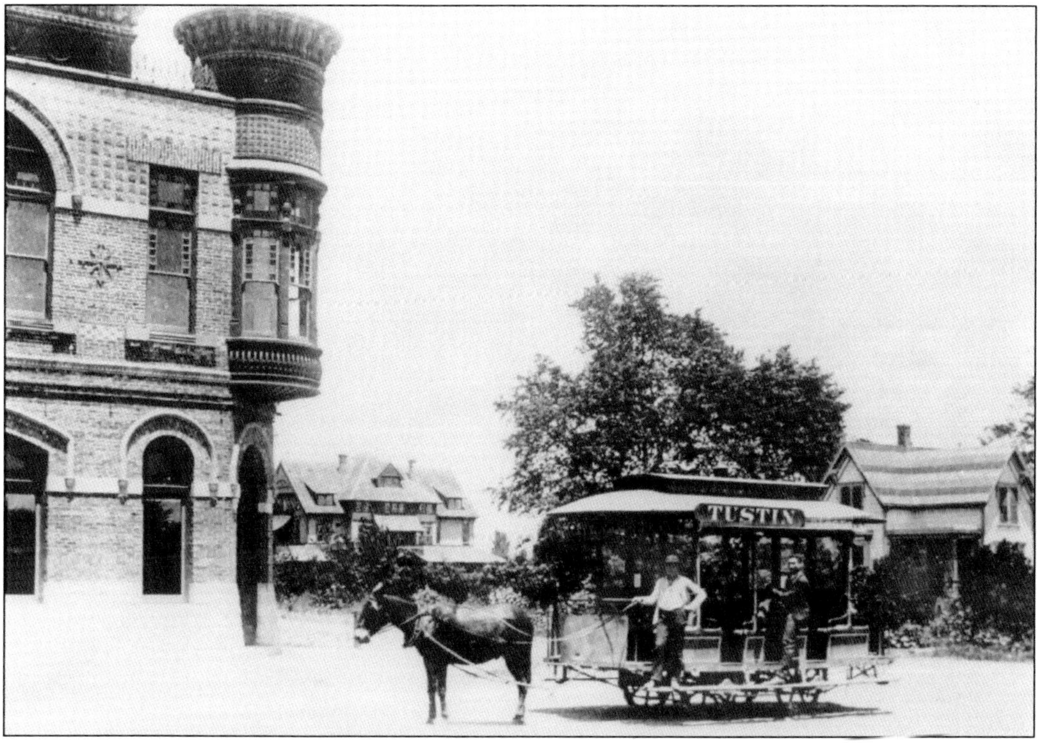

This cart will be bound for Santa Ana running on Main Street in Tustin, and then on to Lyon, First, and Main Streets in Santa Ana. (Courtesy of the Orange County Archives.)

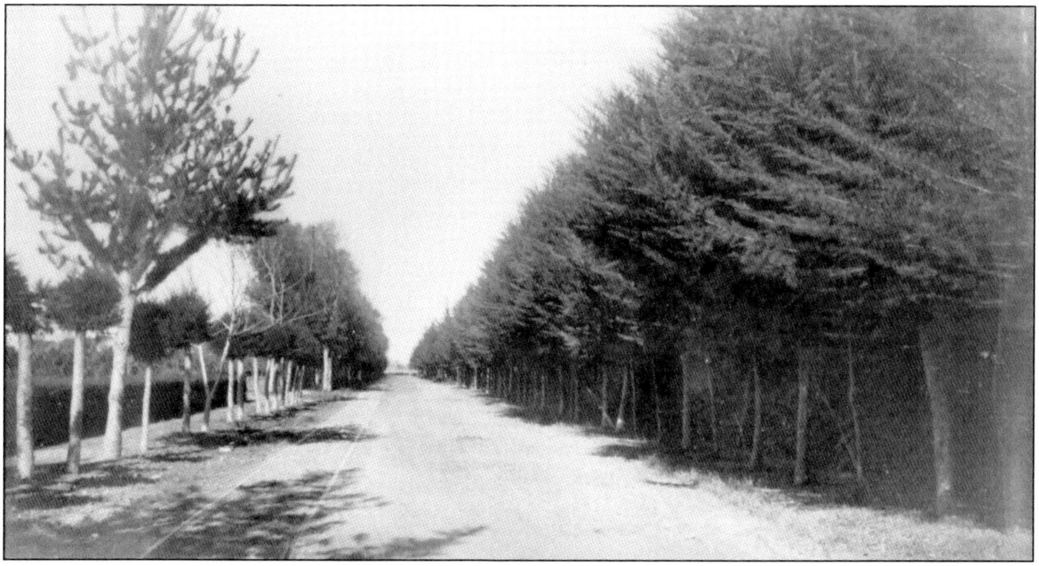

In the 1870s and 1880s, steam-driven trains had been a fact of life in what is now Orange County for just a few short years. Horsepower in those days sometimes relied on horses. A horse-drawn streetcar line connected Tustin to Santa Ana and Santa Ana with the city's Southern Pacific depot and the City of Orange. This view looks north on Lyon Street from Chestnut Avenue. To the left, one can see the tracks for the horse-drawn carts running between Santa Ana and Tustin. (Courtesy of the Santa Ana History Room, Santa Ana Public Library.)

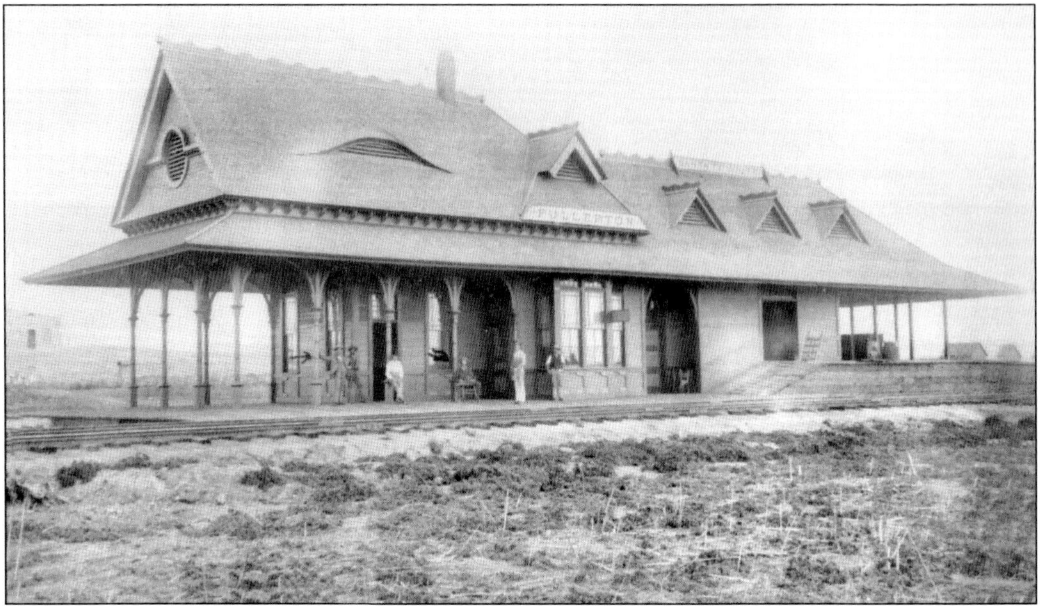

Here is a quiet afternoon at the Fullerton Santa Fe depot. This photograph was taken shortly after the depot was opened in 1888. (Courtesy of the Fullerton Public Library.)

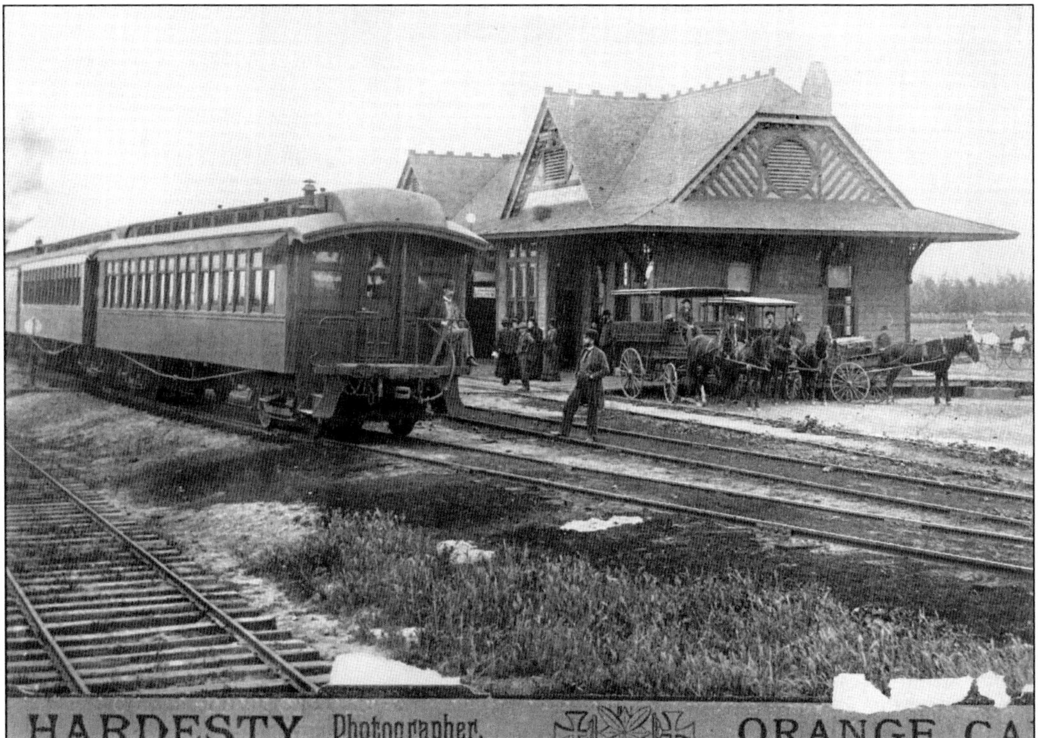

The Orange Santa Fe depot was built in 1888 and was torn down 50 years later. The most important arrival in Orange to this point was a special train for Pres. Benjamin Harrison on April 23, 1891. When the Placentia cut off was built in 1910 between Fullerton and Atwood, some mainline trains bypassed Orange. (Courtesy of the Orange History Center, Orange Public Library.)

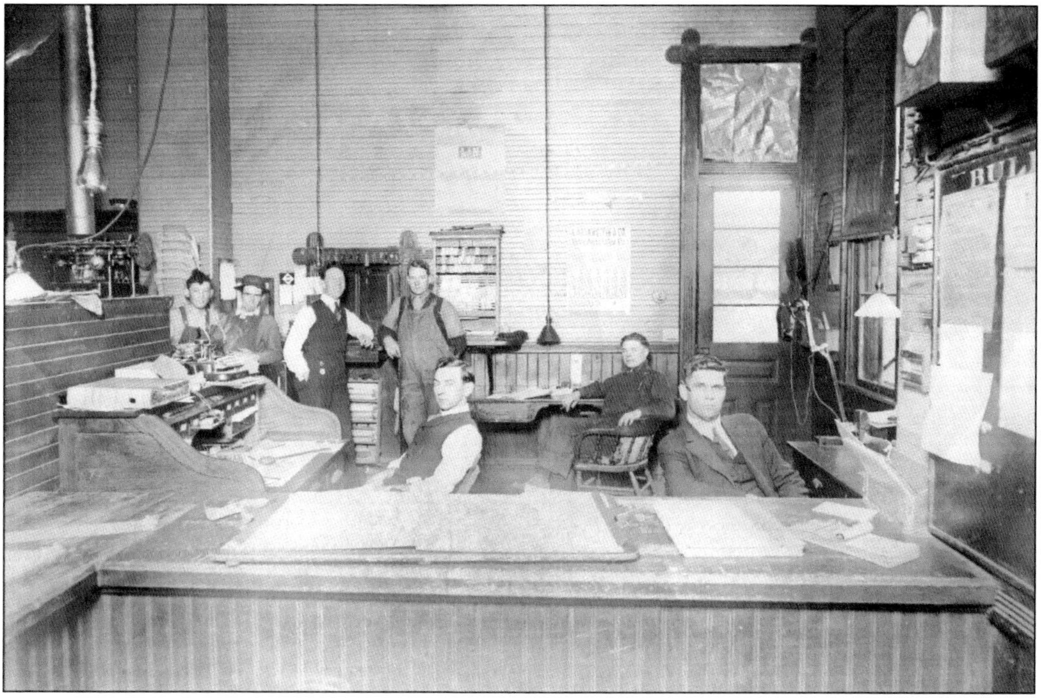

The staff pauses for a picture of those present in the office of the Orange Santa Fe depot in March 1915. George Leichtfuss, on the right, was the station manager. At this time, the small depot was the center of small town life since the important comings and goings happened here. News on the telegraph line came here first, and the small town depot acted as a town's front door to the world. (Courtesy of the Orange History Center, Orange Public Library.)

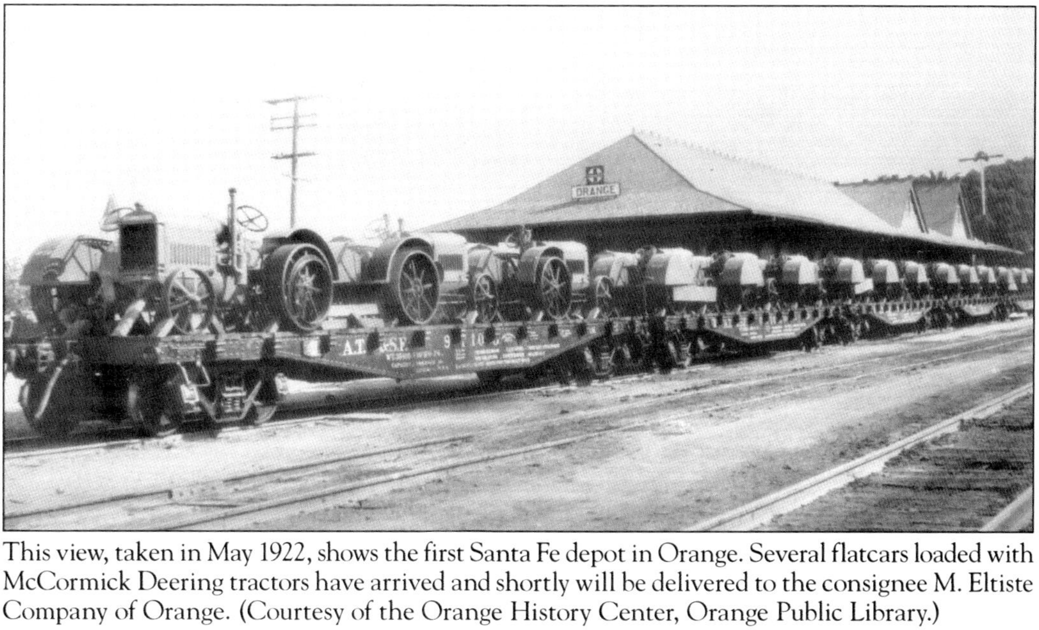

This view, taken in May 1922, shows the first Santa Fe depot in Orange. Several flatcars loaded with McCormick Deering tractors have arrived and shortly will be delivered to the consignee M. Eltiste Company of Orange. (Courtesy of the Orange History Center, Orange Public Library.)

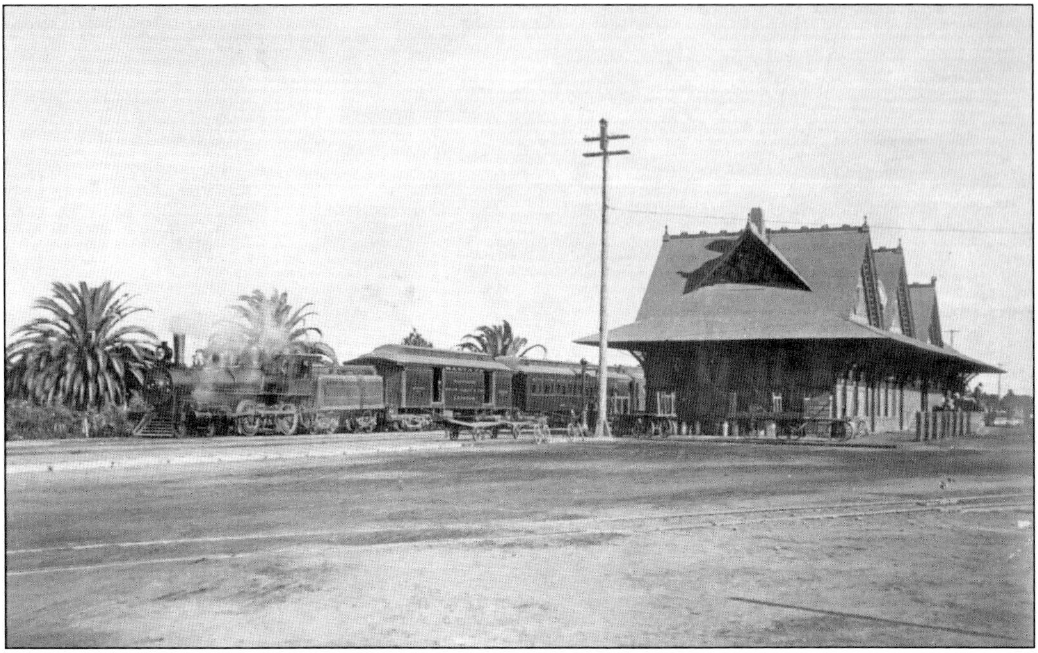

On a late afternoon in about 1895, a Santa Fe 4-4-0 arrives from San Diego. Santa Ana's Santa Fe depot was built in 1887. No motor vehicles are visible in this view. (Courtesy of the author.)

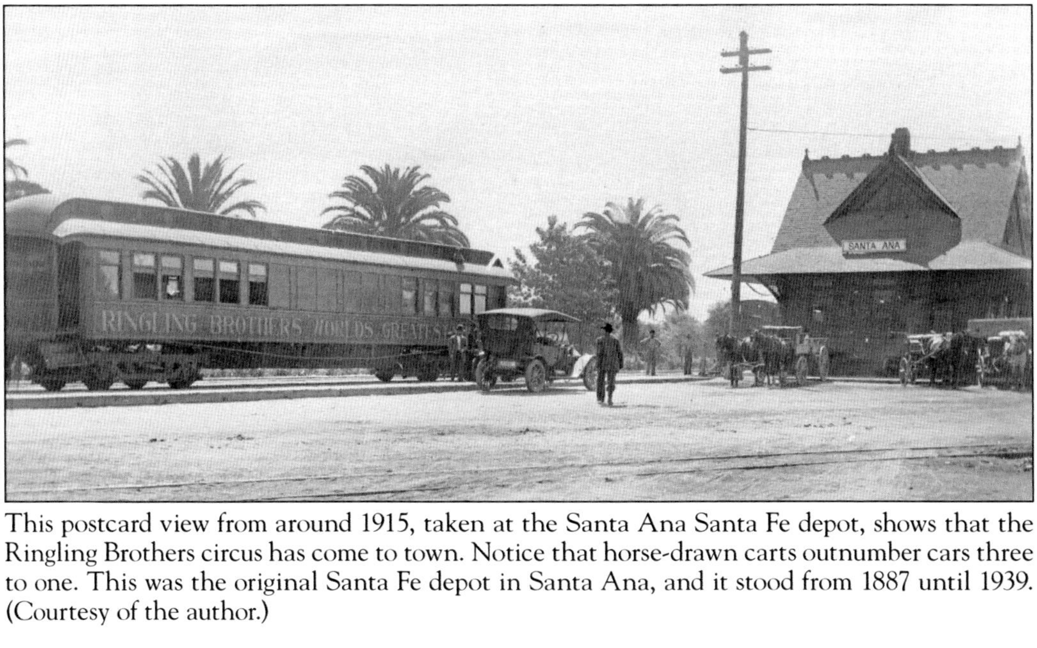

This postcard view from around 1915, taken at the Santa Ana Santa Fe depot, shows that the Ringling Brothers circus has come to town. Notice that horse-drawn carts outnumber cars three to one. This was the original Santa Fe depot in Santa Ana, and it stood from 1887 until 1939. (Courtesy of the author.)

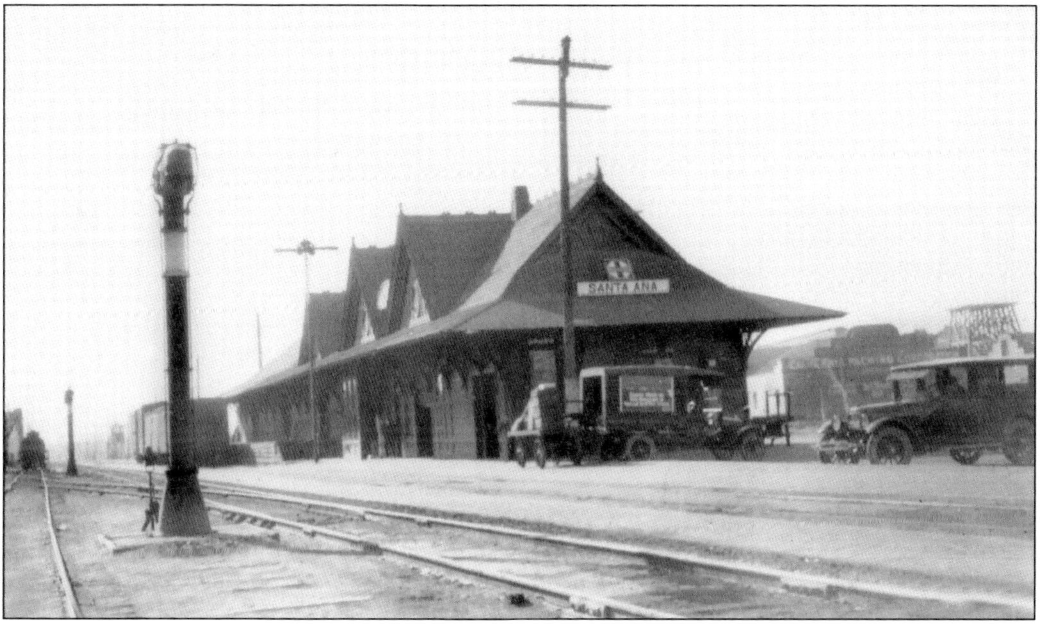

This photograph of the Santa Fe depot in Santa Ana dates from about 1925. In the foreground is one of two tall spouts or plugs that were used to provide water for steam locomotives. If one looks closely, in the distance a grade-crossing tower can be seen; this was for a watchman to protect vehicle traffic and trains from running in to each other at First Street. (Courtesy of the author.)

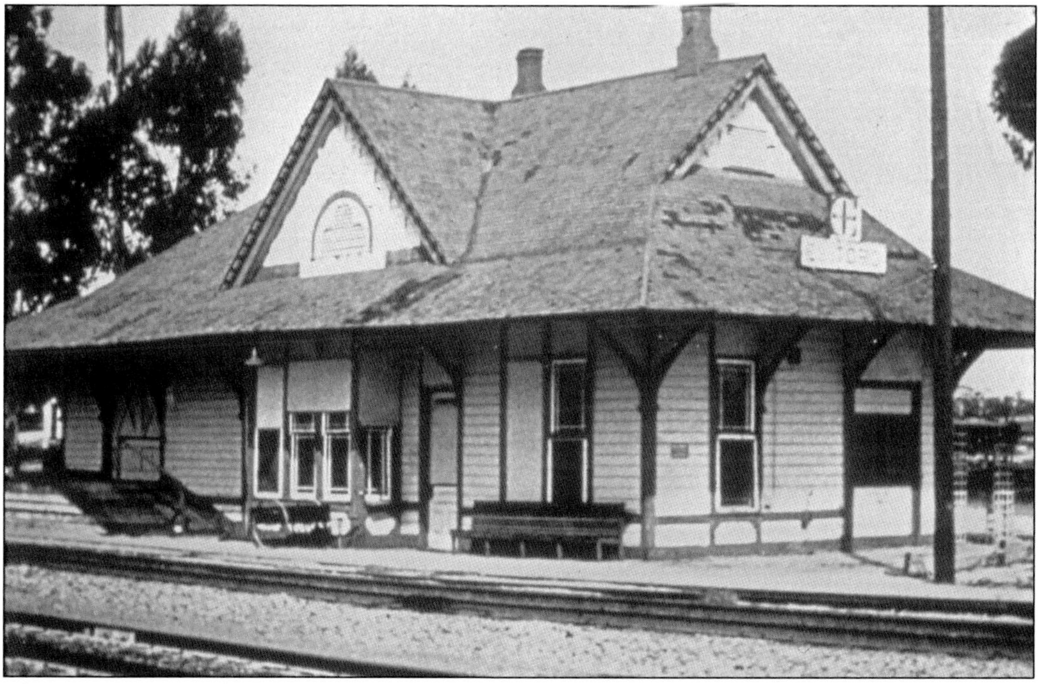

The Santa Fe crossed El Toro Road on its trip toward San Diego. This wood-frame depot is similar to numerous others built during the boom years in the late 1880s. This depot was torn down in 1952. Surviving examples of this style of depot can be found in nearby San Diego County at Carlsbad and Encinitas. (Courtesy of the author.)

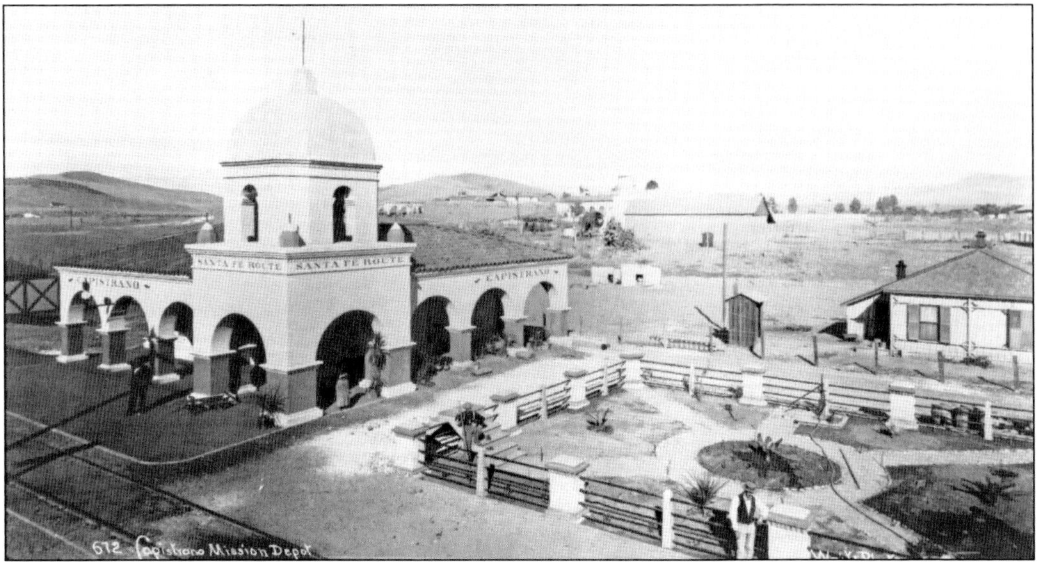

The village of San Juan Capistrano could boast about this brand-new Santa Fe depot, photographed shortly after its construction in 1894. At this time, the location was simply known as Capistrano. (Courtesy of the Orange County Archives.)

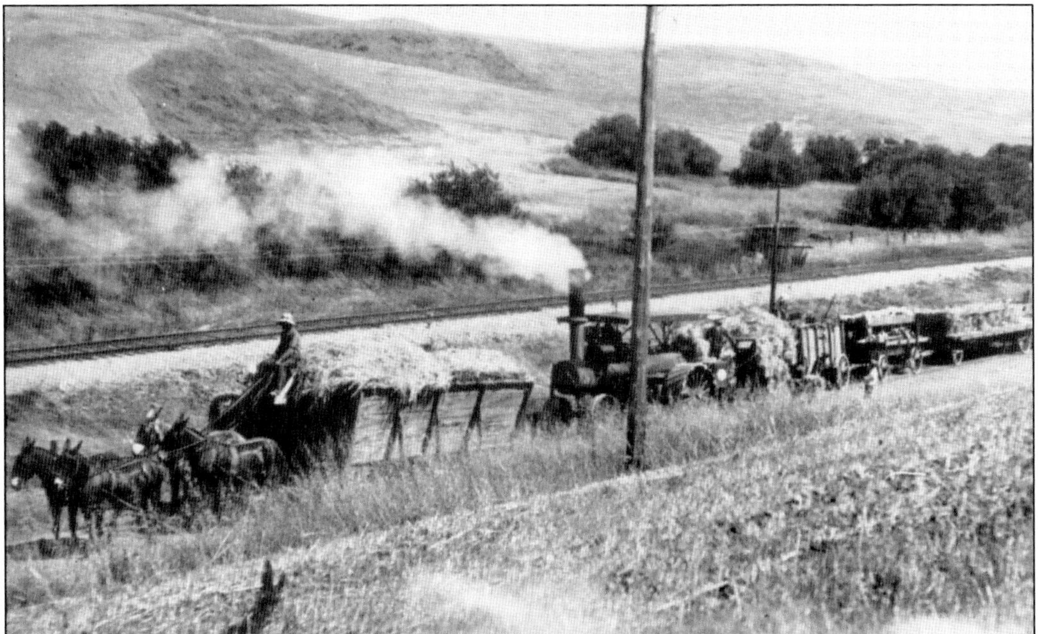

Three of the key features of Orange County's future are seen in this photograph, taken in south Orange County around 1900. Crops of many types became well known as key Orange County moneymakers, including oranges, walnuts, and lima beans. The rich soil and favorable climate helped boost agriculture in the early days. Mechanized equipment helped farmers increase the yield of their farmland and reduce labor costs as well. And finally, the addition of the Santa Fe Railway broke the SP monopoly in Orange County and California, and offered a predictable means to ship harvested crops to distant markets. (Courtesy of the Santa Ana History Room, Santa Ana Public Library.)

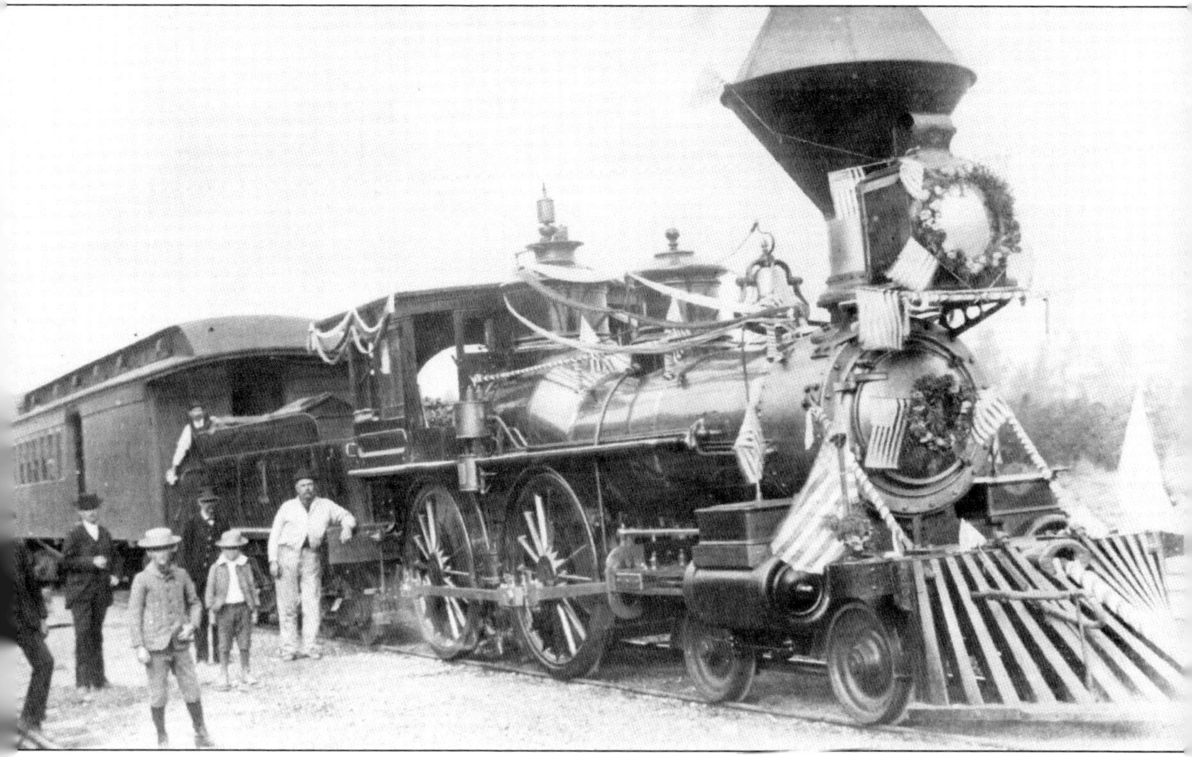

The pride of the Santa Ana and Newport Railroad (SA&N) is ready for a trip to Newport Beach from Santa Ana. This view dates from around 1895. The SA&N left Santa Ana from a convenient location between the Santa Fe and SP depots. The SA&N was completed around 1891 and would be taken over by SP in 10 years time. (Courtesy of the Bowers Museum, Santa Ana, CA.)

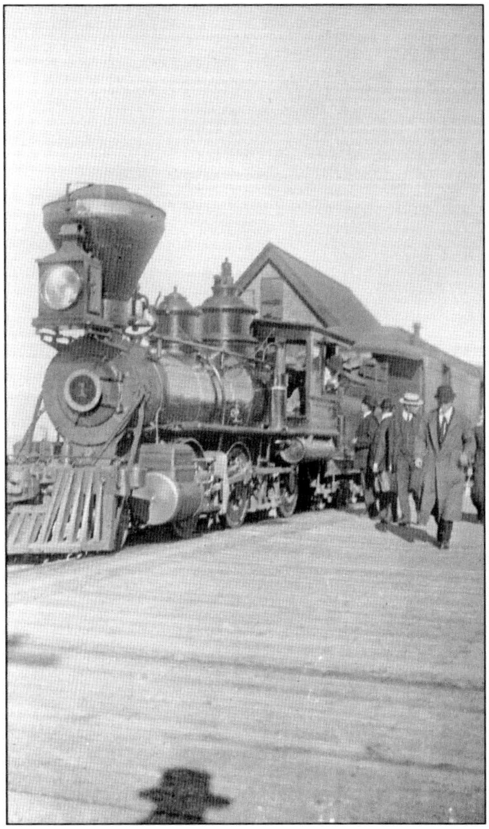

This image depicts a sunny morning on McFadden's Wharf in Newport Beach. The well-dressed men are walking away from the SA&N's 2-4-0 locomotive. This photograph dates from around 1895. The SA&N's former right-of-way became Newport Avenue and later the 55 Freeway, so the remaining portion of this pioneer railroad remains south of First Street to just south of Warner Avenue. It was purchased by SP and is now owned by Union Pacific. (Courtesy of the Tustin Area Historical Society.)

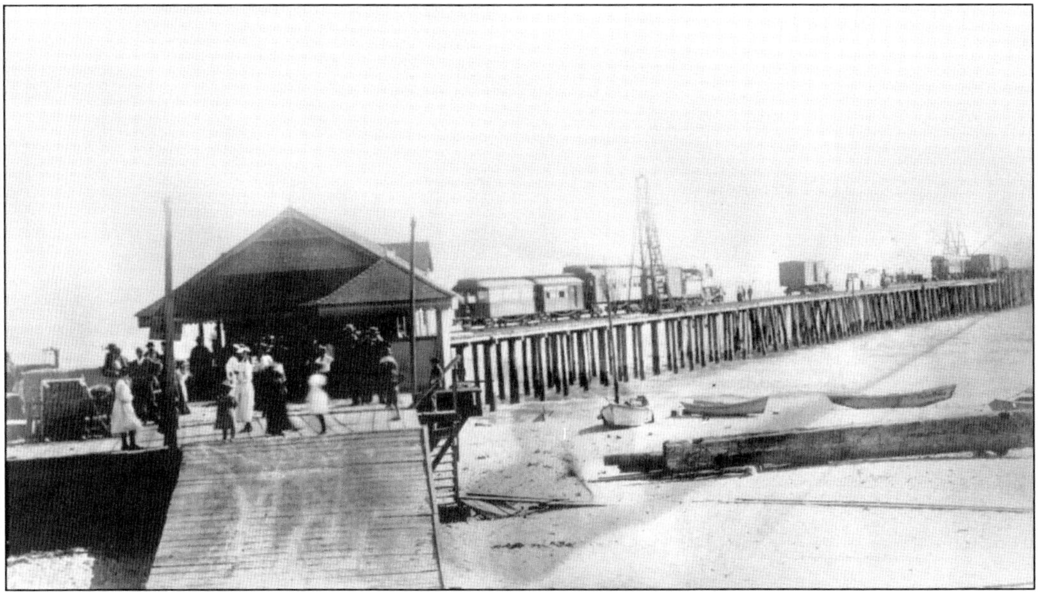

For many years, McFadden's Wharf at Newport Beach served as an important point for the delivery of goods to the budding populations of what was a rapidly growing area. The SA&N connected the coast with Santa Ana. On the right foreground are boats belonging to the dory fishermen of Newport Beach. (Courtesy of the Santa Ana History Room, Santa Ana Public Library.)

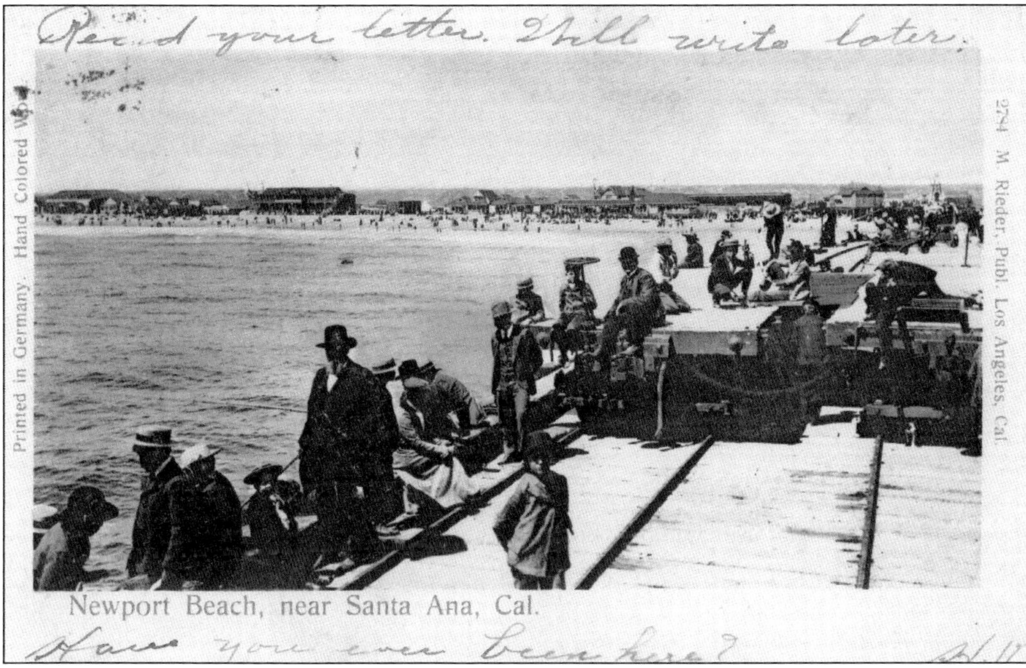

It is hard to imagine that the mix of business and recreation activities on McFadden's Wharf were safe. The photograph for this card was likely taken on a weekend day. (Courtesy of the Orange County Archives.)

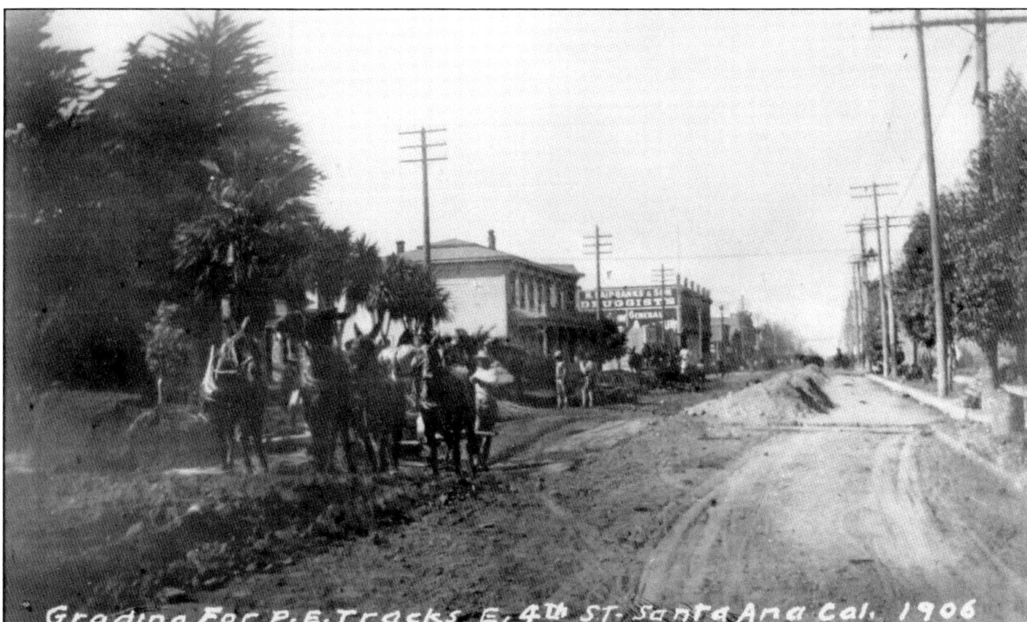

This scene shows an unpaved Fourth Street being graded for the new Pacific Electric (PE) tracks in 1906. The horse-drawn crew is working in the 400 block of East Fourth Street. The completion of the PE would offer Santa Anans a third route by rail to get to Los Angeles. (Courtesy of the Santa Ana History Room, Santa Ana Public Library.)

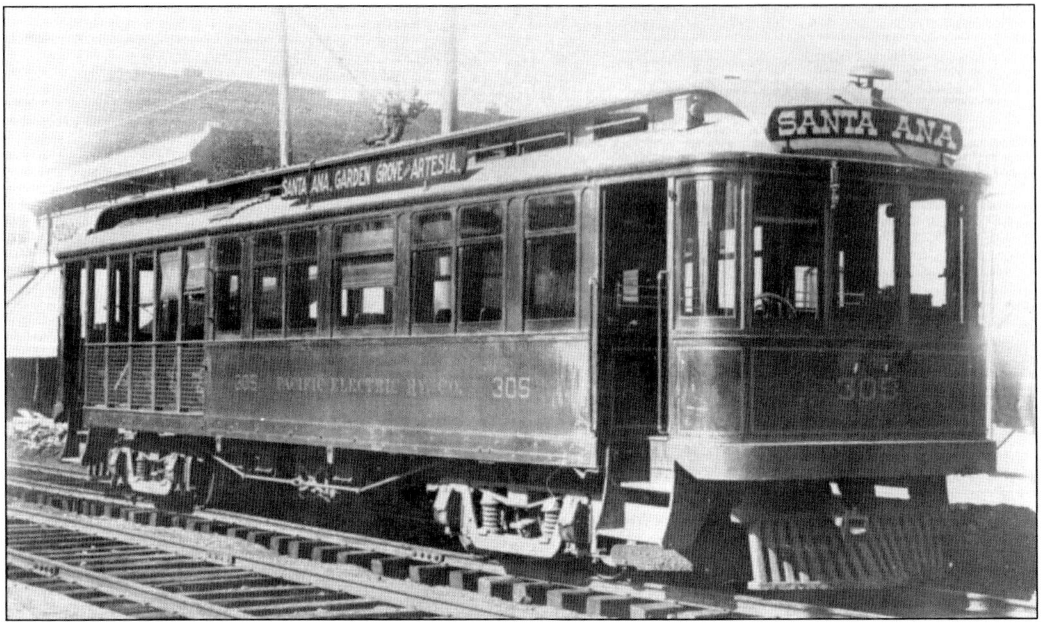

Reportedly, the first PE trolley to reach downtown Santa Ana is shown in this view from 1905. The double track line was laid on the roadbed of an as-yet unpaved street. Note the unballasted ties in this shot. (Courtesy of the Bowers Museum, Santa Ana, CA.)

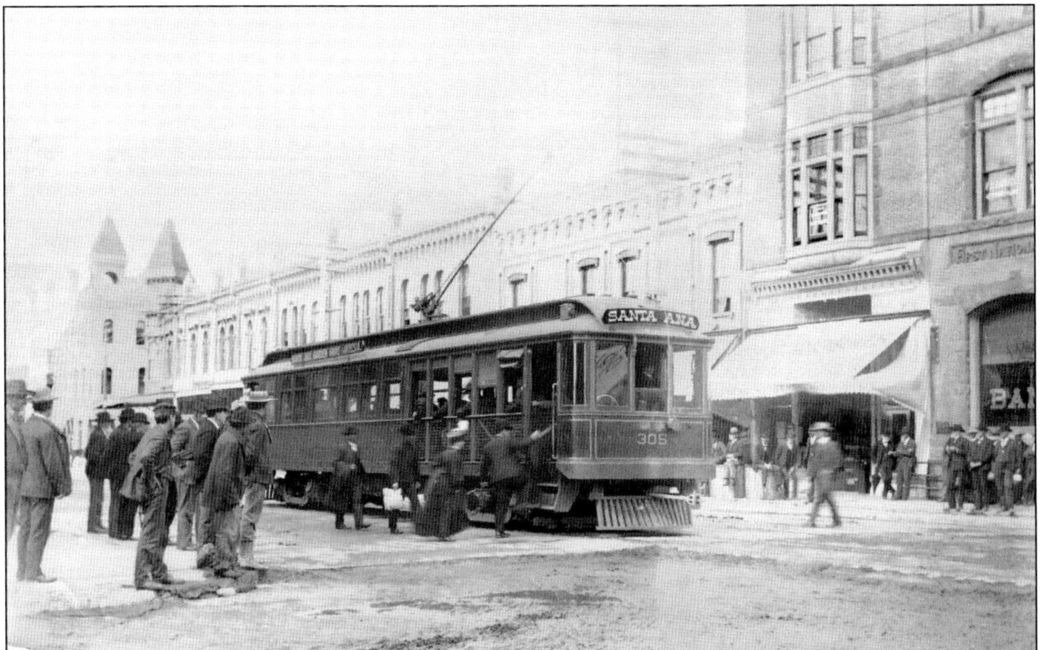

A Los Angeles–bound PE car boards on West Fourth Street just beyond Main Street. This photograph dates from around 1910, so PE service was still relatively new. Just a few years earlier, folks standing on the corner on the left could have boarded a horse-drawn cart for Tustin. Progress had been rapid for the budding county seat city of Orange County. (Courtesy of the Bowers Museum, Santa Ana, CA.)

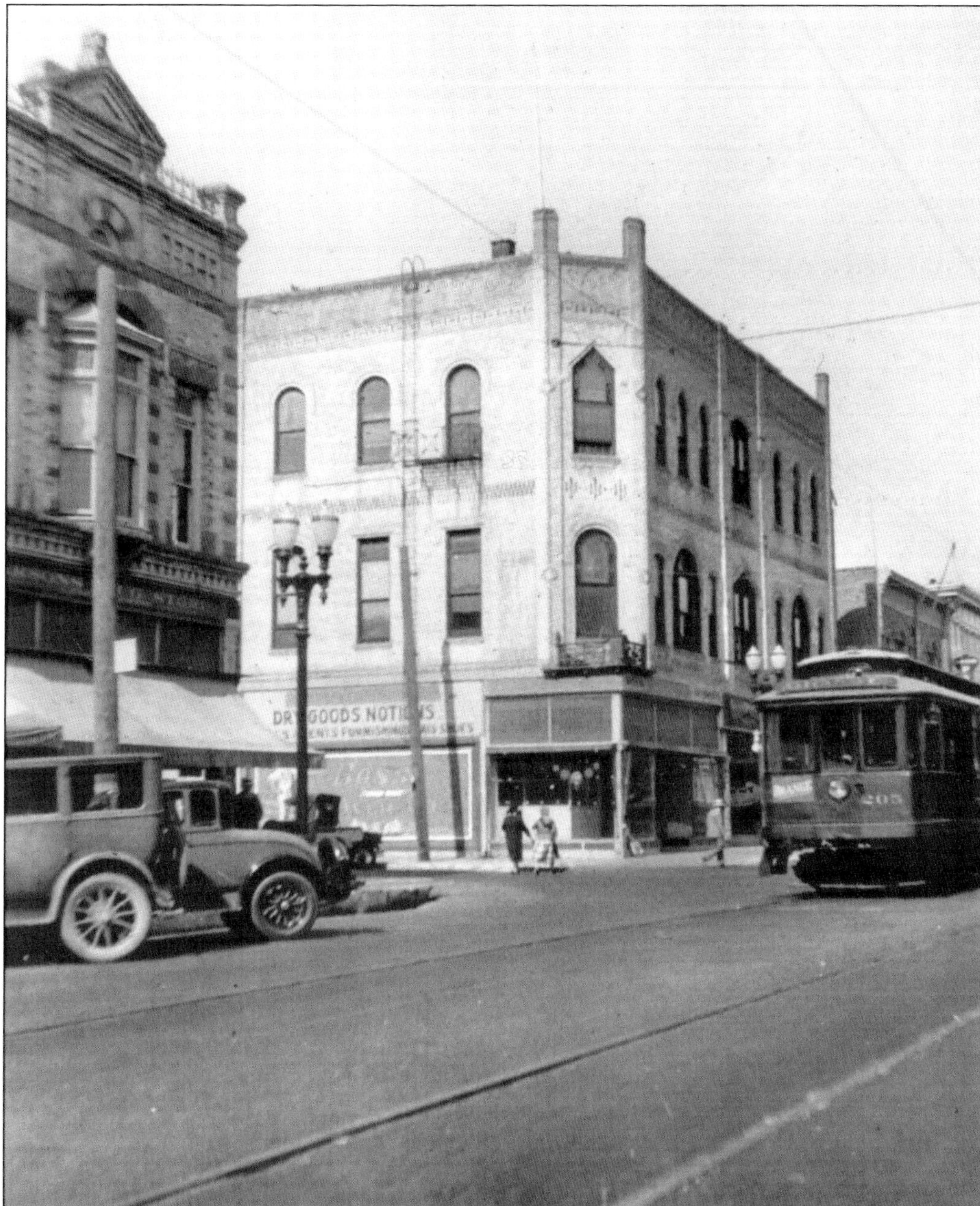

A PE streetcar is westbound on Fourth Street crossing Bush Street. This car is bound for Orange and will use the track branching north up Main Street to reach that city. The imposing building in the background is the Grand Opera House, pictured around 1920. (Courtesy of the Santa Ana History Room, Santa Ana Public Library.)

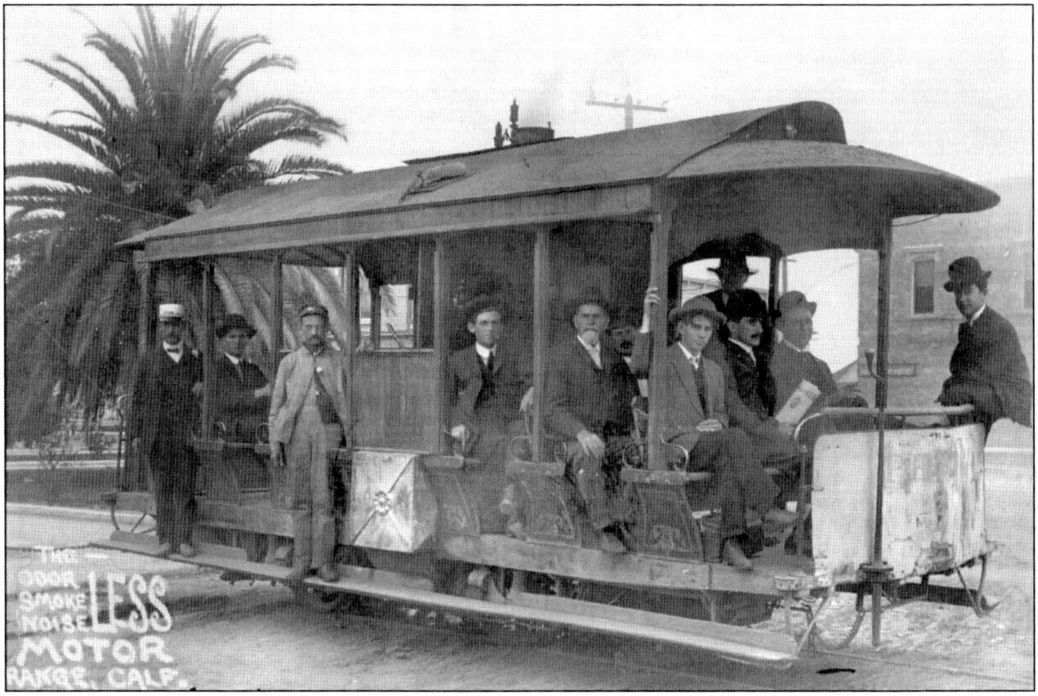

The "odorless, smokeless, noiseless" cars of the Santa Ana and Orange Motor Company ran along Main Street between the two towns. Eventually this line was turned over to the Los Angeles Interurban and then the PE. The line north of Santiago Creek continued as a motor line until that portion was electrified in 1914; the segment south of Santiago Creek was electrified in 1906. (Courtesy of the Bowers Museum, Santa Ana, CA.)

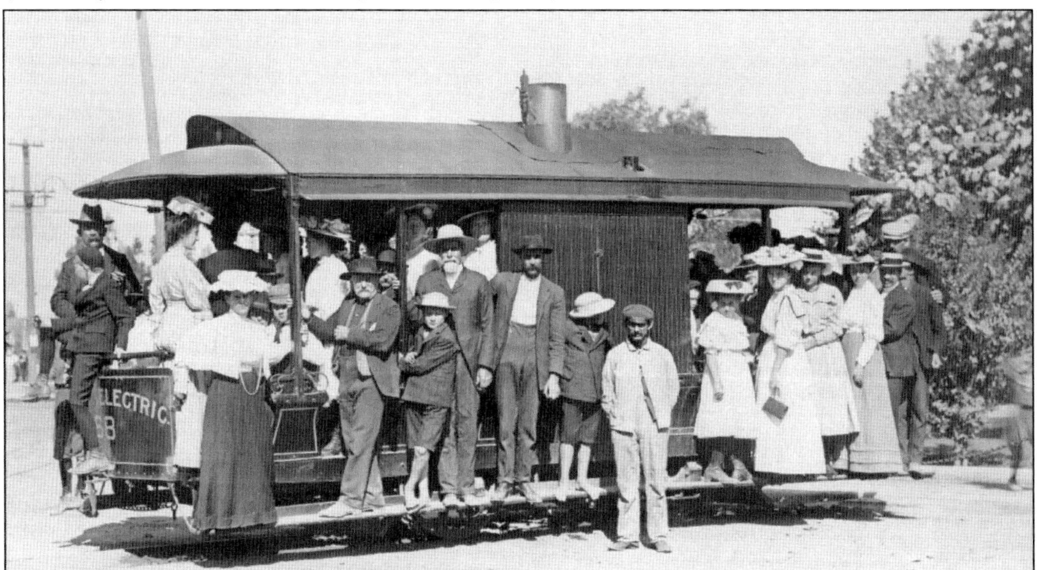

The Santa Ana and Orange Motor cars were taken over by PE, which continued operating motorcars until 1914, when the segment between the Santiago Creek and Orange was electrified. (Courtesy of the Orange History Center, Orange Public Library.)

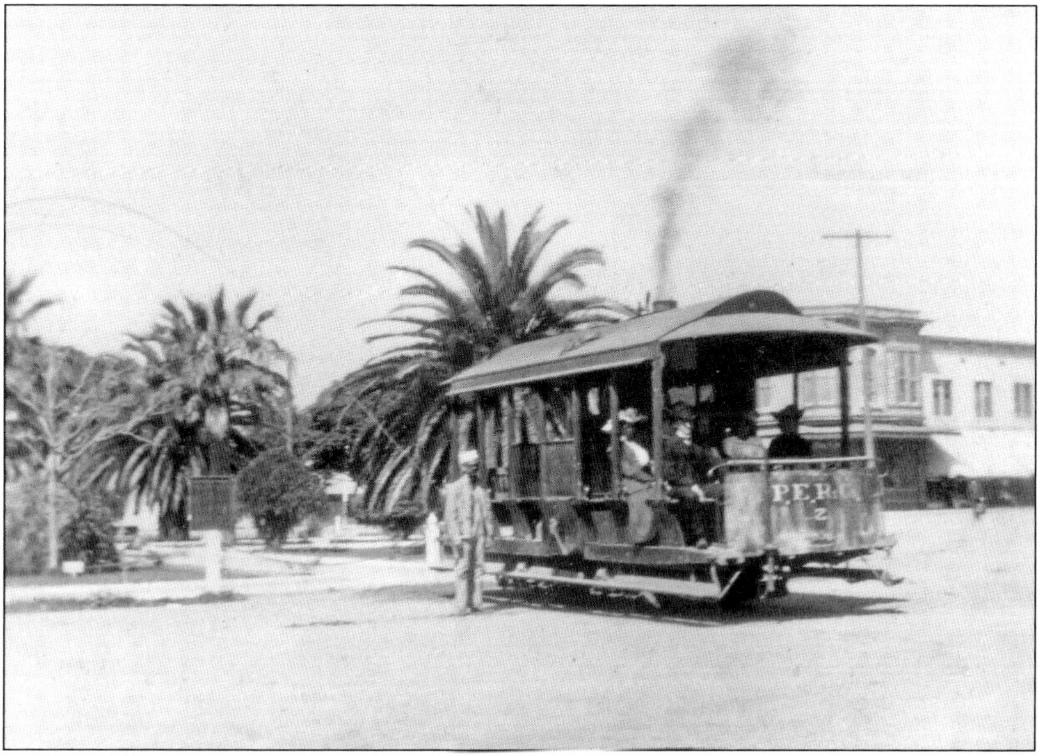

In about 1910, a PE motorcar prepares to depart toward Santa Ana from the plaza in Orange. At the Santiago Creek, passengers will transfer to an electrified trolley for the final trip to central Santa Ana. (Courtesy of the Santa Ana History Room, Santa Ana Public Library.)

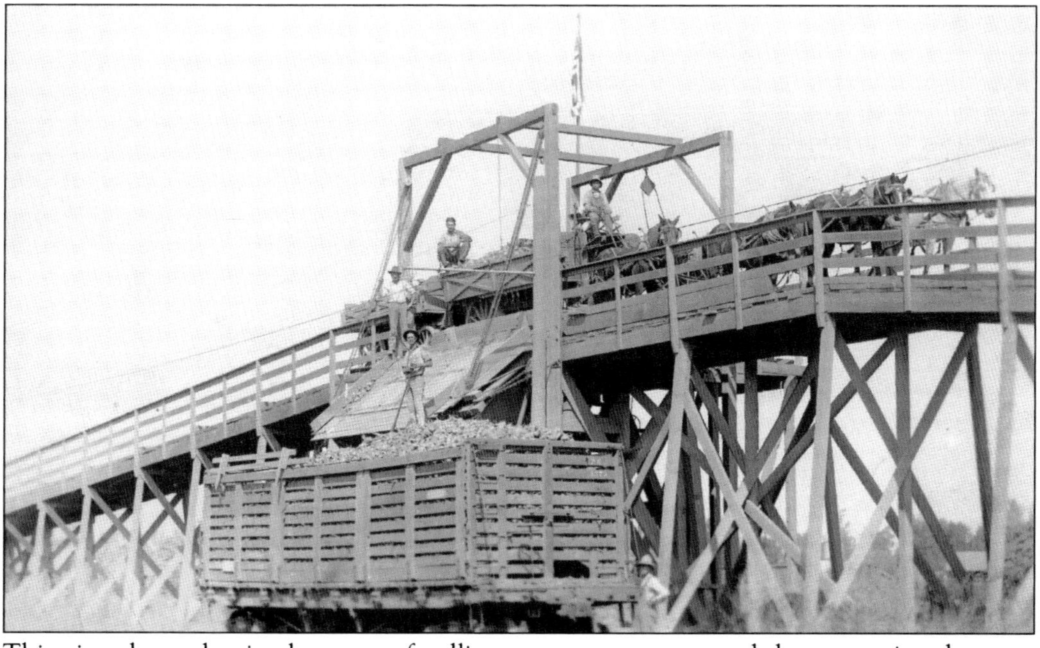

This view shows the simple means of pulling wagons up a ramp and then emptying the sugar beets into a waiting railroad car. (Courtesy of the Orange County Archives.)

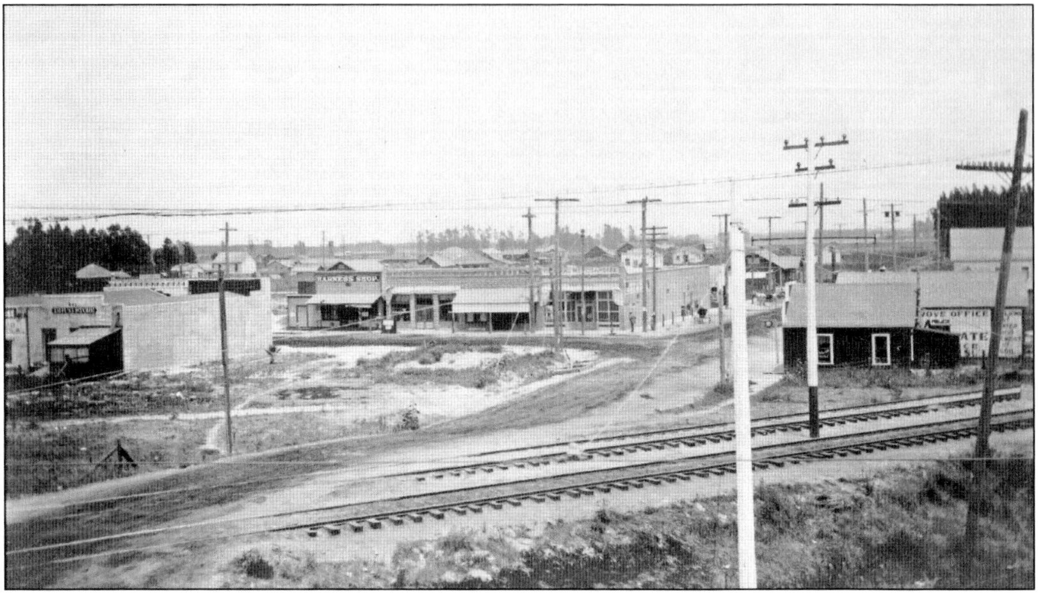

The village of Garden Grove looked like this in 1909. The brick commercial buildings in the background are on Main Street. In the foreground is the double-track mainline of the PE Santa Ana line. (Courtesy of the Garden Grove Historical Society.)

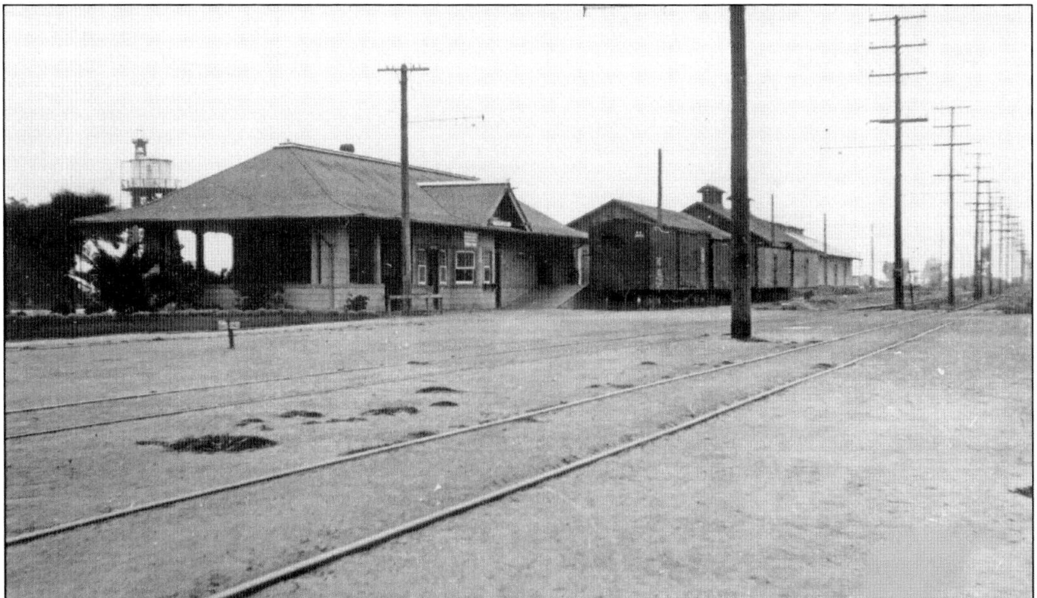

The PE depot in Garden Grove is seen here as it looked in 1921. Although freight was never a big driver on this part of the railway, Garden Grove did provide heavy freight business for the PE. This was likely due in part to the fact that in several other cities served by the PE the major freight railroads were already established. (Courtesy of the Garden Grove Historical Society.)

Two

The Southern Pacific Railroad

America's first transcontinental railway was connected in May 1869. Just six years later, the Southern Pacific (SP) was extended from Los Angeles and Downey to Anaheim. The area destined to become Orange County was now connected to a national web of train lines. Migration to Southern California was enabled by this development, and the growth of the future Orange County was underway. The SP next built southwest to Santa Ana and arrived in that city in 1877. Aside from the Santa Ana extension, additional lines radiated from Anaheim, including Los Alamitos, Stanton, Westminster, and Tustin. In these days, the landscape of Orange County, mostly flat and well drained, was filled with orange and walnut orchards, sugar beets, and lima beans. The SP expanded to serve the agricultural businesses of the day. The SP also bought the SA&N running between Santa Ana and Newport.

By the early 1920s, passenger business became the exclusive work of the Orange County's other rail lines (PE, ATSF, and UP). Freight service, however, continued to grow with the development of numerous agricultural pacing houses, sugar beet processing, and other row crops. By the mid-1950s, steam no longer operated on the SP in Orange County, and soon the SP began to absorb the various PE remnant lines. SP itself looked at merger opportunities, including a potential merger with the Santa Fe. This proposal was not approved, and the SP, shorn of many non-railroad assets, was acquired by the owner of the Denver and Rio Grande Western Railroad and enjoyed a surge of intermodal container business. This was not enough to compete, and ultimately, the SP ended 120 years of service to Orange County and was absorbed by the mighty UP.

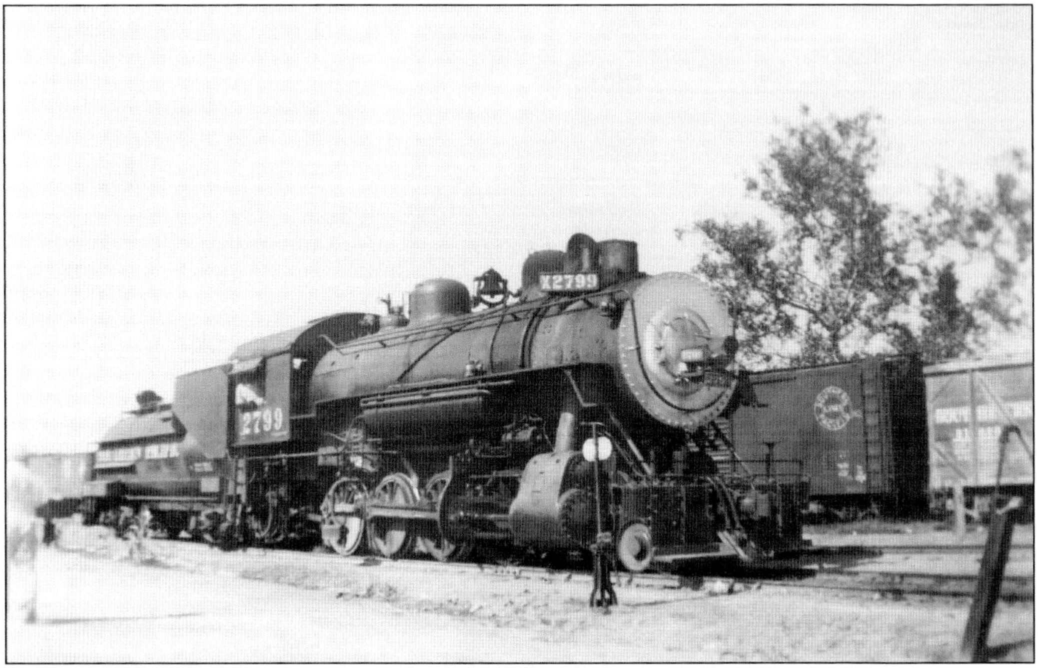

SP was still using steam when this photograph was shot in 1951. SP2799 was a 2-8-0 locomotive. This Baldwin locomotive was one of a group of 79 ordered by the SP. (Photograph by Ed Maring; courtesy of Tom Gildersleeve.)

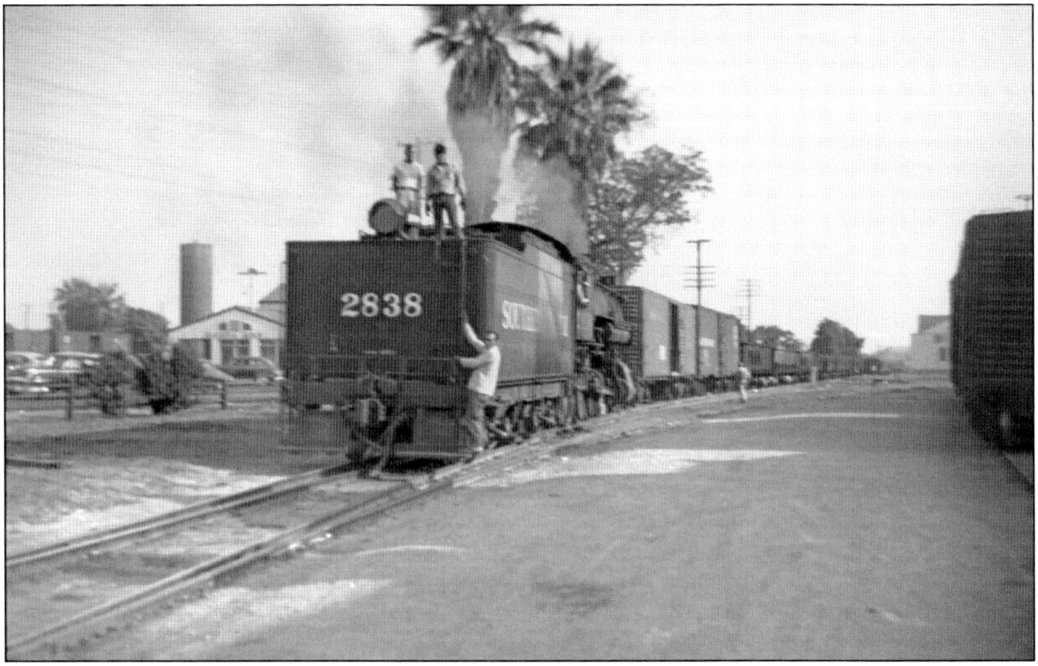

The trackage arrangement around the old Santa Fe and SP depots provided ways for locomotives to turn to face the correct direction. It seemed like there was always some type of activity "down by the depot." Here SP 2-8-0 is backing north past the Santa Ana depot. Note the headlight mounted on the tender. (Photograph by and courtesy of Tom Gildersleeve.)

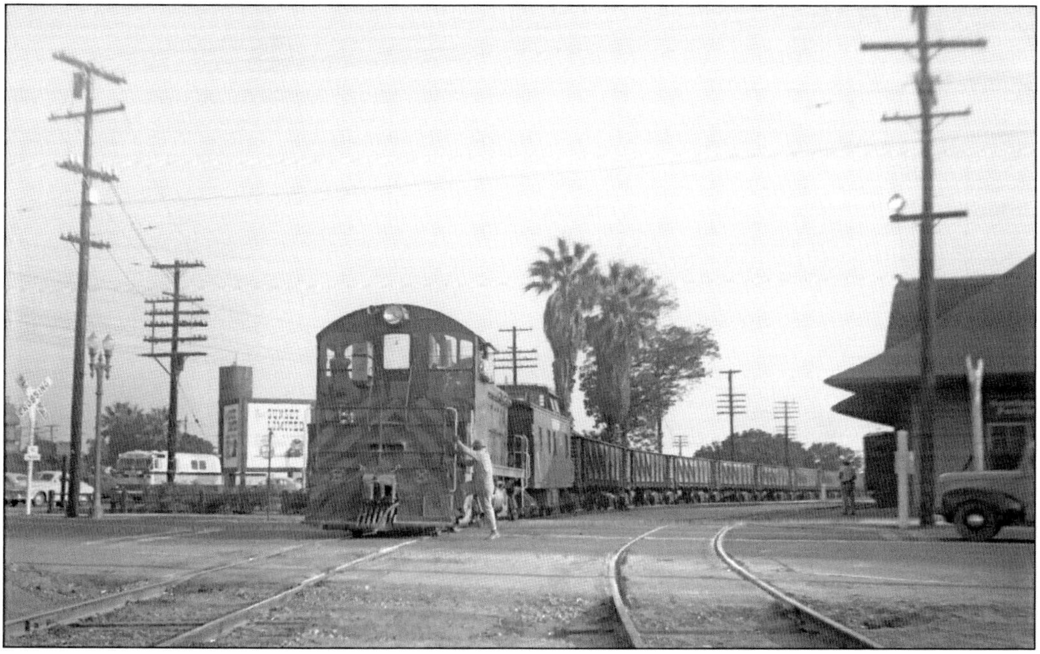

While the SP still operated steam in 1951, it was clear that diesel would be in charge soon. Note the billboard on the left for SP's *Sunset Limited*. This image is from Santa Ana around 1951. (Photograph by and courtesy of Tom Gildersleeve.)

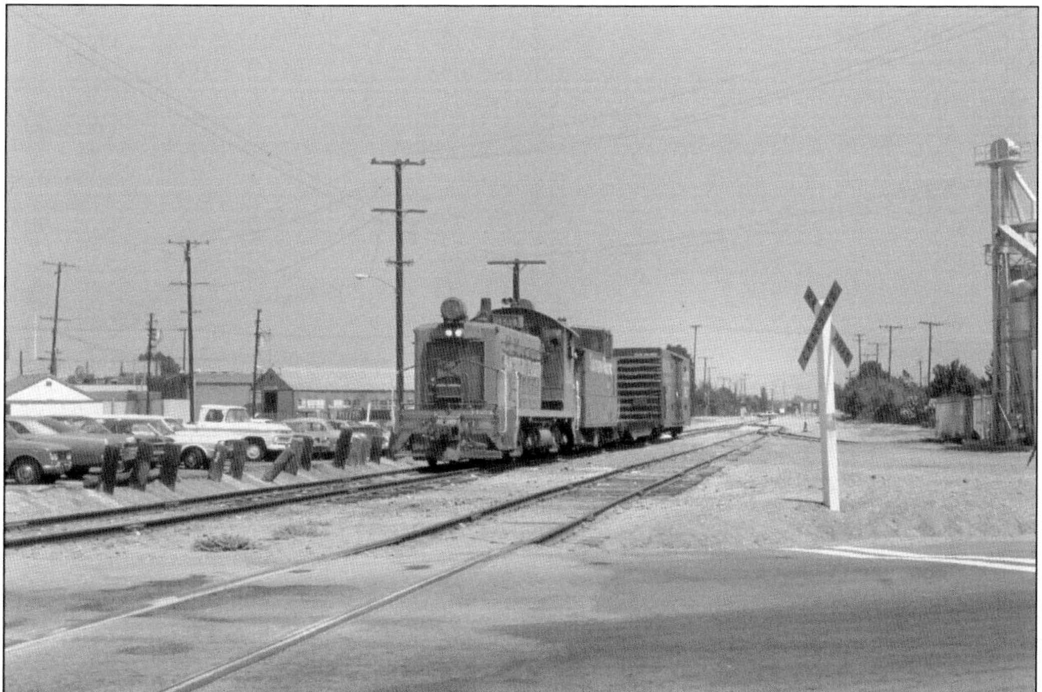

Southern Pacific No. 1124 is shown leaving Garden Grove with just two freight cars and a caboose. This is the former track of the PE. (Photograph by and courtesy of Cliff Prather.)

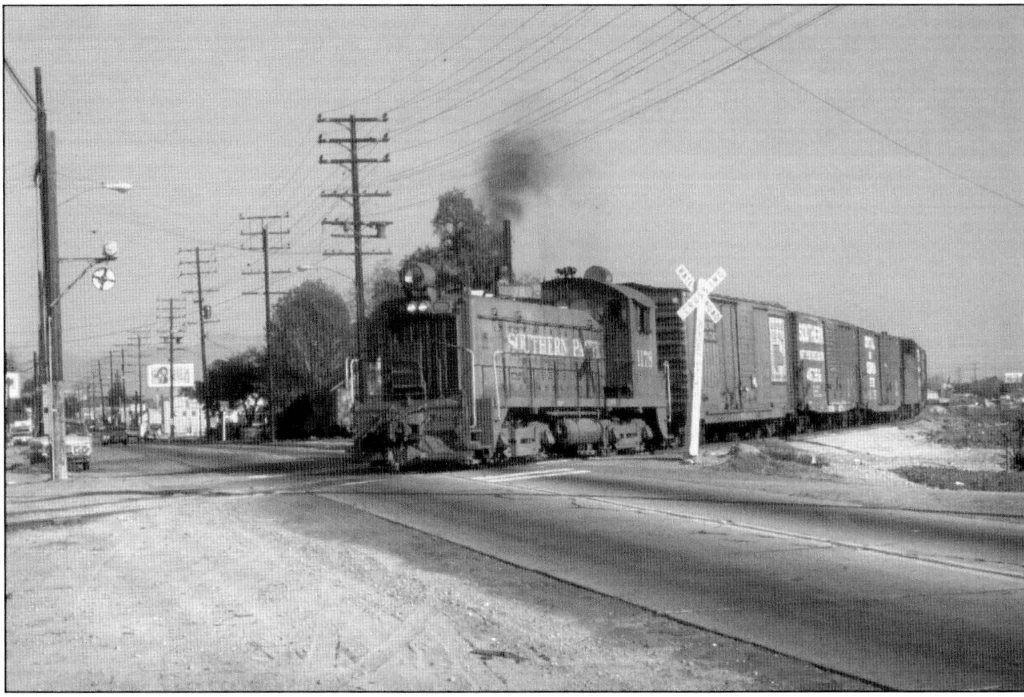

SP No. 1178 trundles across West Fifth Street in Santa Ana. Compare this photograph, taken on February 12, 1972, with the one below. (Photograph by and courtesy of Cliff Prather.)

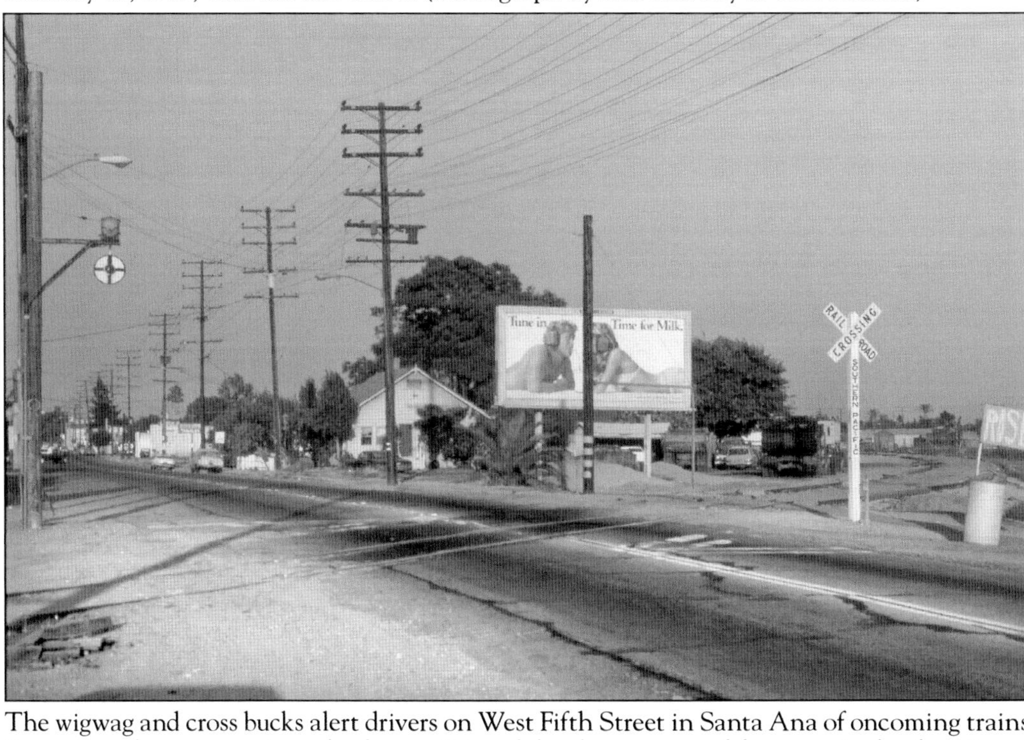

The wigwag and cross bucks alert drivers on West Fifth Street in Santa Ana of oncoming trains. Drivers need not worry since the former PE track has been removed from service by the SP as of this July 30, 1978, shot. (Photograph by and courtesy of Cliff Prather.)

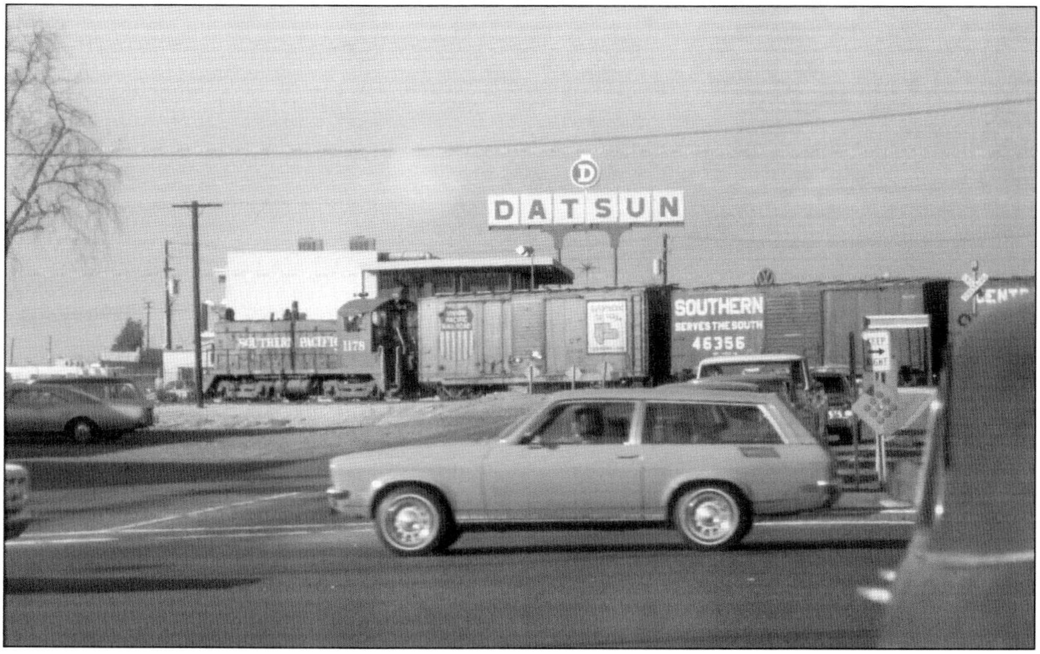

Here Southern Pacific No. 1178 is shown crossing Harbor Boulevard just north of Westminster Avenue in Garden Grove. This train is heading northwest on the former PE line. Today no tracks remain at this location, the Datsun dealership is gone, Harbor Boulevard is now a six-lane super street, and the Vega station wagon in the foreground is also just a memory. (Photograph by and courtesy of Cliff Prather.)

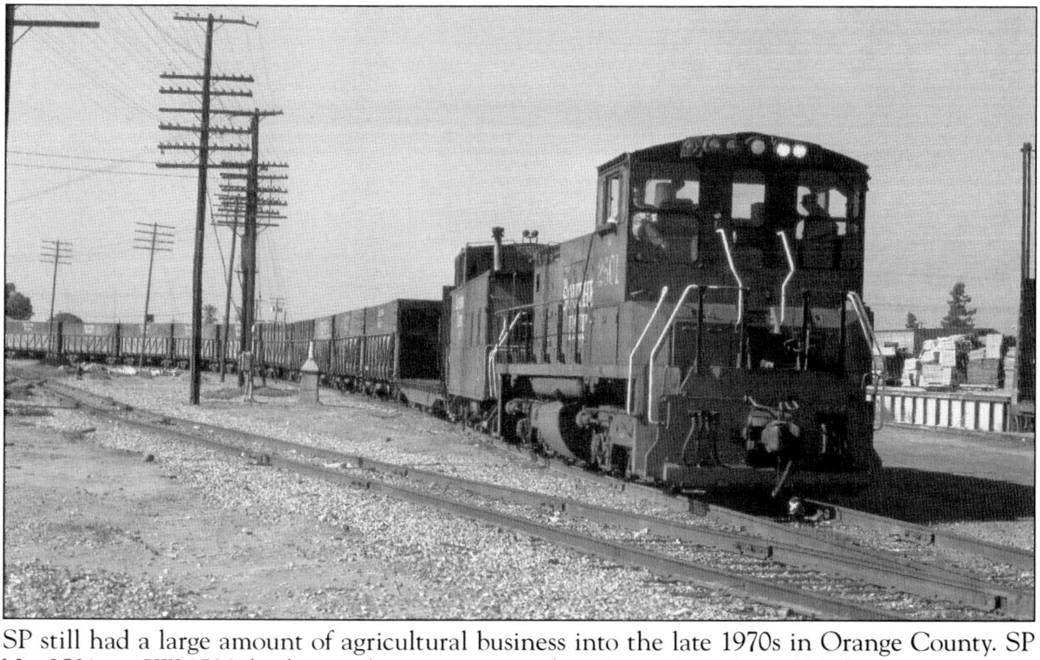
SP still had a large amount of agricultural business into the late 1970s in Orange County. SP No. 2501, an SW 1500, leads sugar beet empties north in Santa Ana. Santa Fe's depot is out of view to the left, and the SP's freight dock is on the right. Inbound sugar beets and outbound empties were a regular sight from the 1950s to the 1970s. (Photograph by and courtesy of Cliff Prather.)

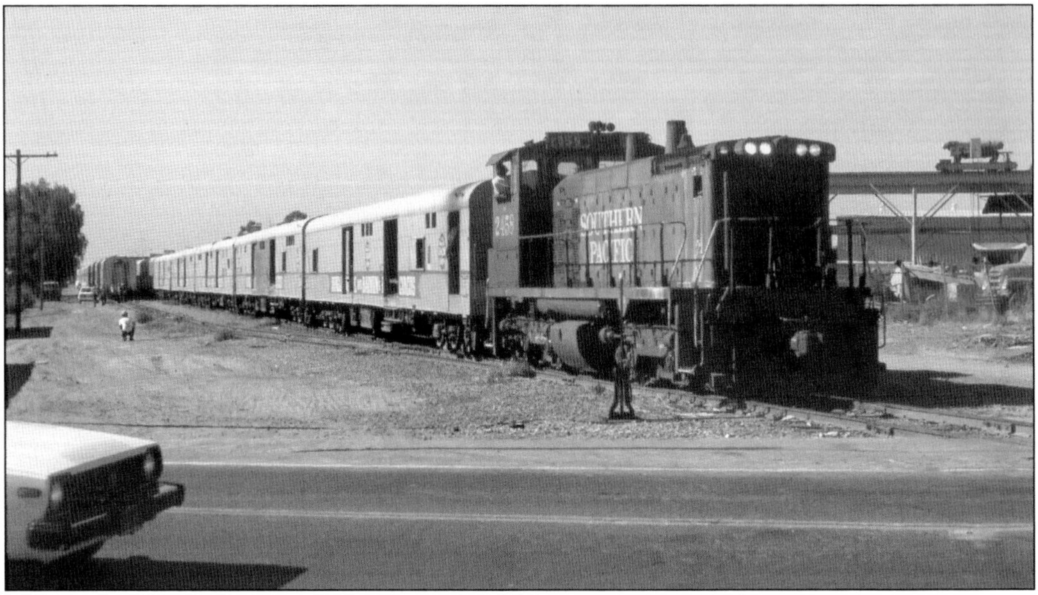

The Ringling Brothers, Barnum, and Bailey Circus travels across the nation via a special train. For many years after unloading the animals in Anaheim, the entire train was spotted on an SP siding in Santa Ana. On August 1, 1973, SP SW-1500 No. 2458 is shown switching circus cars to fit entirely on the two side tracks. The photograph location is Washington Avenue looking north. SP's line south from Anaheim was taken for the widening of the Santa Ana Freeway; the tracks at this location became the new Penn Way. (Photograph by and courtesy of Cliff Prather.)

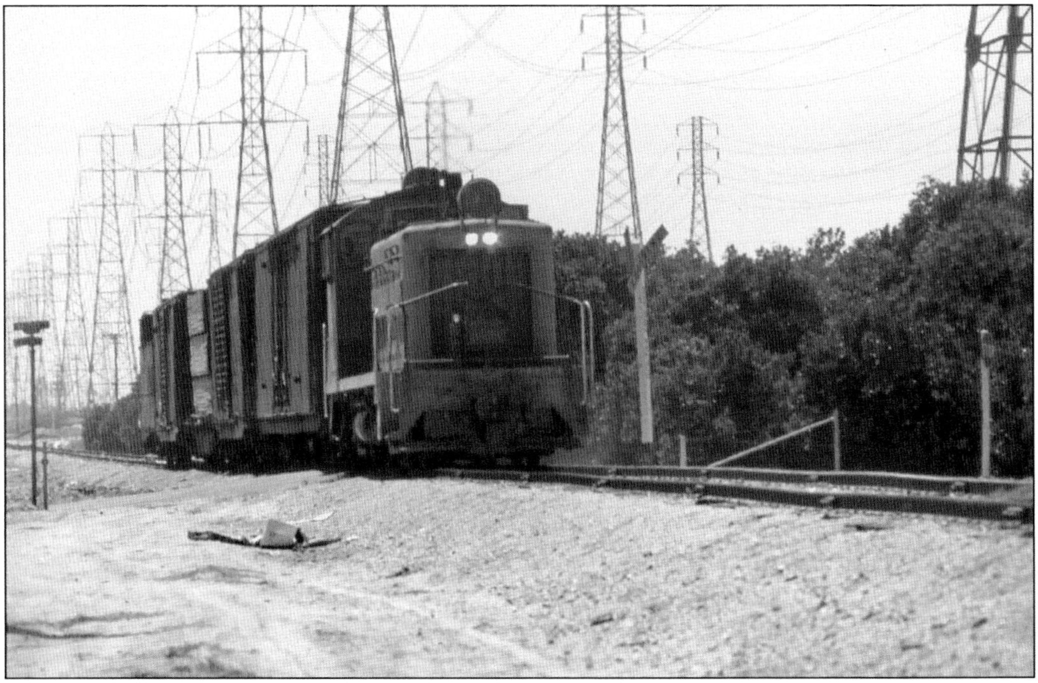

Here an SP local, led by No. 1124, is heading east toward Villa Park. At one time, this SP branch eventually reached Tustin and terminated near Main Street and Newport Avenue. (Photograph by and courtesy of Cliff Prather.)

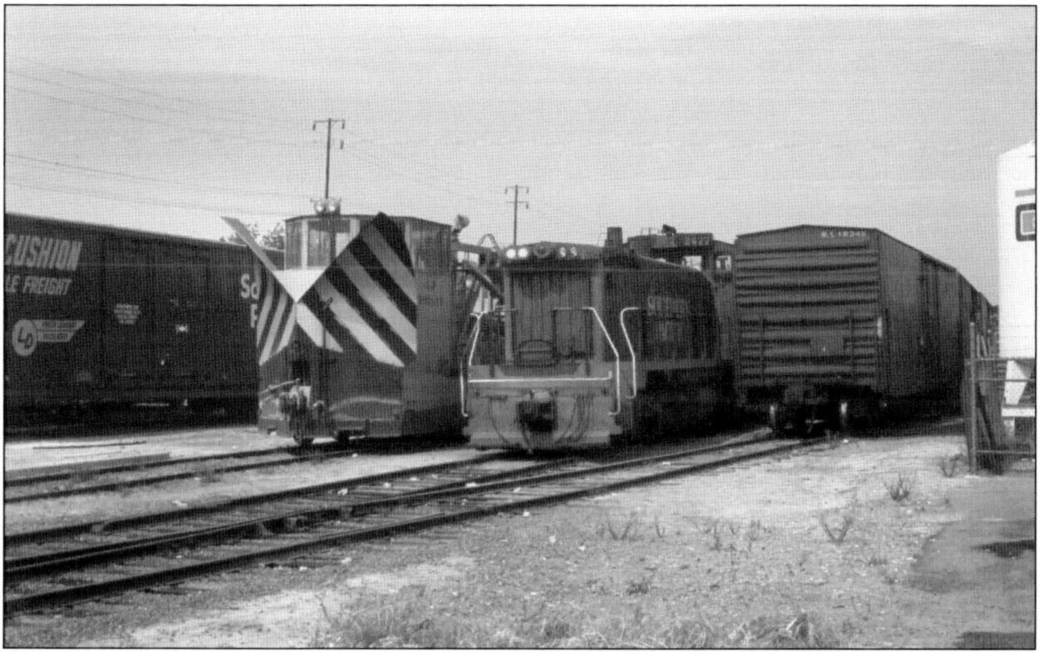

This SP train is using trackage rights granted by the UP as it passes east through Fullerton on August 4, 1971. The locomotive is No. 2477, an SW-1500. The odd looking contraption next to the train is a UP Jordan spreader used for clearing the right-of-way of weeds and other debris. (Photograph by and courtesy of Cliff Prather.)

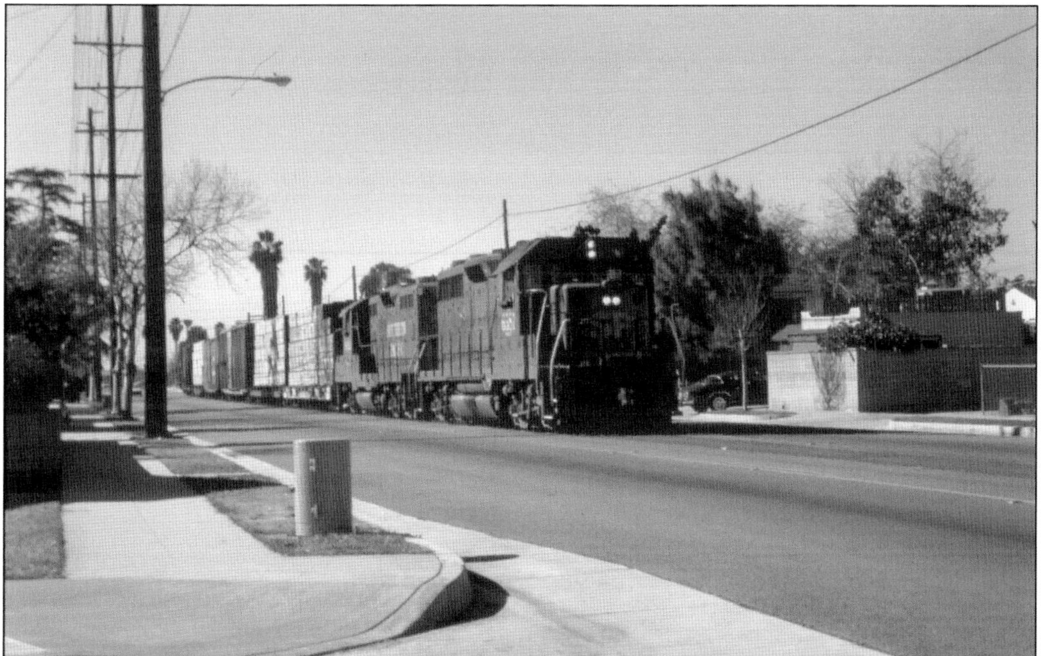

An SP local train heading east on Santa Ana Street and has just left West Anaheim. The day's motive power on January 16, 1989, included SP No. 6567 and No. 3834 (GP-35 and GP-9). (Photograph by and courtesy of the author.)

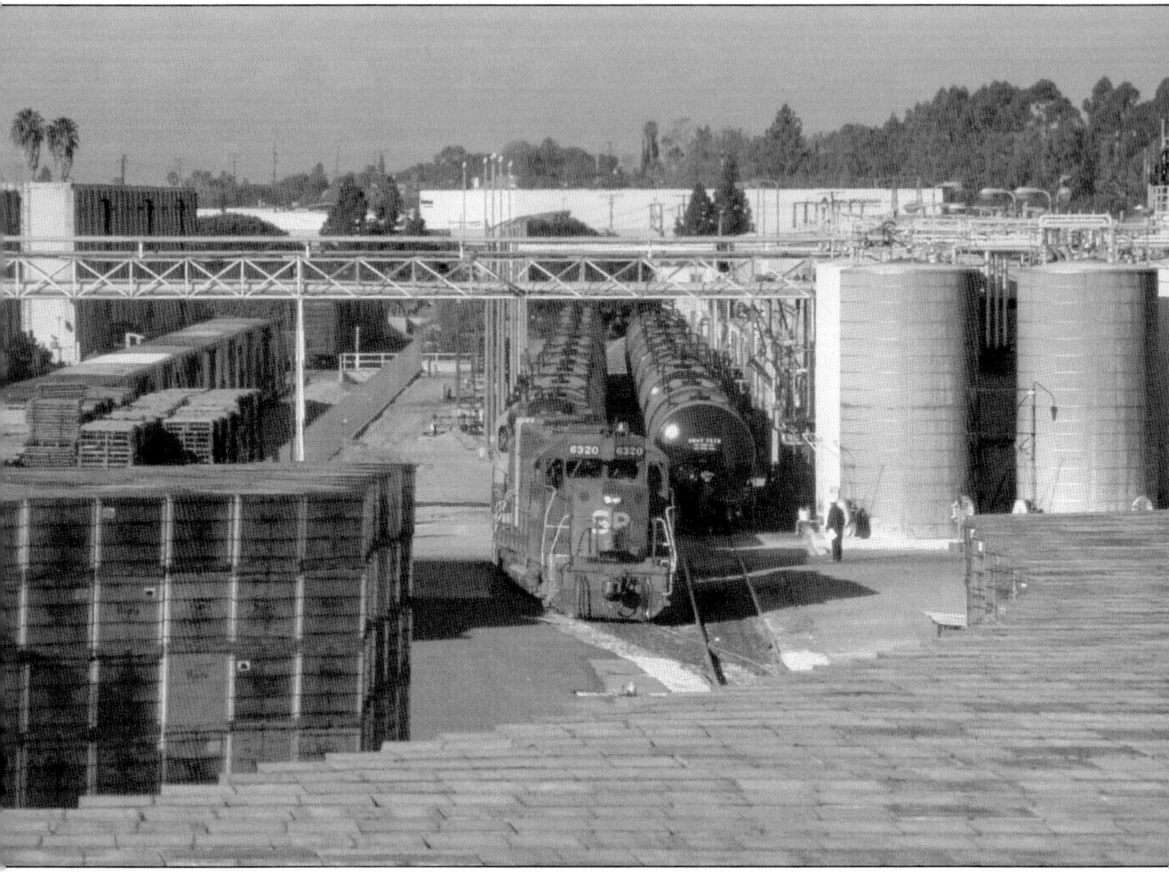

One of the biggest traffic generators for local railroads was the Hunt Wesson plant in Fullerton. The factory was served by the SP and UP railroads. In this photograph, taken on January 15, 1974, SP No. 6320 and an unidentified second locomotive tiptoe through the factory. (Photograph by and courtesy of Cliff Prather.)

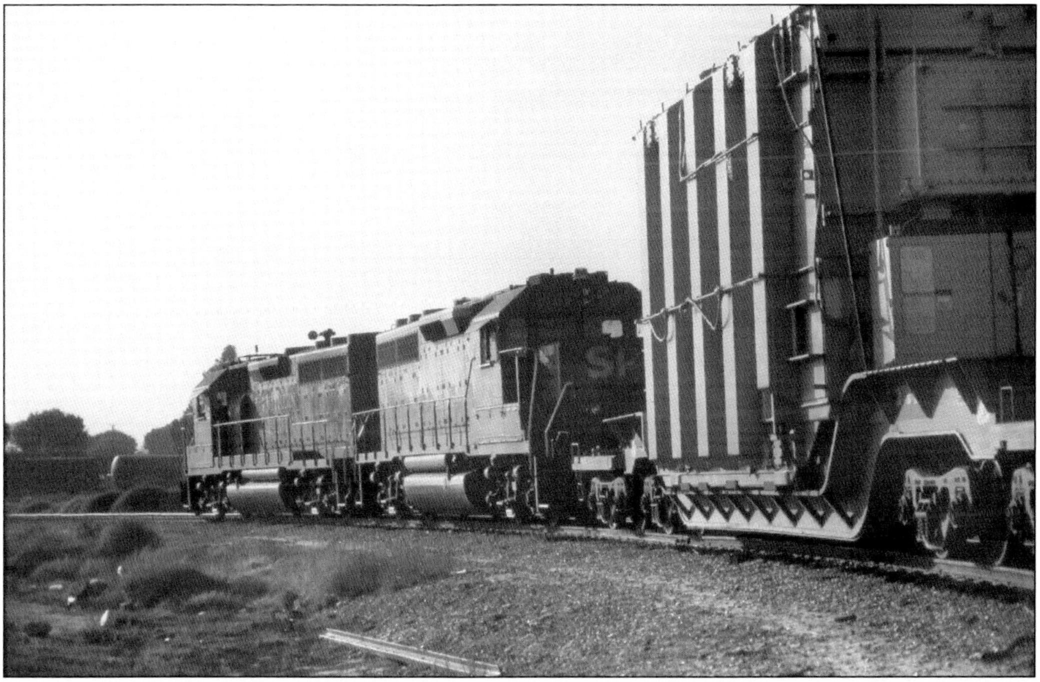

SP GP-40s No. 7102 and No. 7104 lead a freight through Los Alamitos Junction. This train originated from West Anaheim. The unusual lowboy freight car is carrying oversized cargo destined for a Southern California Edison maintenance center. (Photograph by and courtesy of Cliff Prather.)

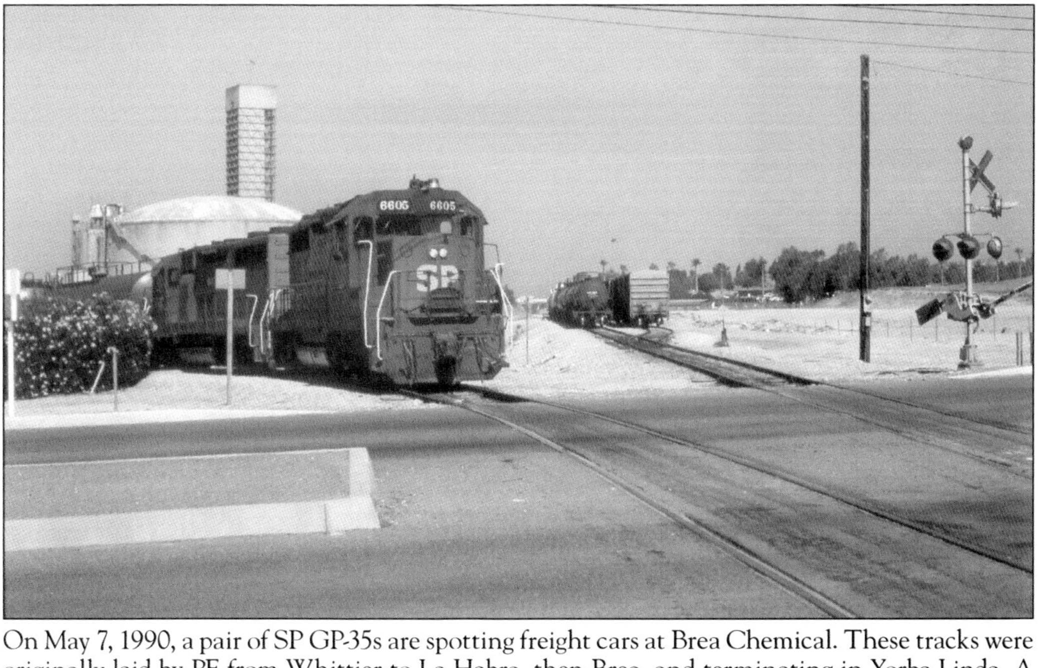

On May 7, 1990, a pair of SP GP-35s are spotting freight cars at Brea Chemical. These tracks were originally laid by PE from Whittier to La Habra, then Brea, and terminating in Yorba Linda. A planned PE extension to Riverside County was never started. (Photograph by and courtesy of Cliff Prather.)

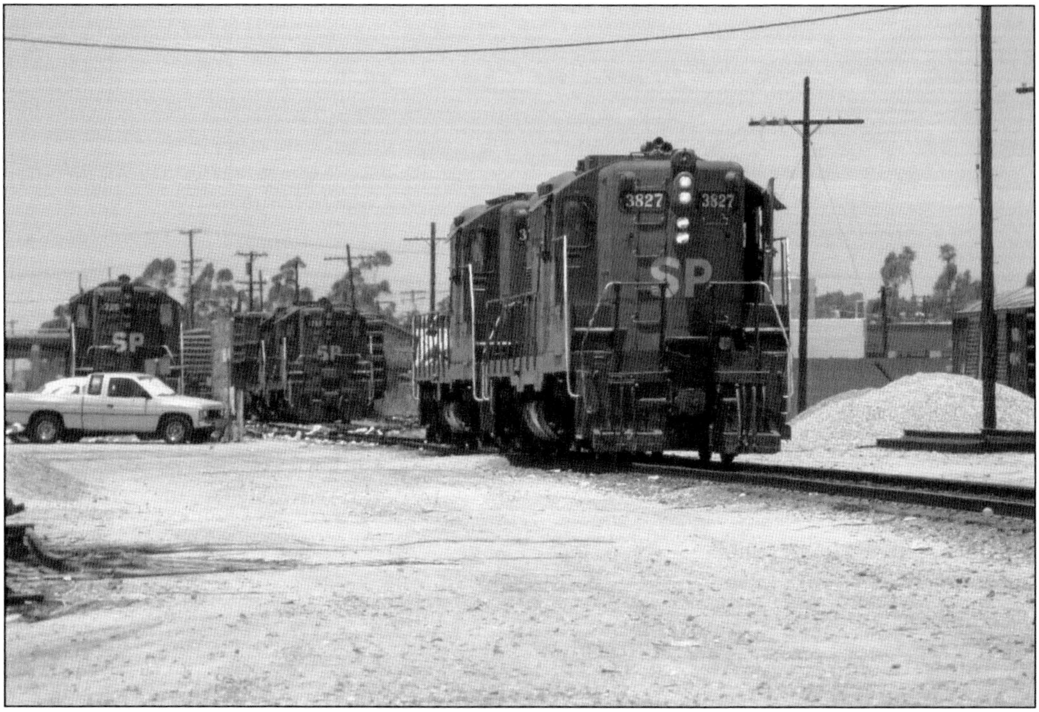

The SP Santa Ana local prepares to leave West Anaheim. Numerous switch jobs were handled from this location, and numerous locomotives are nearly always present. This track is now operated by the UP. (Photograph by and courtesy of the author.)

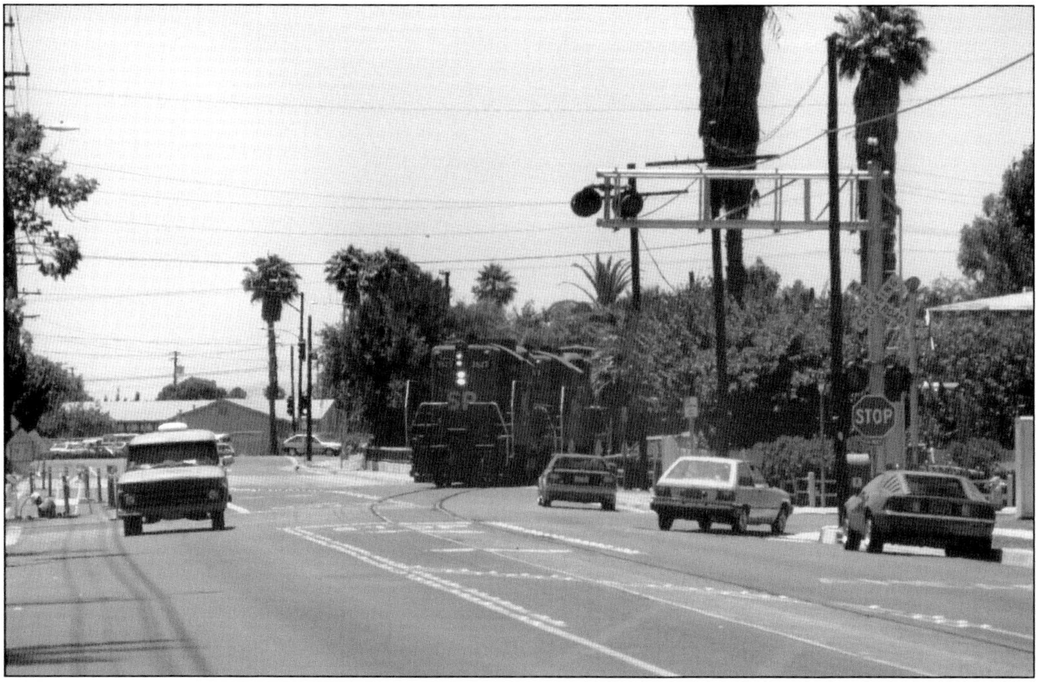

SP No. 3827 and No. 3753 have just crossed over the Santa Ana Freeway and are entering Santa Ana Street in Anaheim. (Photograph by and courtesy of the author.)

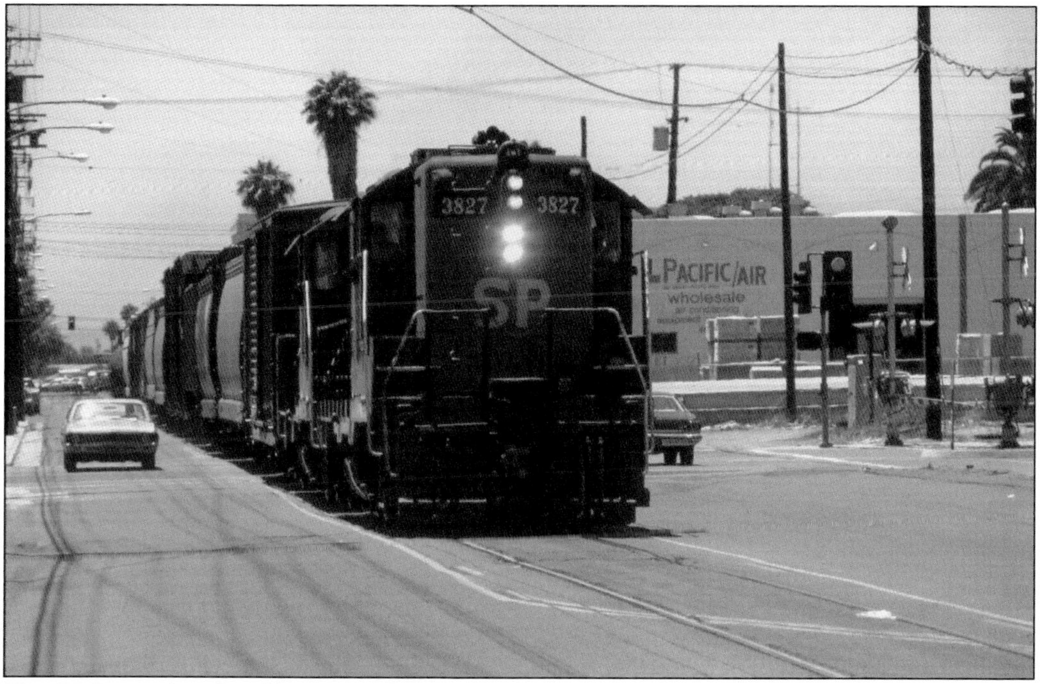

The SP Santa Ana local has just left the West Anaheim depot and will run eastward on Santa Ana Street in downtown Anaheim. This line contains the only street-running railroad in Orange County and is a surprise for the uninitiated driver. This image is from July 1987. (Photograph by and courtesy of the author.)

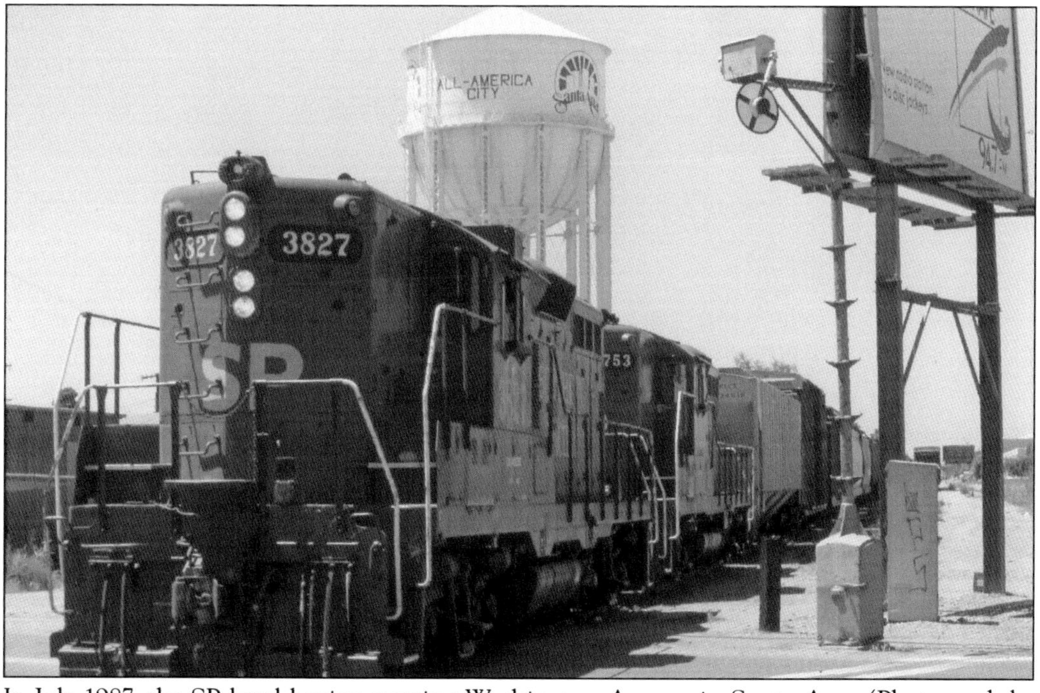

In July 1987, the SP local begins crossing Washington Avenue in Santa Ana. (Photograph by and courtesy of the author.)

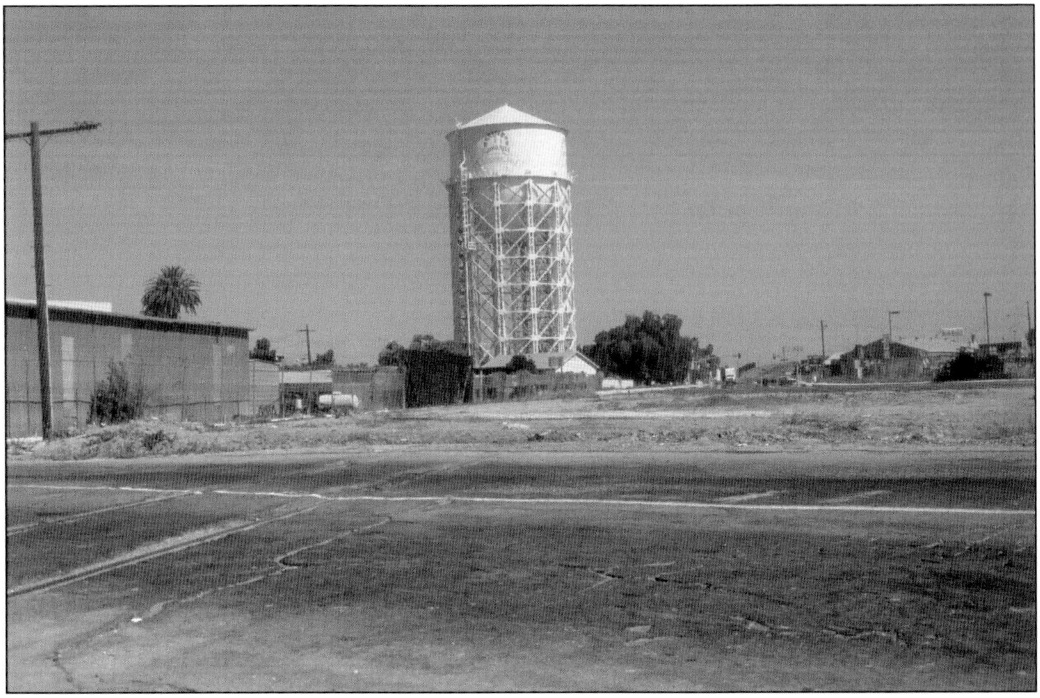

This view looks north up the old SP right-of-way from Washington Avenue in Santa Ana on May 30, 1996. The only track remaining is a small segment still embedded in the street. The landmark Santa Ana water tower looms in the distance at center. Compare this shot with the one taken a showing a train at this location on the previous page. (Photograph by and courtesy of the author.)

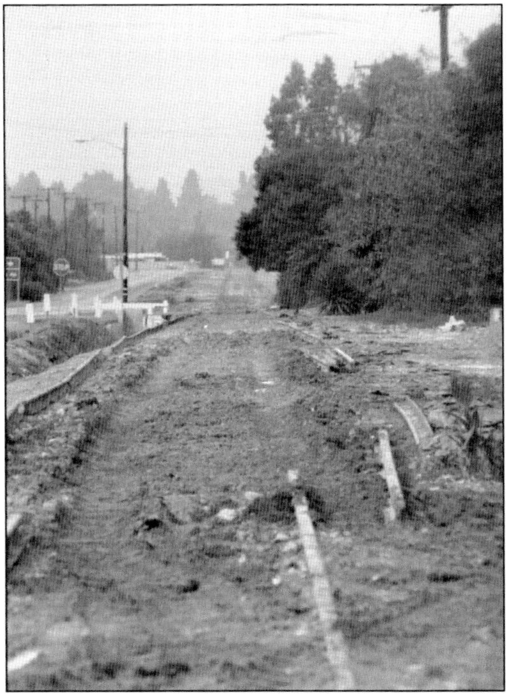

The Tustin branch of the SP has reached the end of the line. The Tustin branch was severed at the Santiago Creek during the heavy rains of February 1969. The force of inertia is powerful, and it was not until January 1973 that the track below the Santiago Creek was pulled up. This photograph looks north along Esplanade Avenue in North Tustin just south of Santa Clara Avenue on January 22, 1973. In the early 1990s, county supervisor Roger Stanton led efforts to acquire the former right-of-way to create Esplanade Park. Supervisor Bill Campbell has spearheaded efforts to acquire additional parts of the right-of-way to add to this recreational element. (Photograph by and courtesy of Cliff Prather.)

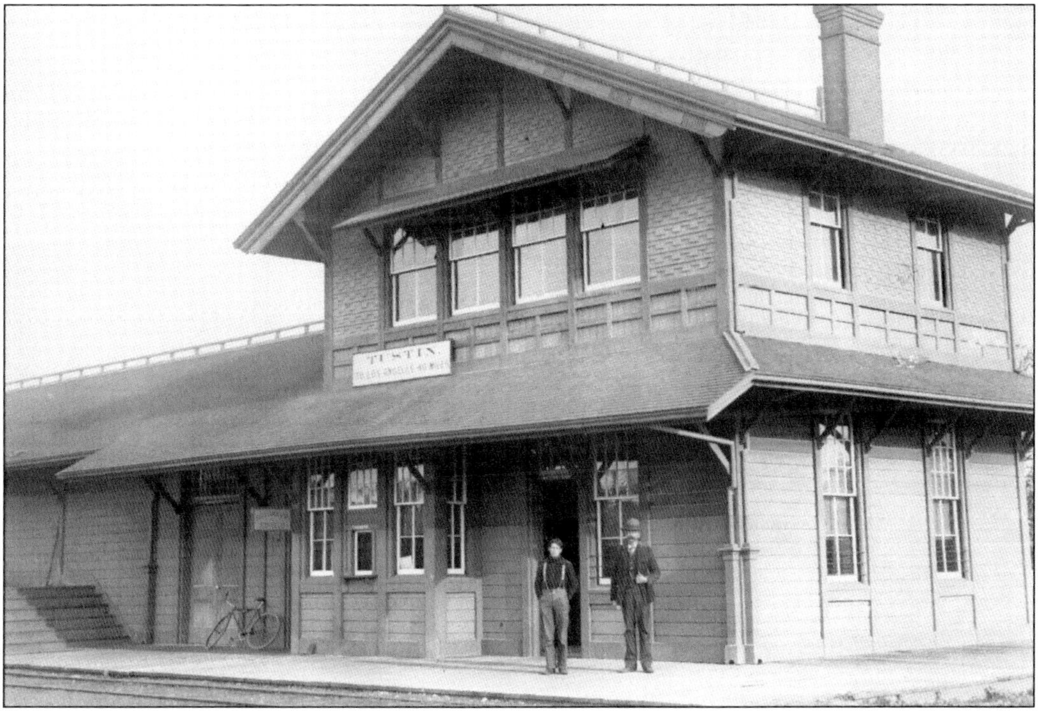

The SP depot was built in Tustin in 1889. The SP had intended for the Tustin line to continue south across the Irvine Ranch and eventually target San Diego. James Irvine was opposed to the SP's move, so this became the end of the line. Meanwhile, nearby Santa Ana raised the necessary cash for the SP to extend the Anaheim line south in 1877. SP, together with the Santa Fe, helped launch the early commercial prominence of Santa Ana. This depot was built to a SP standard plan used elsewhere in California, including Crafton (north of Redlands), Downey, Morgan Hill, Mountain View, San Pedro, and Whittier. (Courtesy of the Tustin Area Historical Society.)

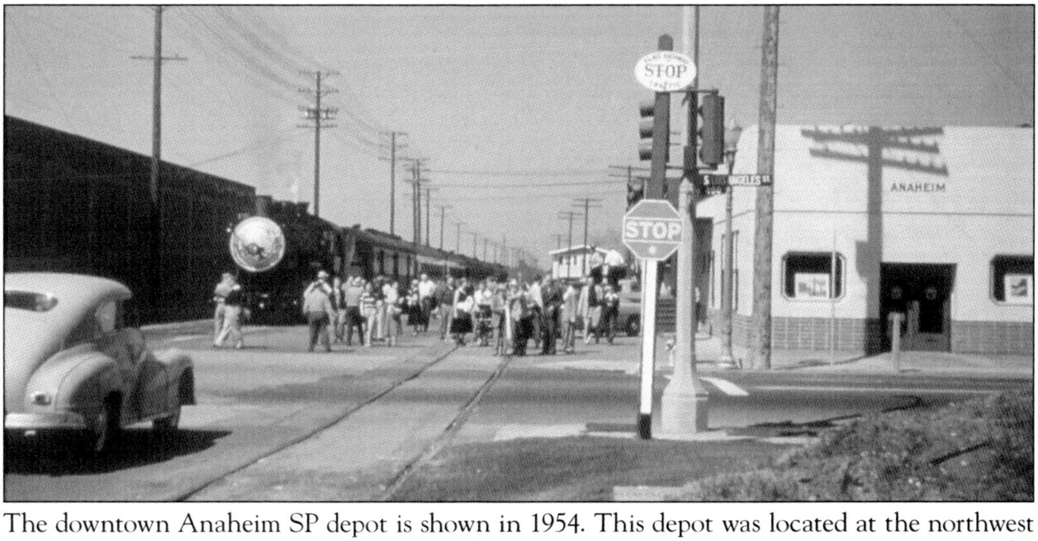

The downtown Anaheim SP depot is shown in 1954. This depot was located at the northwest corner of Los Angeles (Anaheim Boulevard) and Santa Ana Streets. The SP train sitting in the center of Santa Ana Street is a special excursion train. (Photograph by E. W. Freer; courtesy of Cliff Prather.)

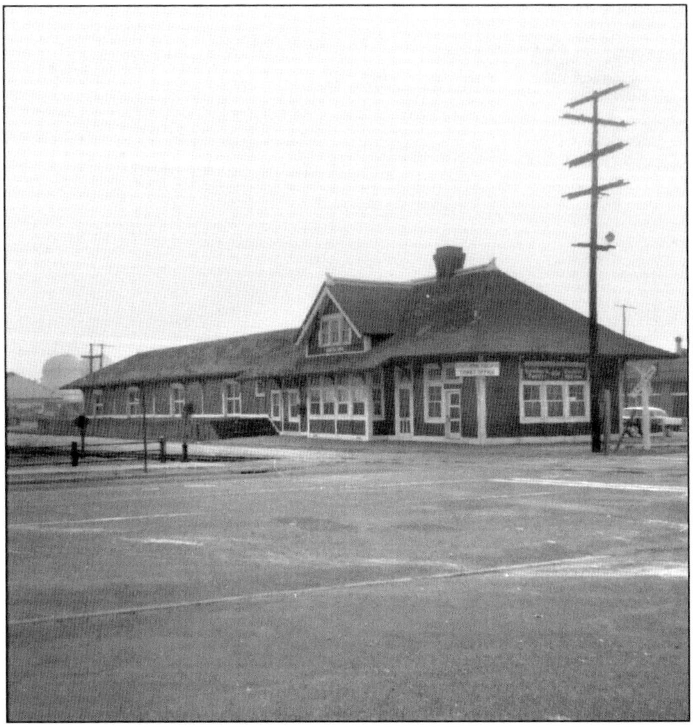

This photograph shows the second SP depot located at the southeast corner of Fourth and Breeden Streets. At one time, trains of the Santa Ana and Newport Railroad departed here for Newport Beach; this railroad was later merged with the SP and terminated just below Dyer Road in Santa Ana. The 1903 depot still looked good in 1965. (Photograph by and courtesy of Cliff Prather.)

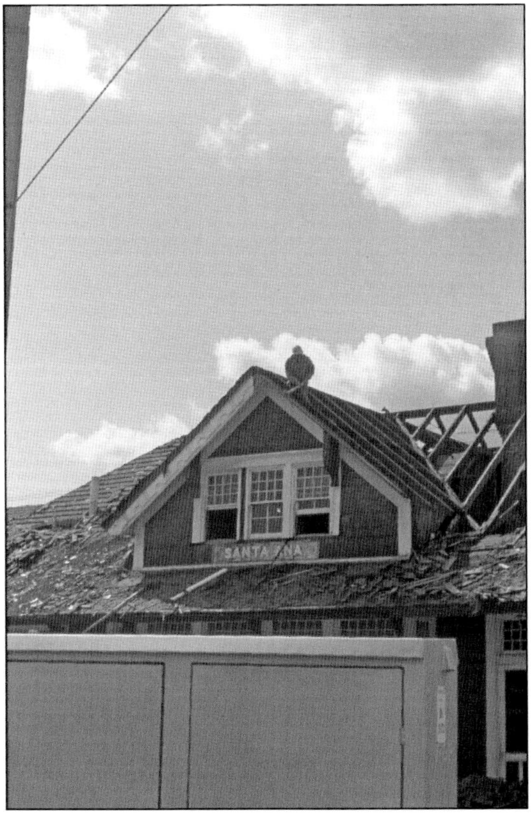

Demolition was a familiar conclusion for most of Orange County's original train depots. A workman is shown here removing the roof from SP's Santa Ana depot in February 1969. (Photograph by and courtesy of Cliff Prather.)

Three

The Atchison, Topeka, and the Santa Fe Railway

The Atchison, Topeka, and the Santa Fe Railway (Santa Fe) built its rail line from Riverside to Santa Ana and San Juan in 1887. The following year, the Santa Fe extended a new line from Orange to Los Angeles and extended south from San Juan to Oceanside and San Diego. The addition of the Santa Fe gave Orange County a new outlet for its various crops and led directly to the land boom experienced in Southern California in the late 1880s. In 1910, the gap between Fullerton and Atwood was closed and linked the great "Transcon" mainline between Los Angeles and Chicago.

The Santa Fe operations in Orange County's rich agricultural farmlands and small towns fostered continued growth into the 1940s. World War II tested America's rail system to the limit. During these years, the Santa Fe helped serve the nation's war needs by hauling troops and material to the various bases in Orange County and San Diego. In the postwar period, Orange County's population skyrocketed, and over time, the population growth and changing business environment altered the Santa Fe. As more houses were built on agricultural fields, the need to haul crops diminished, and finished goods, manufacturing raw materials, and construction materials dominated the freight lines.

In 1971, most passenger rail companies, including the Santa Fe, turned over passenger service to Amtrak. As time marched on, fewer people knew or cared about freight railroading. In the mid-1990s, the Santa Fe became the Burlington Northern Santa Fe (BNSF). BNSF carries on the tradition of railroading in Orange County, and its daily trains funnel goods to and from the Port of Los Angeles/Long Beach and San Diego to points east. Most of the former Santa Fe lines in Orange County are either double or triple track to handle the increased volumes of traffic.

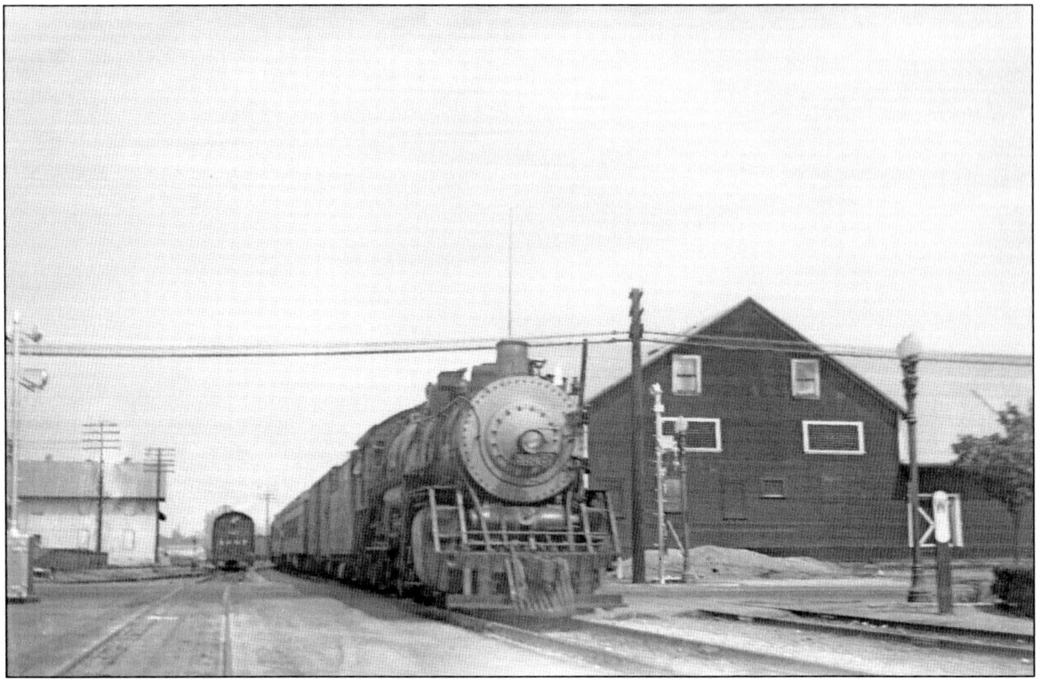

During the early 1950s, numerous troop trains ran through Santa Ana as a result of the Korean War. On this day in 1951, a Santa Fe (2-8-2 No. 3243) locomotive leads a troop train across Fourth Street in Santa Ana. The photographer remembers this train because a soldier gave him a letter to mail since the soldier could not leave the train. (Photograph by and courtesy of Tom Gildersleeve.)

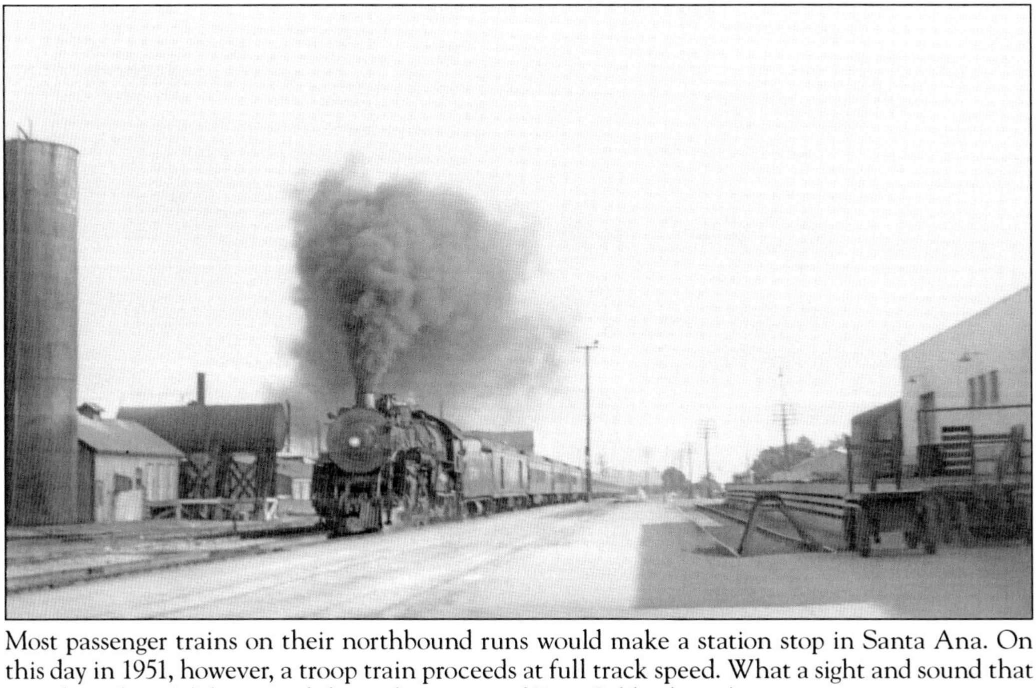

Most passenger trains on their northbound runs would make a station stop in Santa Ana. On this day in 1951, however, a troop train proceeds at full track speed. What a sight and sound that must have been! (Photograph by and courtesy of Tom Gildersleeve.)

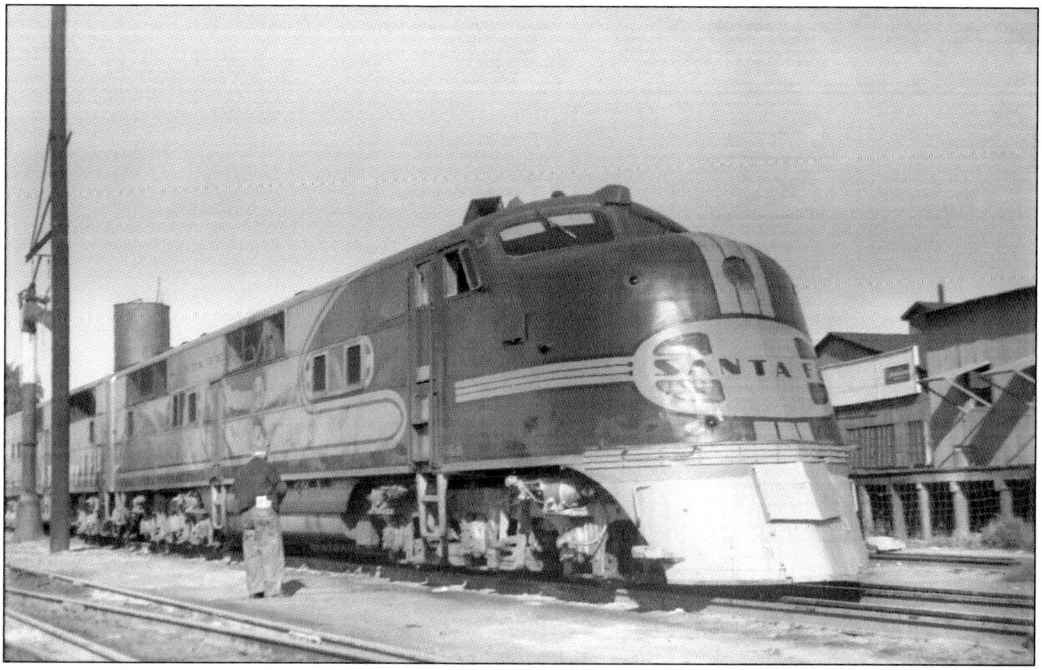

Some say that the E unit was the most beautiful locomotive ever built by EMD General Motors. The engineer is conducting a once-over inspection of his locomotive in Santa Ana in 1951. (Photograph by and courtesy of Tom Gildersleeve.)

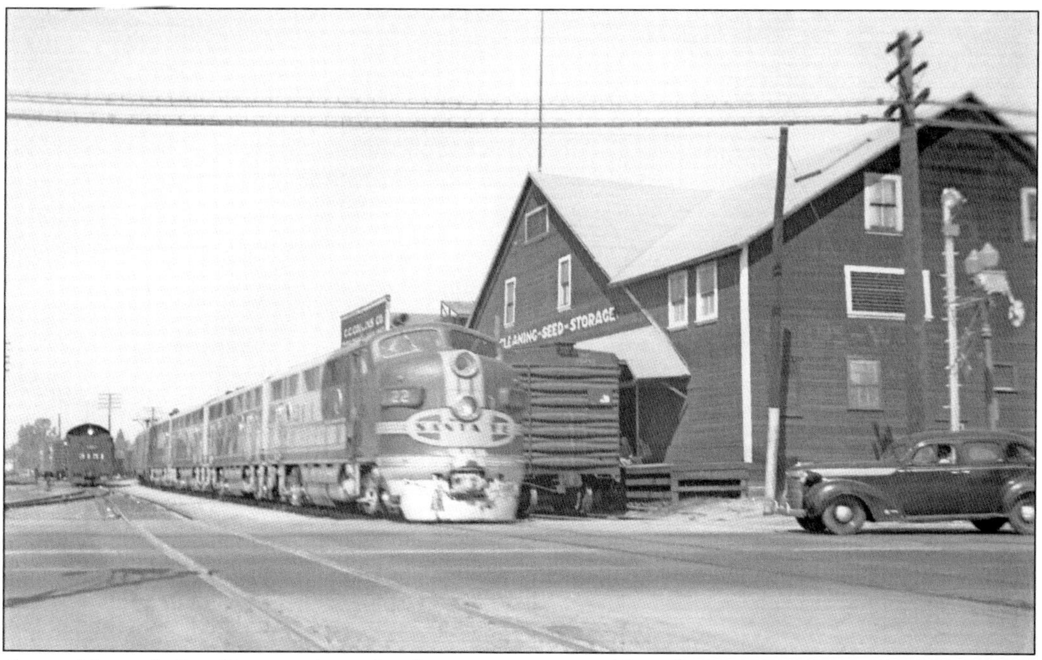

A southbound San Diegan slows for the station stop at Fourth Street in Santa Ana. At about this moment, the driver at the car on the right is putting the gear in reverse. Wigwag signals and good judgment were the only protections from oncoming trains. (Photograph by and courtesy of Tom Gildersleeve.)

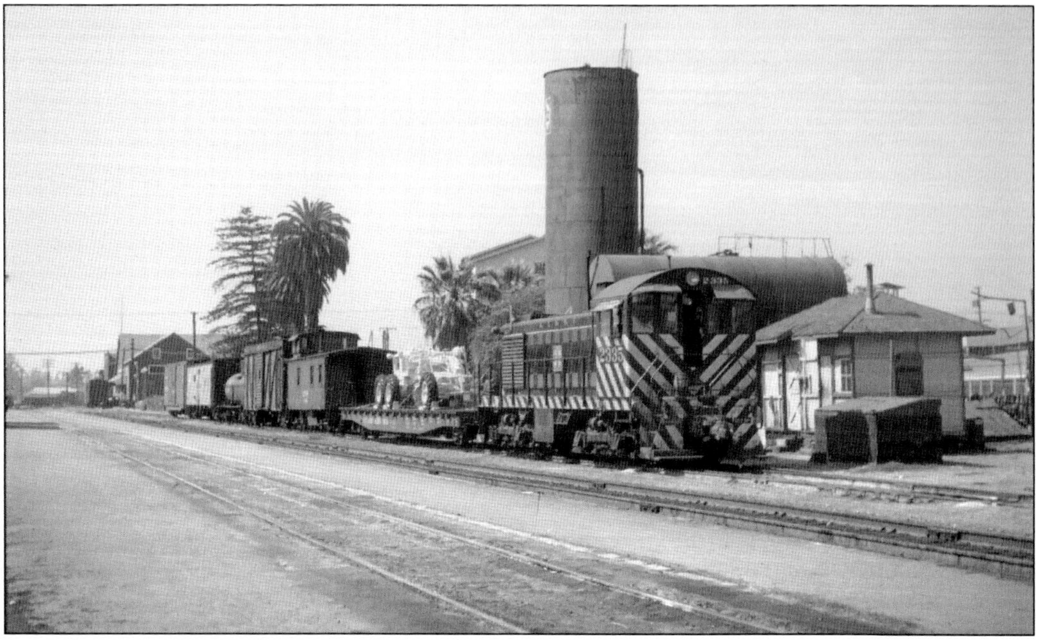

On July 12, 1951, an Alco Santa Fe switcher is working the sidings in Santa Ana. The initial Santa Fe freight diesels were delivered in the black-and-white, zebra-stripe livery. (Photograph by and courtesy of Tom Gildersleeve.)

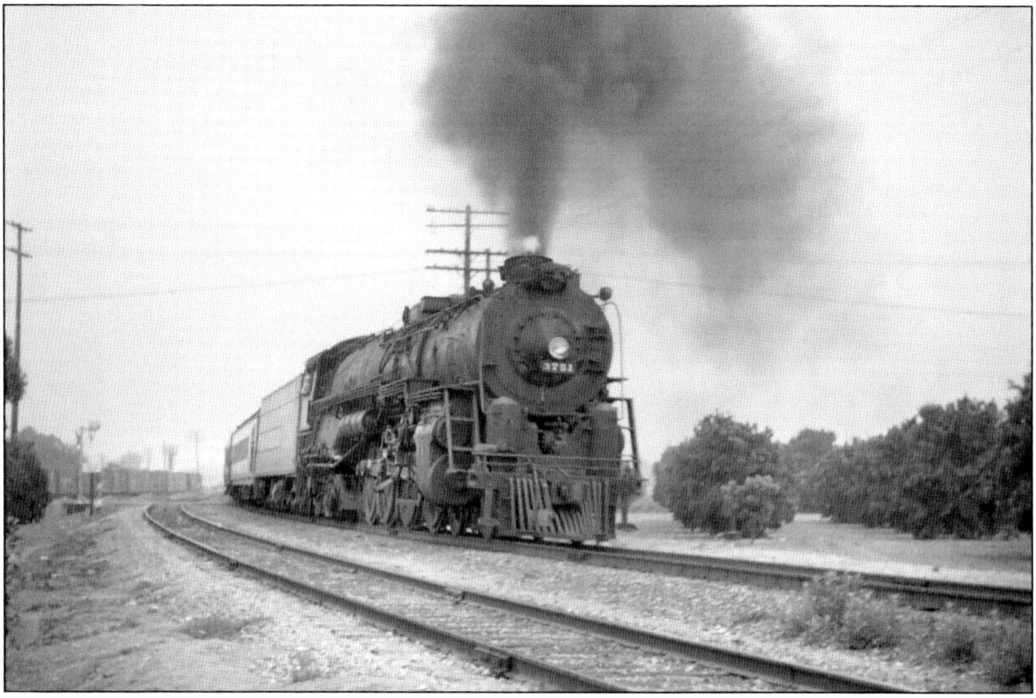

On July 25, 1951, Santa Fe's No. 3751 leading a Del Mar Race special can be seen. This train is just entering the curve after crossing Chestnut Avenue and will be galloping down the Fourth District straight away. It has been a pleasure to see the No. 3751 travel on this line once again in recent years. (Photograph by and courtesy of Tom Gildersleeve.)

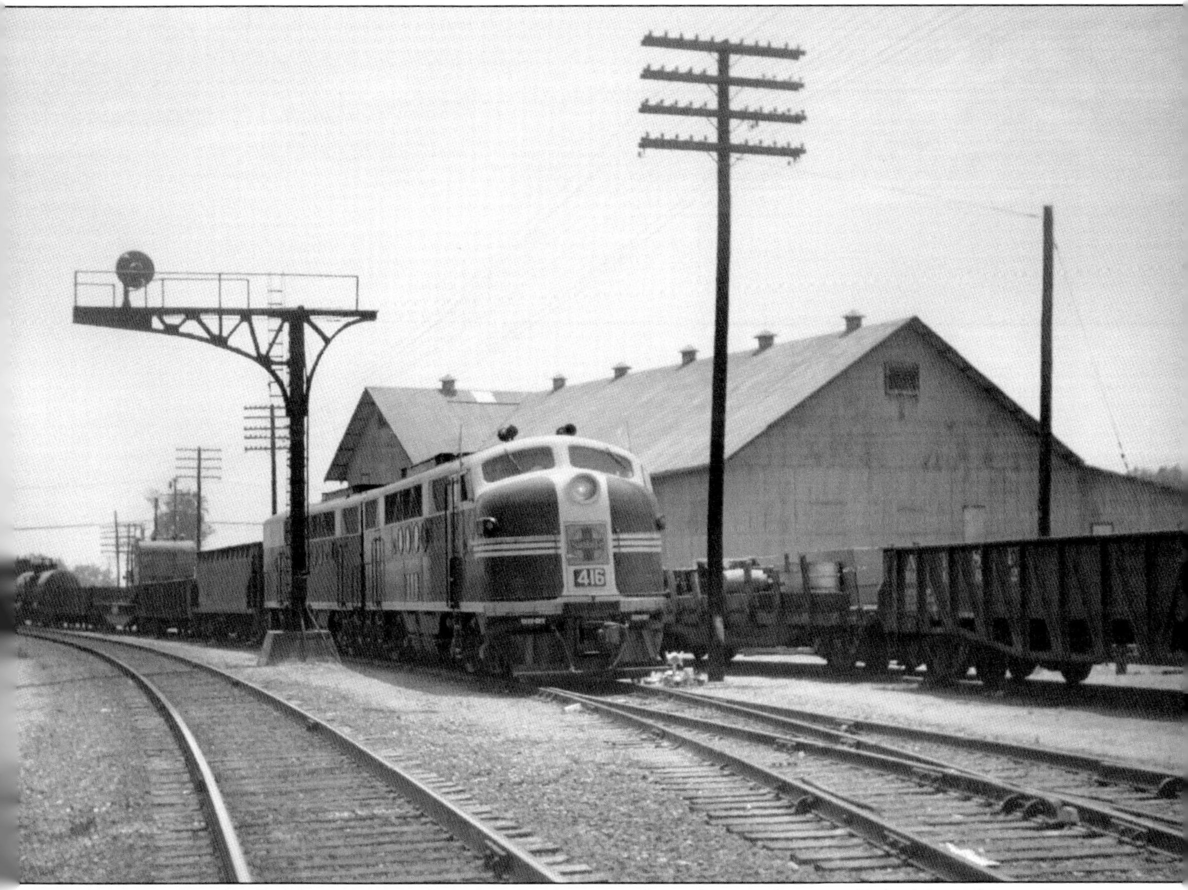

A Santa Fe freight led by two FTs has finished its work in Santa Ana on July 25, 1951, and is preparing to enter the main track heading north. This location is about two blocks north of the Santa Fe depot at 1038 East Fourth Street. (Photograph by and courtesy of Tom Gildersleeve.)

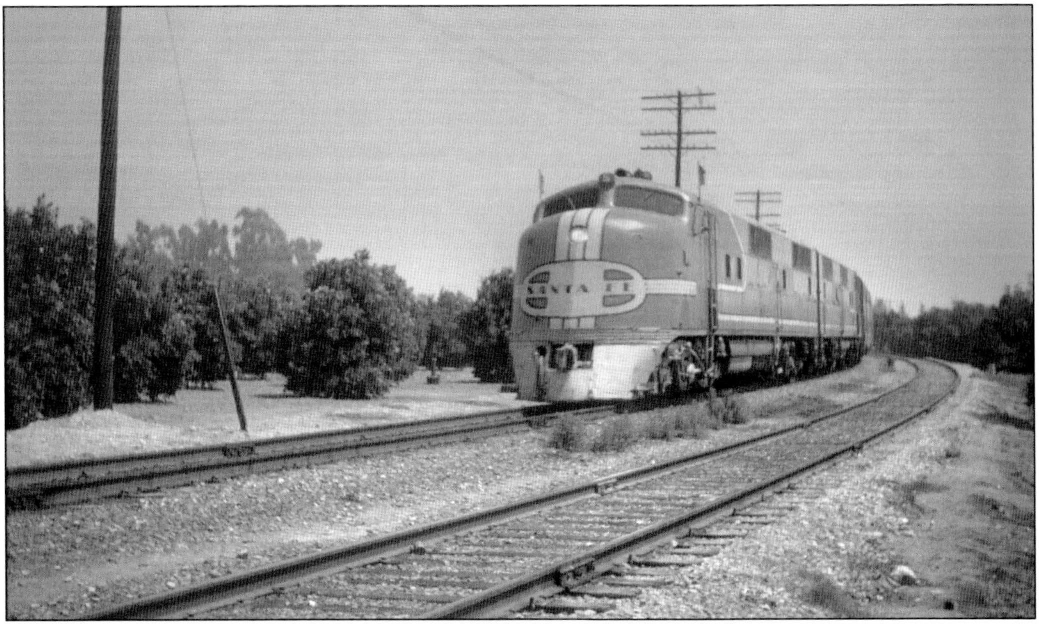

This northbound San Diegan is led by E2 No. 5 on July 26, 1951. Yes, those are orange trees on both sides of the tracks between Chestnut and Grand Avenues in Santa Ana (Photograph by and courtesy of Tom Gildersleeve.)

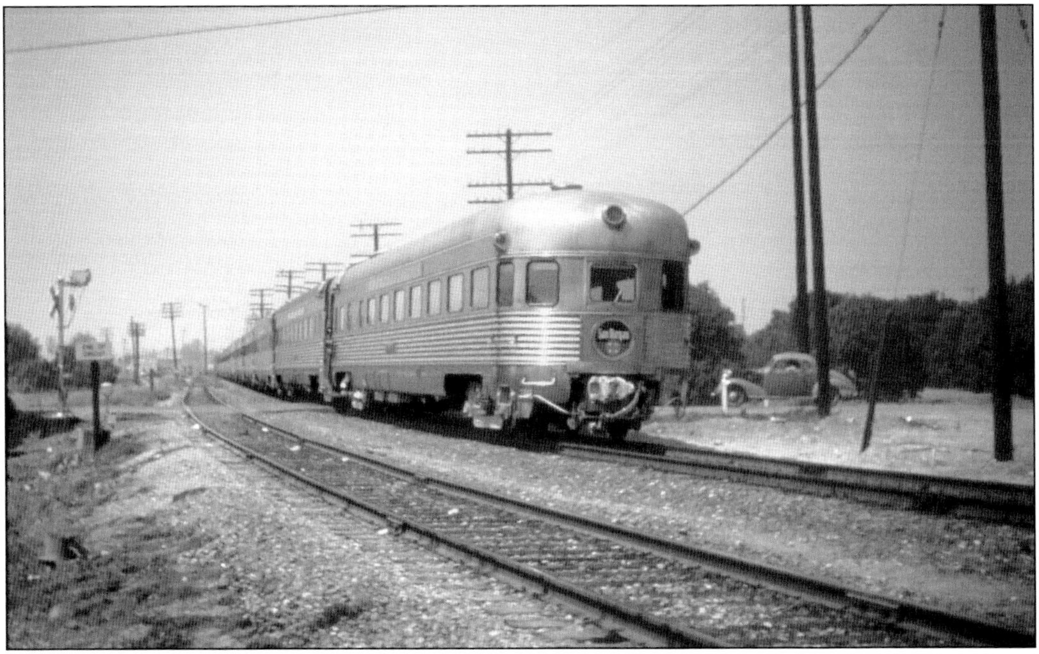

A northbound San Diegan is shown heading to the Santa Ana station in July 1951. The drumhead on the observation car identifies the train name. This day's San Diegan has an elegant observation car to end a completely streamlined passenger train. On the right, one can see one of the numerous orange groves from the 1950s. The location is the Chestnut Avenue crossing of the Santa Fe tracks just west of McClay Street in Santa Ana (now Grand Avenue). (Photograph by and courtesy of Tom Gildersleeve.)

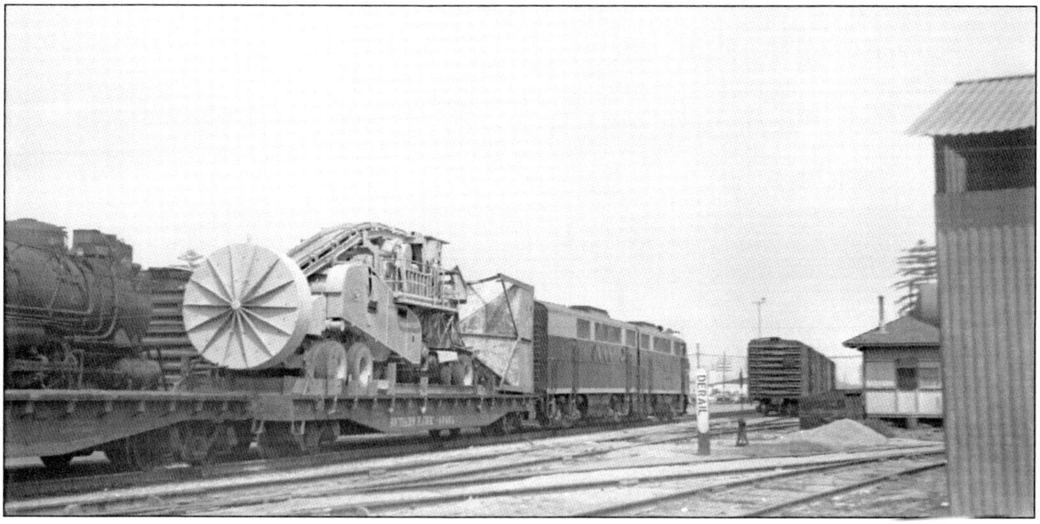

A pair of diesel locomotives moves freight north through Santa Ana in 1951. Note the steam locomotive (ATSF No. 4007) on the left next to the freight. (Photograph by and courtesy of Tom Gildersleeve.)

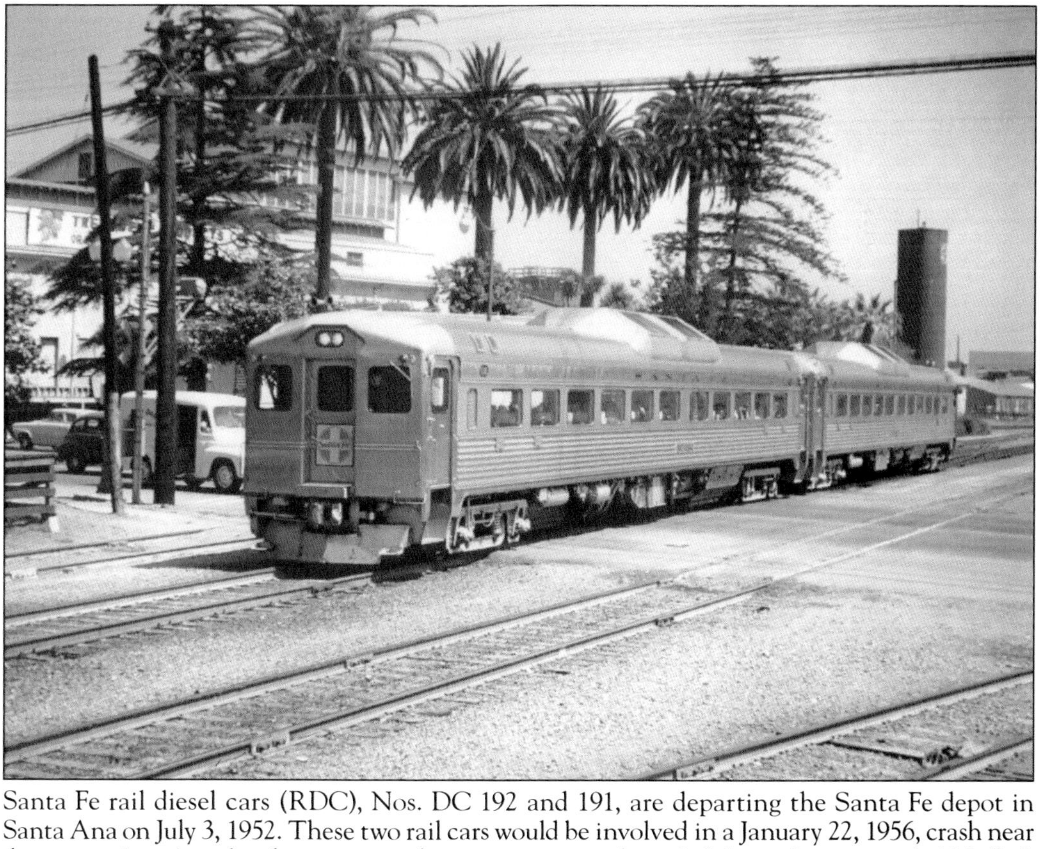

Santa Fe rail diesel cars (RDC), Nos. DC 192 and 191, are departing the Santa Fe depot in Santa Ana on July 3, 1952. These two rail cars would be involved in a January 22, 1956, crash near downtown Los Angeles that remains the worst train crash in California history, with 30 killed. Behind the train is the old depot park and beyond, the Treesweet Juice Factory. (Photograph by and courtesy of Tom Gildersleeve.)

In this scene from 1952, a San Diegan led by an E unit holds the main line while ATSF No. 3849 waits on the No. 2 track. The two trains and the car on the left are all waiting to enter First Street. The steam locomotive is a 2-10-2. The Santa Ana Santa Fe depot can be seen in the distance on

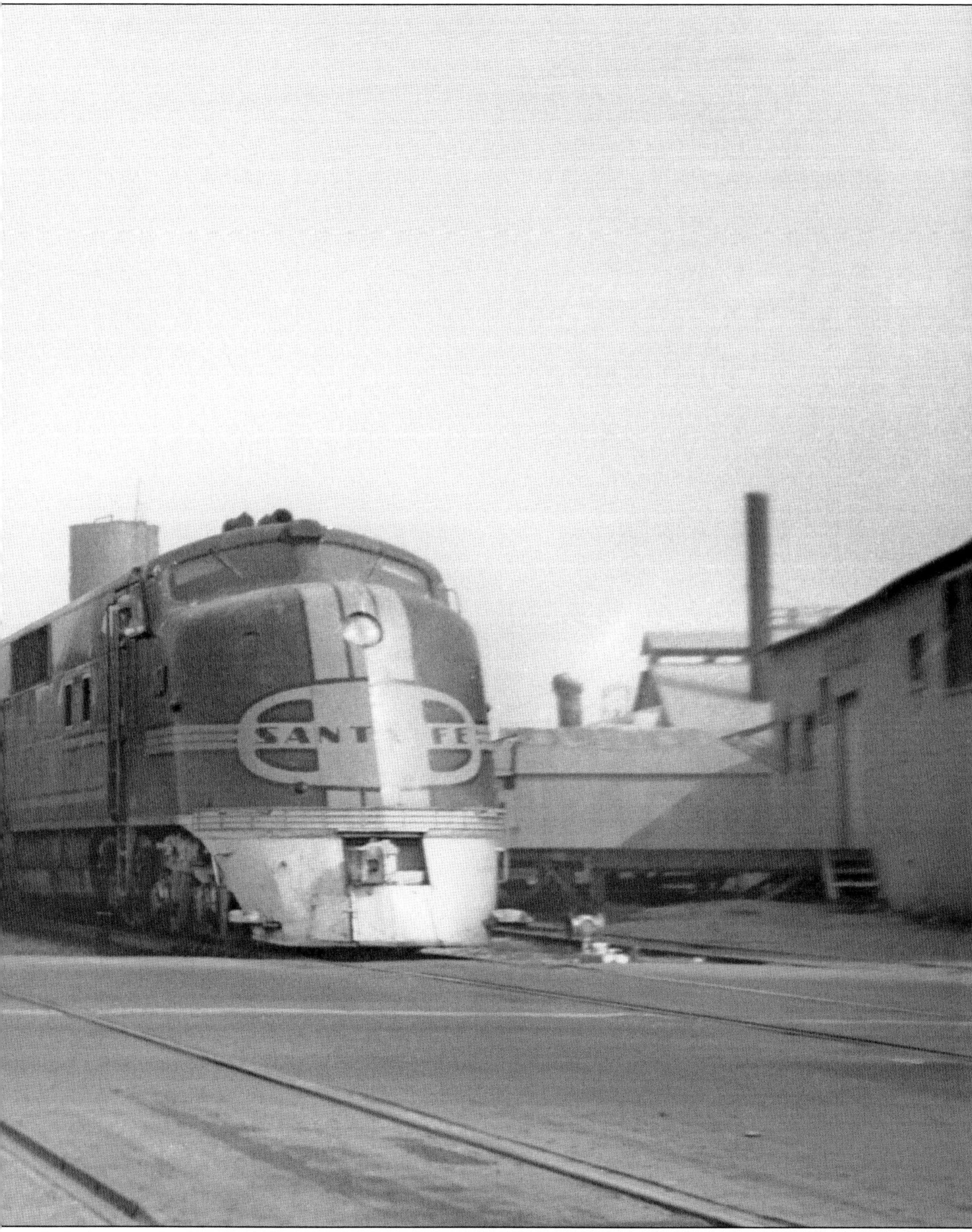

the left along with a woody station wagon. It looks like all three are prepared to race. (Photograph by and courtesy of Tom Gildersleeve.)

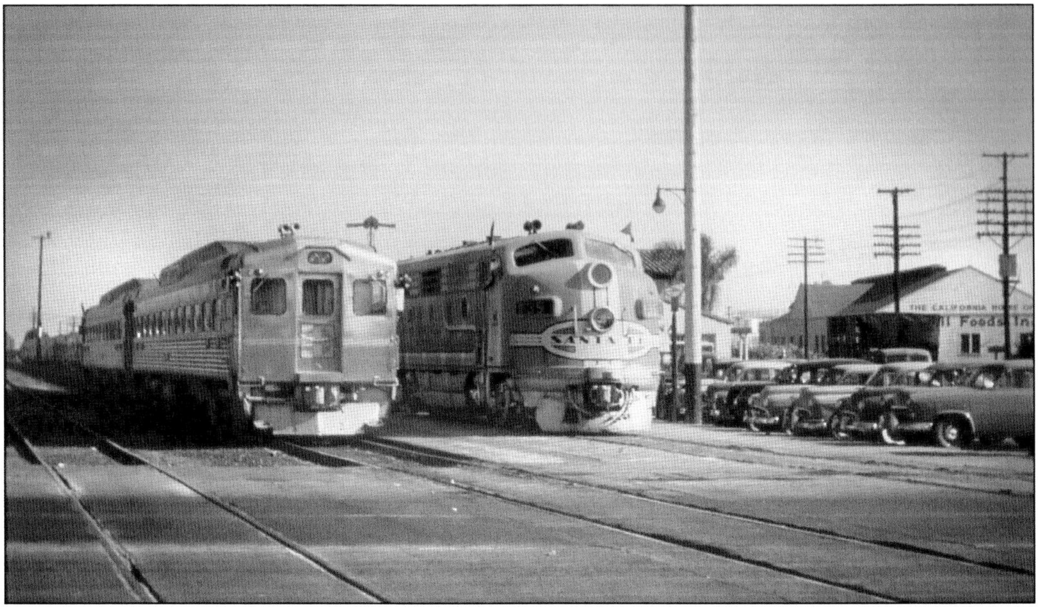

Santa Fe San Diegans hold both main tracks at the Santa Ana depot. On the near track is a pair of RDCs (rail diesel cars). A conventional F-7 stands on the far track on July 3, 1952. Several of this series of photographs were taken on the same date and demonstrate the variety of equipment in use during this steam-to-diesel transition. (Photograph by and courtesy of Tom Gildersleeve)

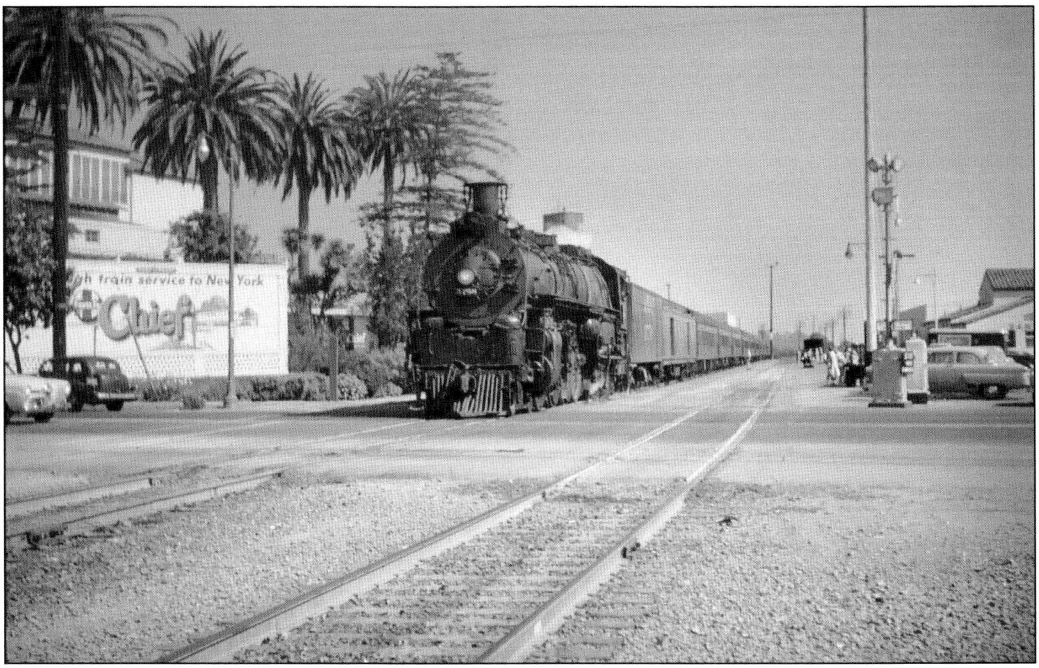

This is a beautiful view of Santa Fe No. 3758 arriving at Santa Ana on July 3, 1952. The big 4-8-4 locomotive is pulling a train that appears to be entirely heavyweight cars. (Photograph by and courtesy of Tom Gildersleeve.)

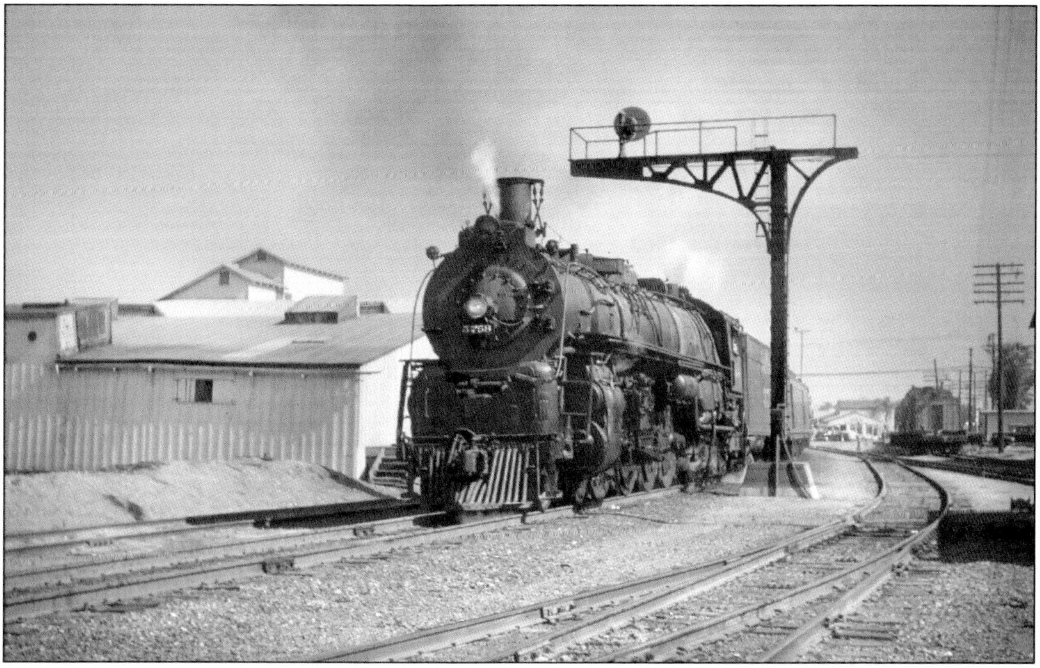

This photograph was also taken on July 3, 1952. Regular steam service on the Santa Fe will end in one year's time. The San Diegan will be led by No. 3758 on this bright afternoon. (Photograph by and courtesy of Tom Gildersleeve.)

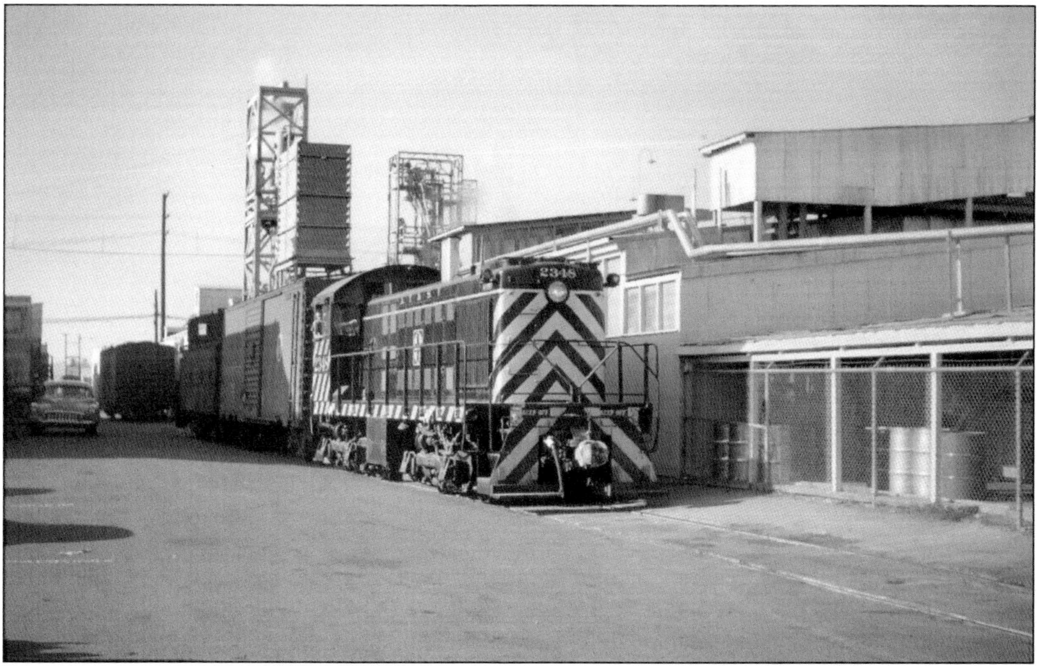

A Santa Fe Alco S-2 switches at the Treesweet plant in Santa Ana on July 3, 1952. Treesweet was a big Santa Fe customer into the 1970s. (Photograph by and courtesy of Tom Gildersleeve.)

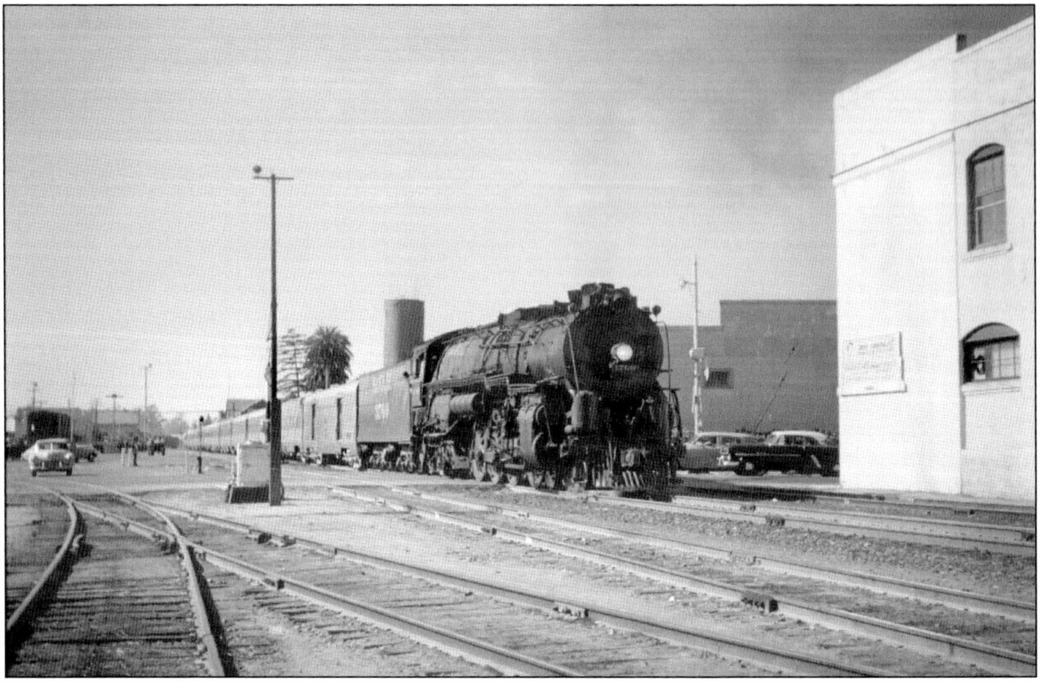

Santa Fe No. 3760, a 4-8-4, gets under way with a southbound San Diegan crossing First Street in Santa Ana. This image is from July 3, 1952. (Photograph by and courtesy of Tom Gildersleeve.)

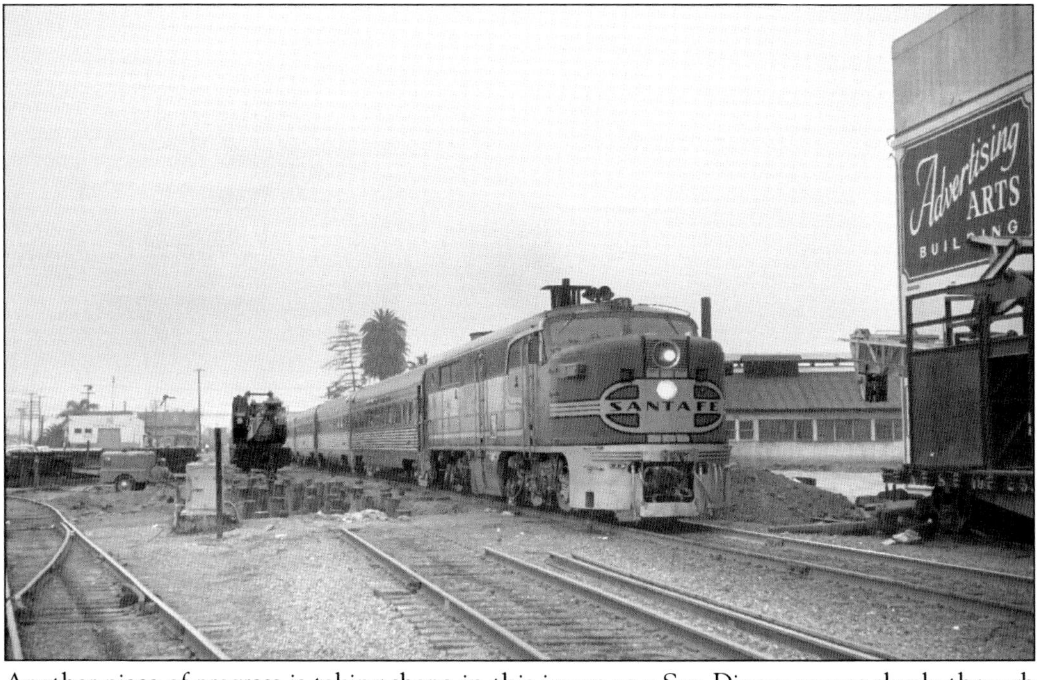

Another piece of progress is taking shape in this image as a San Diegan moves slowly through the construction site of the new First Street grade separation. The Santa Fe depot can be seen on the left in the distance. Today's train (June 20, 1964) must be light since only a single PA-4 locomotive is needed. (Photograph by and courtesy of Tom Gildersleeve.)

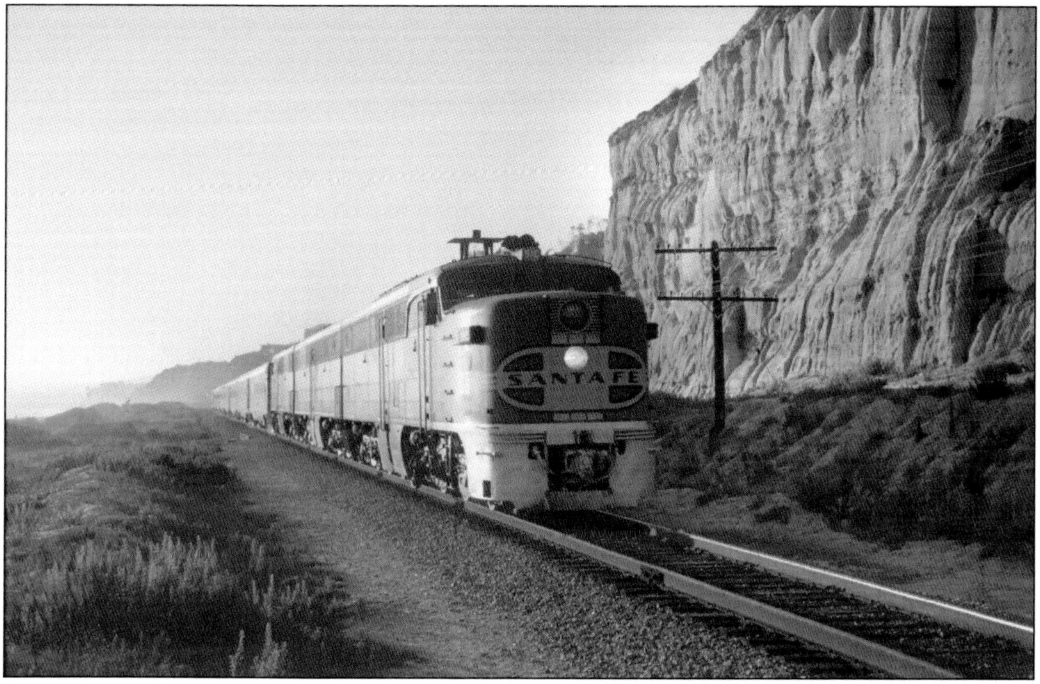

On Independence Day in 1964, a San Diegan train heads south along the coast to its final destination of San Diego. (Photograph by and courtesy of Tom Gildersleeve.)

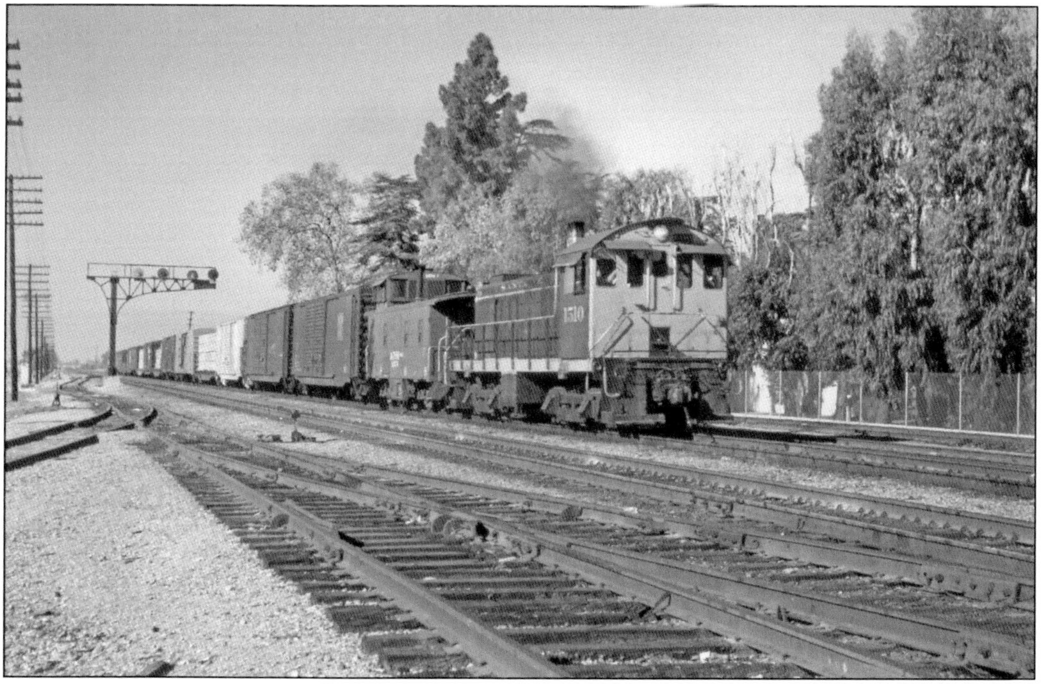

In this 1965 view, a Santa Fe S-4 Alco locomotive is leading a Fullerton switch back to the Fullerton depot. This locomotive was part of a group delivered to the Santa Fe Railway in 1952. Note that the black-and-white zebra paint scheme has been replaced with blue and yellow. (Courtesy of the author.)

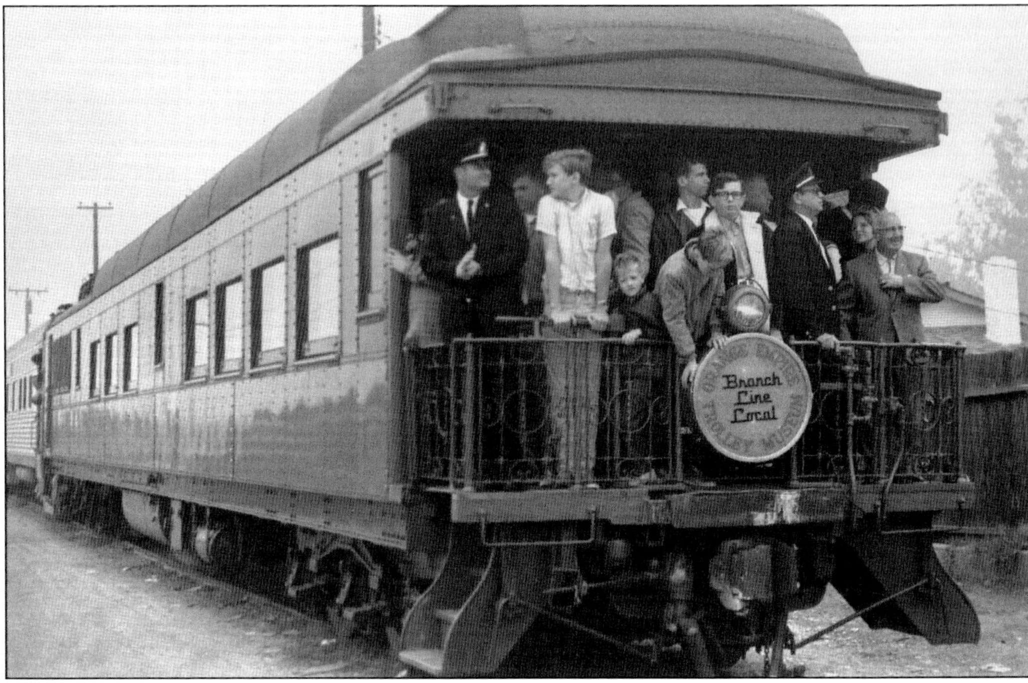

The date is November 5, 1966, and the Orange Empire Trolley Museum has arranged a rare mileage train excursion on board the *Branch Line Local.* This train was operated by the Santa Fe Railway and is near the railroad siding of Tustin. Citrus packinghouses were located at this spot, which is just southeast of Irvine Boulevard and Newport Avenue, where Ruby's is now located. The young man with glasses standing on the deck of the observation car is Cliff Prather. (Courtesy of the Tustin Area Historical Society.)

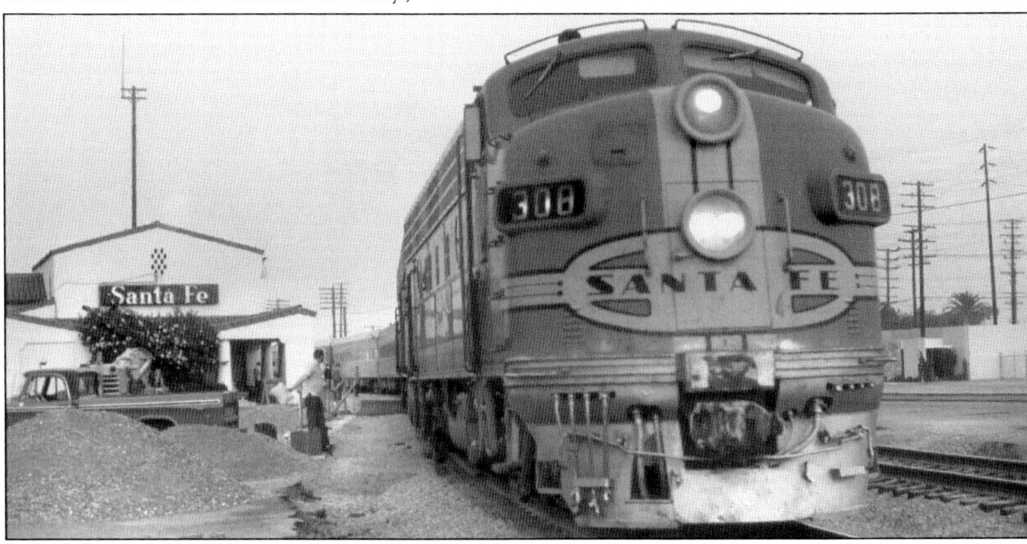

In 1969, a grade separation of Santa Fe tracks was built in Fullerton. Because the business of the railroads is 24 hours per day, a temporary shoofly track was laid across the depot parking lot. Here a northbound San Diegan carefully navigates the temporary track. While most drivers and the railroads welcome grade separations, true train fans lament this kind of progress. (Photograph by and courtesy of Cliff Prather.)

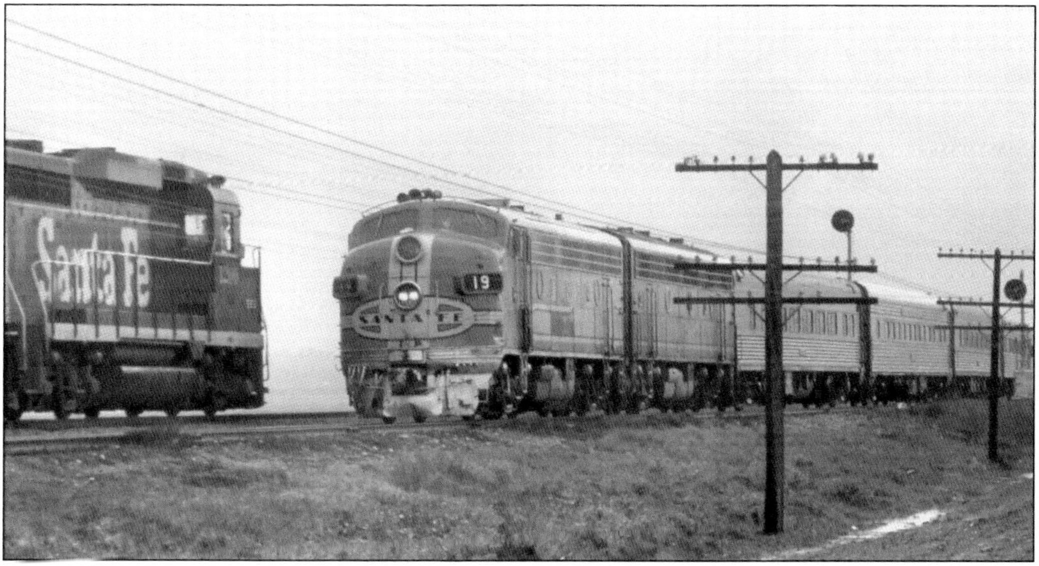

A mainline meet between two Santa Fe trains is seen here in March 1970. Train No. 75 is to arrive at Santa Ana at 1:25 p.m. to drop off and pick up passengers. The Santa Fe freight is bound for San Diego and is led by GP-30 No. 1200. This meet was at the new Irvine station, which was located next to Edinger Avenue just north of Marine Corps Air Station (MCAS) Santa Ana. (Photograph by and courtesy of Cliff Prather.)

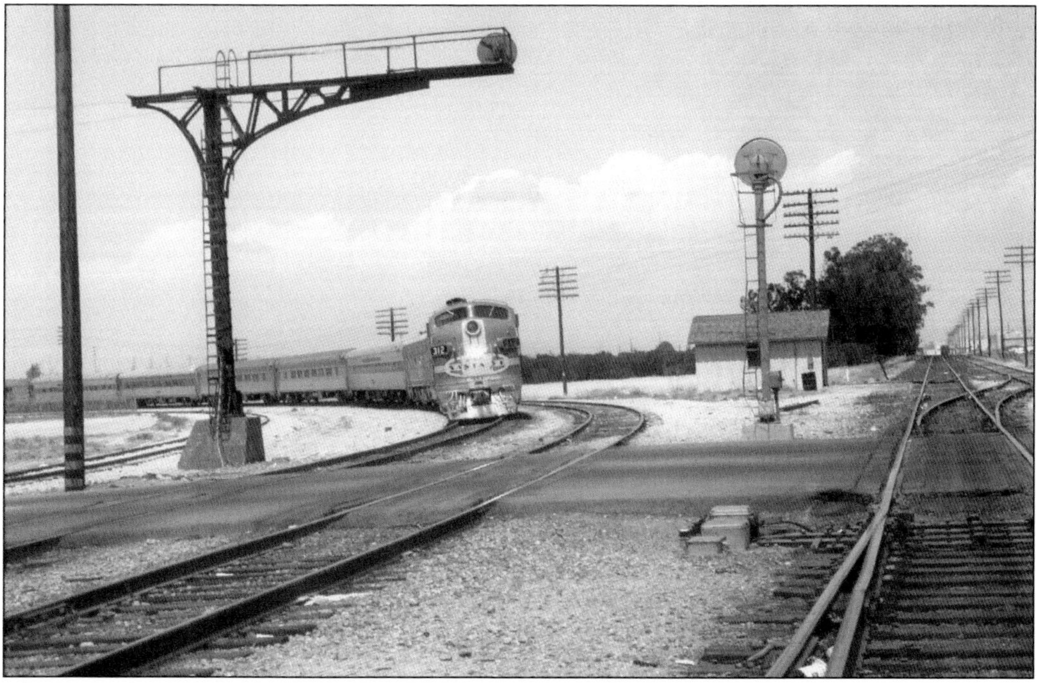

The City of Orange was the junction point of the Santa Fe's Fourth District mainline and the Olive District. In this April 1970 scene looking north, a southbound San Diegan rounds the curve just before crossing Walnut Street. This train entered the Fourth District at Fullerton. The track to the right is the Olive District, which junctions with the Santa Fe Third District in Atwood after running along Orange-Olive Road. (Photograph by and courtesy of Cliff Prather.)

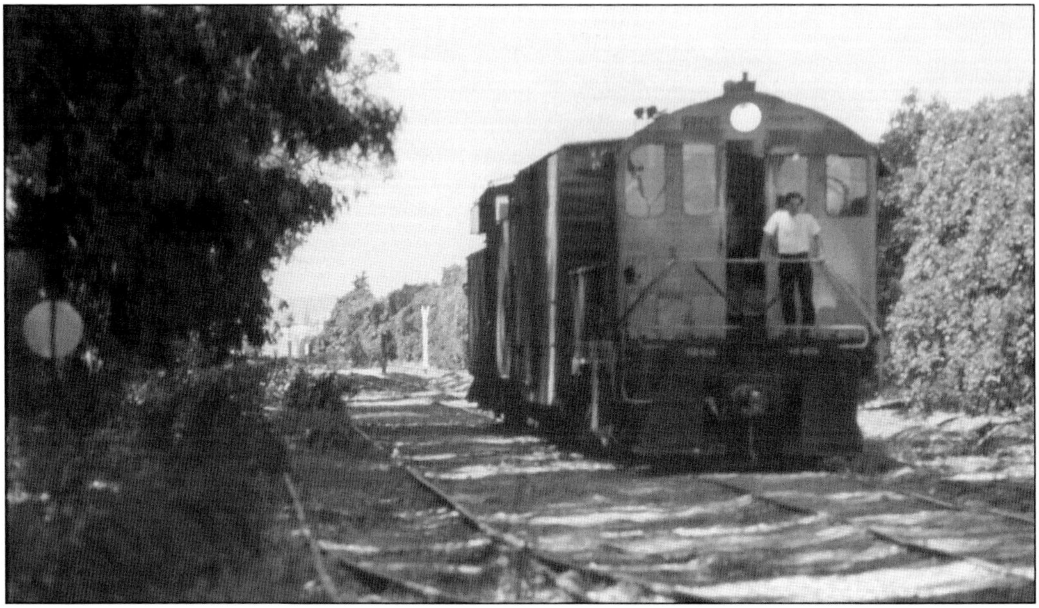

Santa Fe was the leading originator of citrus freight in Orange County. Here a Santa Fe Alco switcher leads on a refrigerator car and a caboose at Frances on June 28, 1970. This track, part of what was known as the Irvine Spur, meandered from the Fourth District main line near MCAS Santa Ana (Tustin) and traveled through the fertile citrus belt of the Irvine Ranch with sidings at Browning, Frances, and Kathryn. Another segment of this spur reached packinghouses in Tustin near Irvine Boulevard and Newport Avenue. (Photograph by and courtesy of Cliff Prather.)

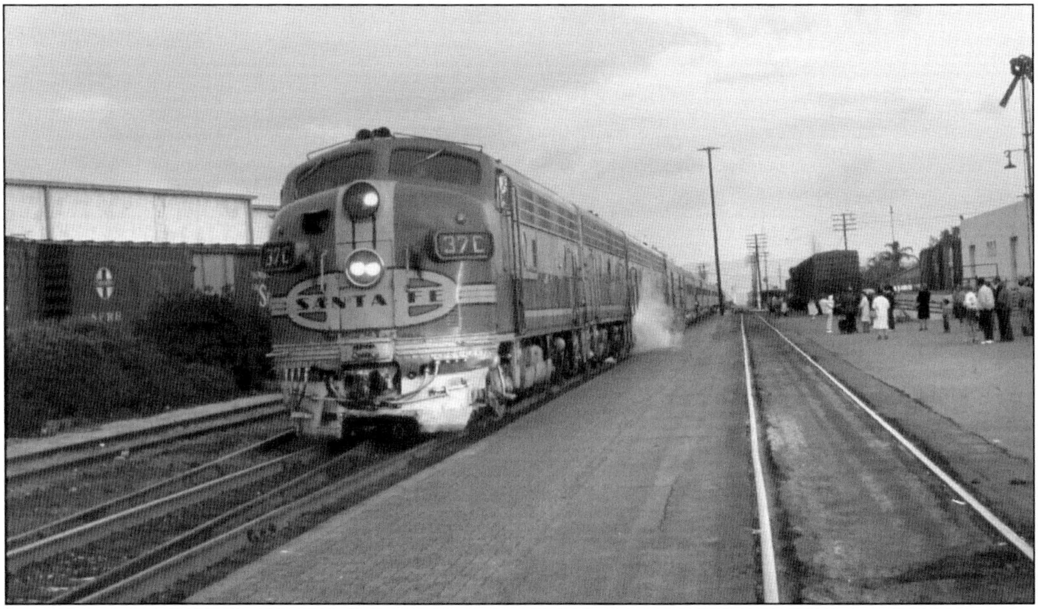

On April 25, 1971, the arrival of San Diegan train No. 77 in Santa Ana looked much the same as it had for the past 25 years. In just five days, passenger service operated by the Santa Fe Railway would end, and Amtrak would take over on May 1, 1971. The freight car shown on the left was spotted at a loading door for the Treesweet juice factory. (Photograph by and courtesy of Cliff Prather.)

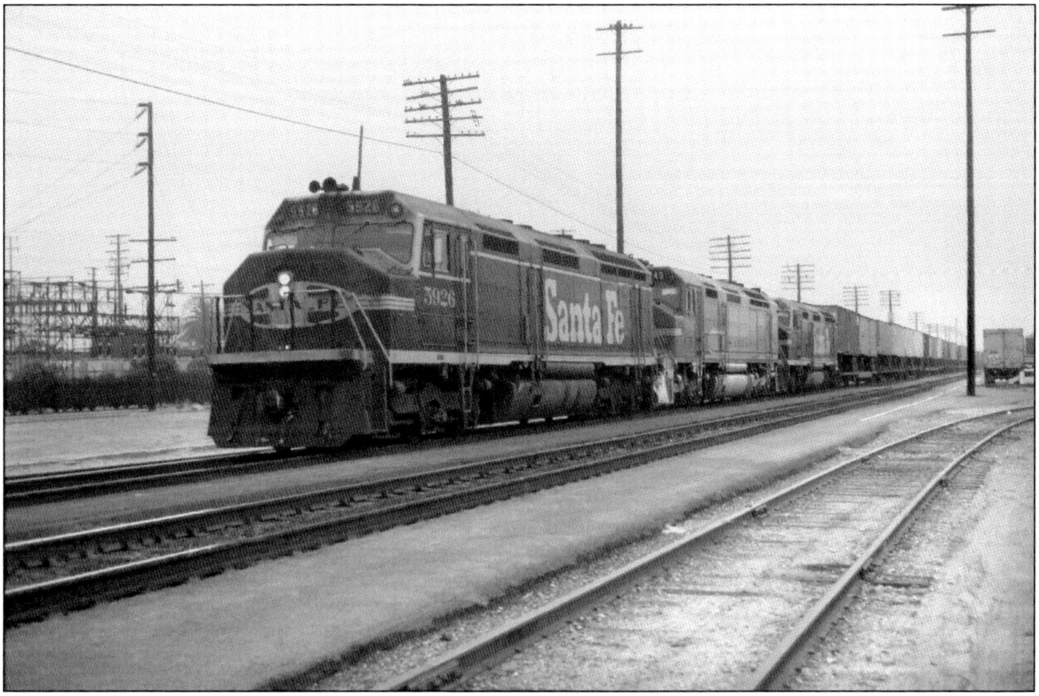

Three big F-45 engines (Nos. 5926, 5945, and 5920) have the *Super* C train in tow at Fullerton on November 24, 1972. The second locomotive still wears red and silver from its passenger service before Amtrak. (Courtesy of the author.)

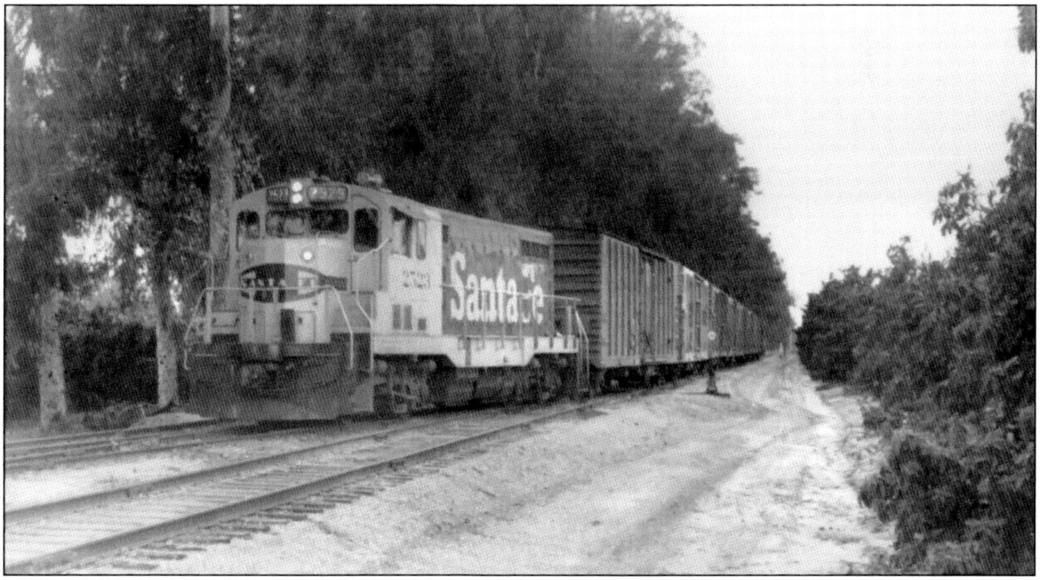

This scene can no longer be duplicated in Orange County. ATSF No. 2523 is approaching the end of the Kathryn Spur. Today's group of refrigerator cars is rather long. The reefers, as refrigerated cars were known, are mechanical. Prior to mechanical cars, reefers had bunkers at either end of the car and were loaded with large blocks of ice. These freight cars were painted orange; the old iced reefers advertised Santa Fe–named passengers trains. (Photograph by and courtesy of Cliff Prather.)

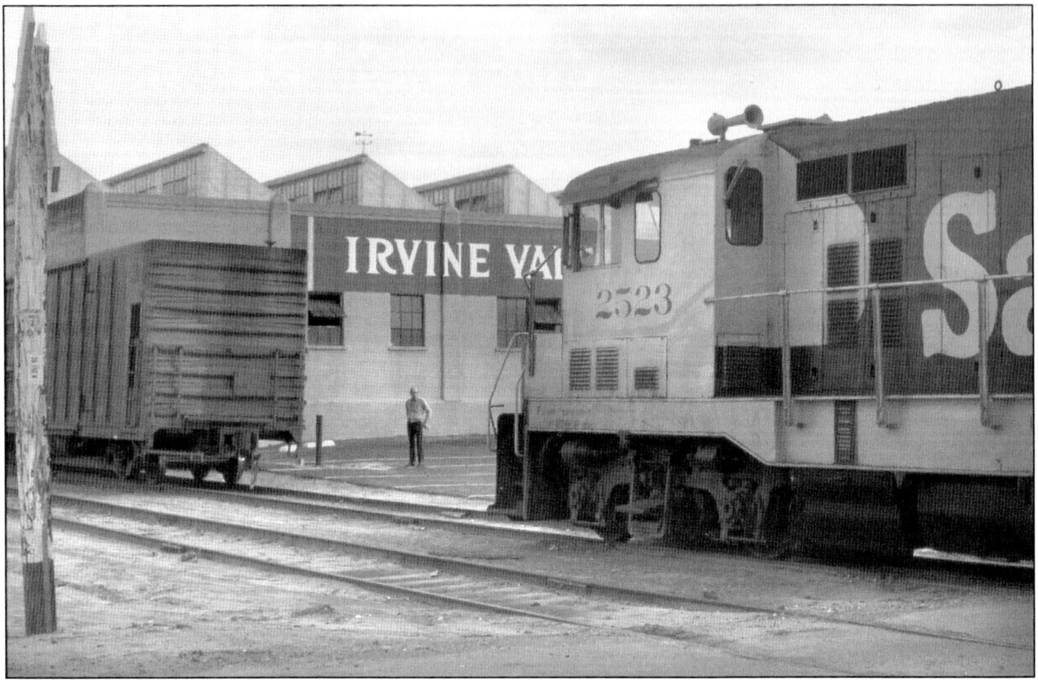

The Irvine Valencia packinghouse was located at the end of the Kathryn Spur on the Irvine Ranch. CF 7 No. 2523 is switching cars before returning to Santa Ana. (Photograph by and courtesy of Cliff Prather.)

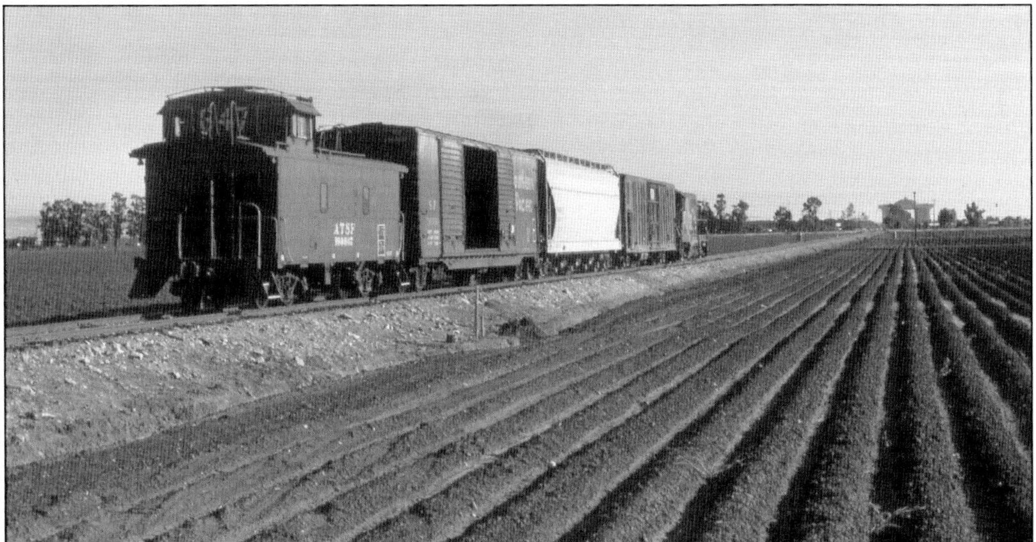

An interesting scene from the 1960s shows a Santa Fe local with three freight cars and a caboose heading south on the Kathryn Spur. The flat, well-drained characteristics of this land made the shift from agriculture to either residential or commercial use especially attractive. As time progressed, orchards were often replaced by row crops. Looming in the distance is one of two giant hangars at Marine Corps Air Station in Santa Ana; the base would be renamed Tustin following that city's successful annexation of the base in 1973. (Photograph by and courtesy of Cliff Prather.)

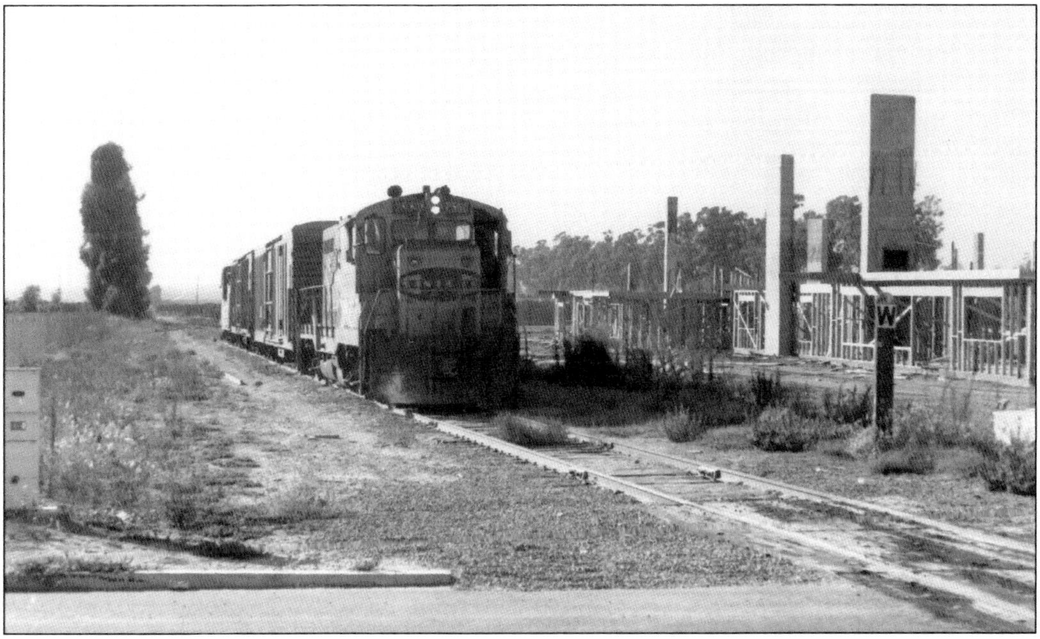

One could not find a much better illustration of the changes in Orange County from the 1960s and 1970s than this shot on the Irvine Ranch. Santa Fe No. 2550 is heading back to the mainline along the Kathryn Spur. Orange trees are rapidly giving way to new homes. (Photograph by and courtesy of Cliff Prather.)

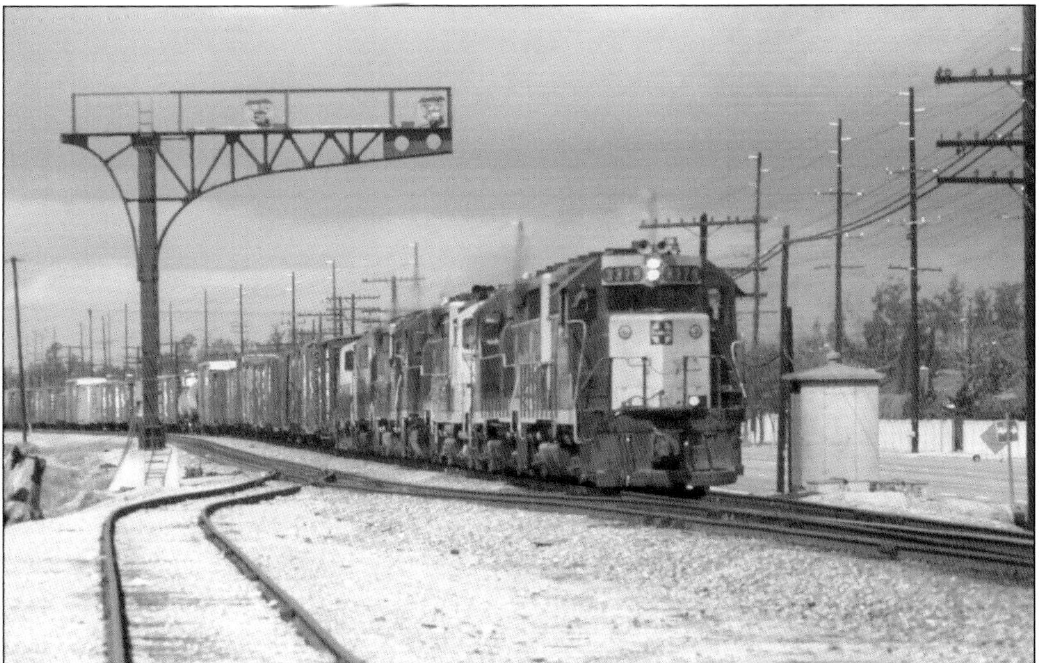

Here is some mainline freight action as Extra 3379 east and five other locomotives roll east toward San Bernardino at Atwood on March 18, 1979. The Santa Fe's Third District and Olive District met at this point. (Photograph by and courtesy of Cliff Prather.)

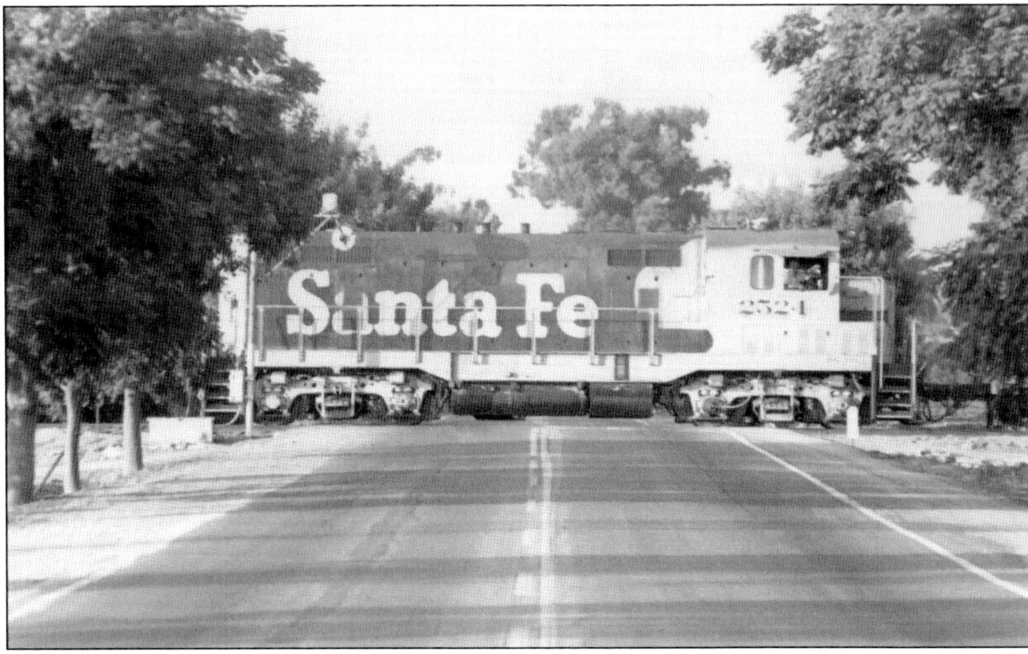

On a tranquil afternoon on August 14, 1979, the quiet is broken by the "kling-klang" of the wigwag signal and Santa Fe CF-7 No. 2524 heading off the Kathryn Spur. This location has been paved over by the twin Irvine and Tustin Marketplace Shopping Centers along Jamboree Boulevard north of the Santa Ana Freeway. (Photograph by and courtesy of Cliff Prather.)

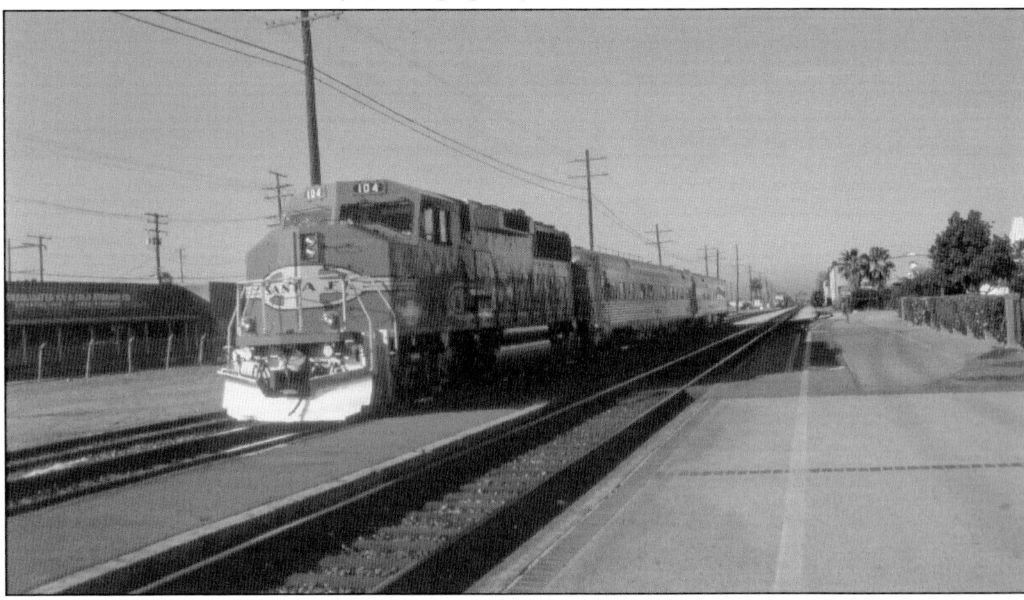

It is November 25, 1991, and red and silver GP 60 No. 104 is leading a special train into Fullerton that originated in Los Angeles. This train, with two coaches, will run east on Santa Fe's Third District to San Bernardino and then return to Los Angles via the Second District through Pasadena. Passengers on this special train received information concerning the planned sale of Santa Fe trackage to regional transportation agencies for commuter rail service. (Photograph by and courtesy of the author.)

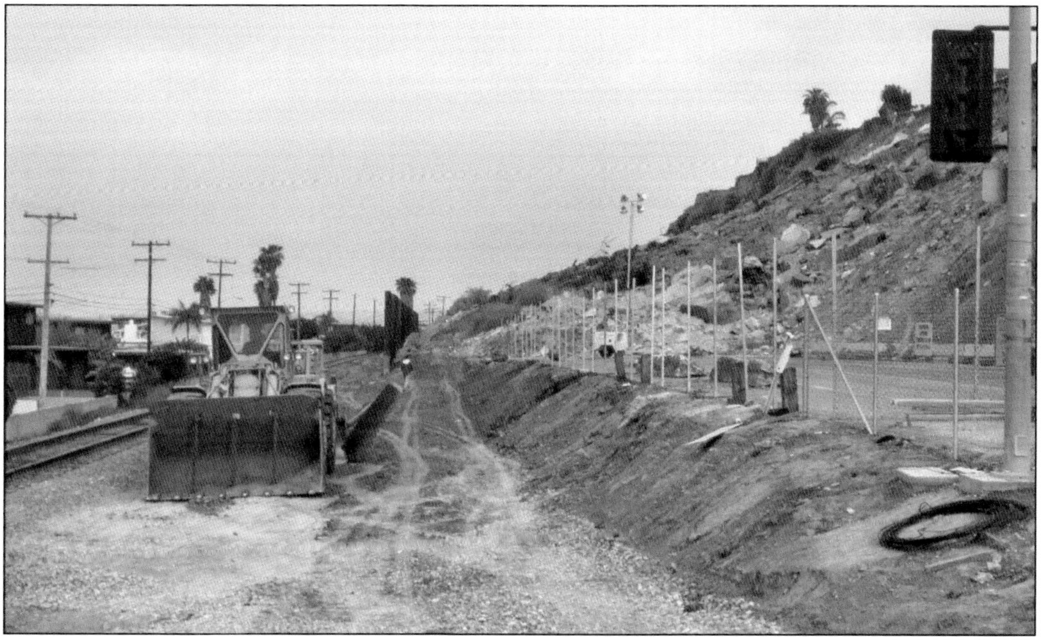

The railroads often must battle nature. The Santa Fe's rail line near Dana Point and San Clemente is confined to a relatively narrow right-of-way. Here crews are clearing a landslide off the rails at Poche. The roadway to the right is still covered with mud and rocks on March 20, 1993. (Photograph by and courtesy of Cliff Prather.)

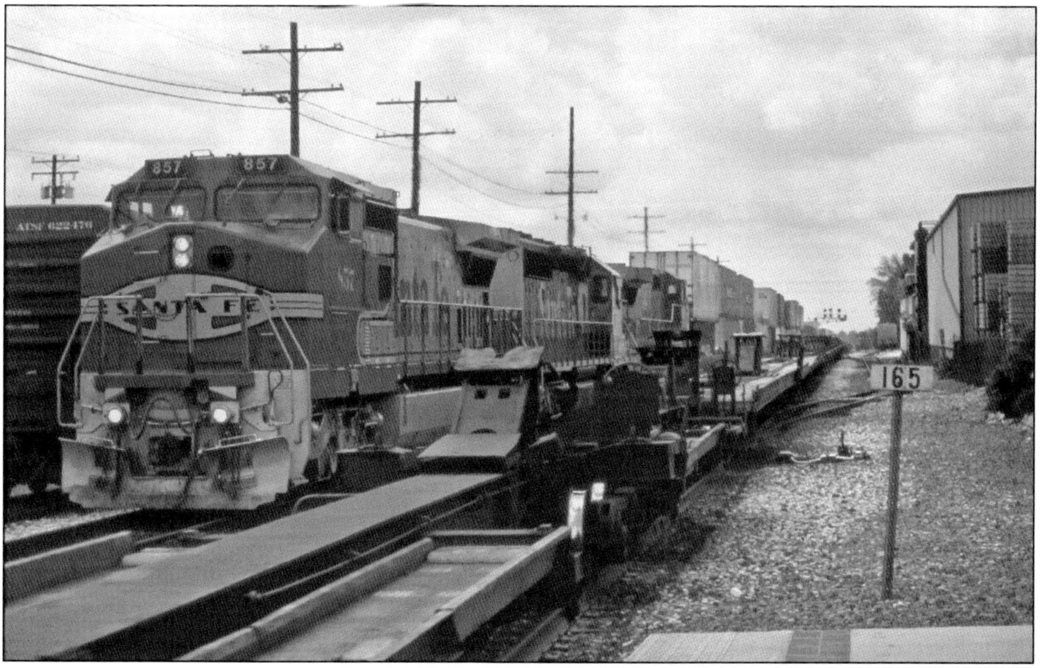

Two Santa Fe trains have met at track speed just west of the Fullerton station on April 9, 1994. ATSF No. 857 is leading an eastbound piggyback train across Harbor Boulevard. The other train is a "bare table" train shifting unloaded intermodal cars to a location where they will be loaded for the next trip. (Photograph by and courtesy of the author.)

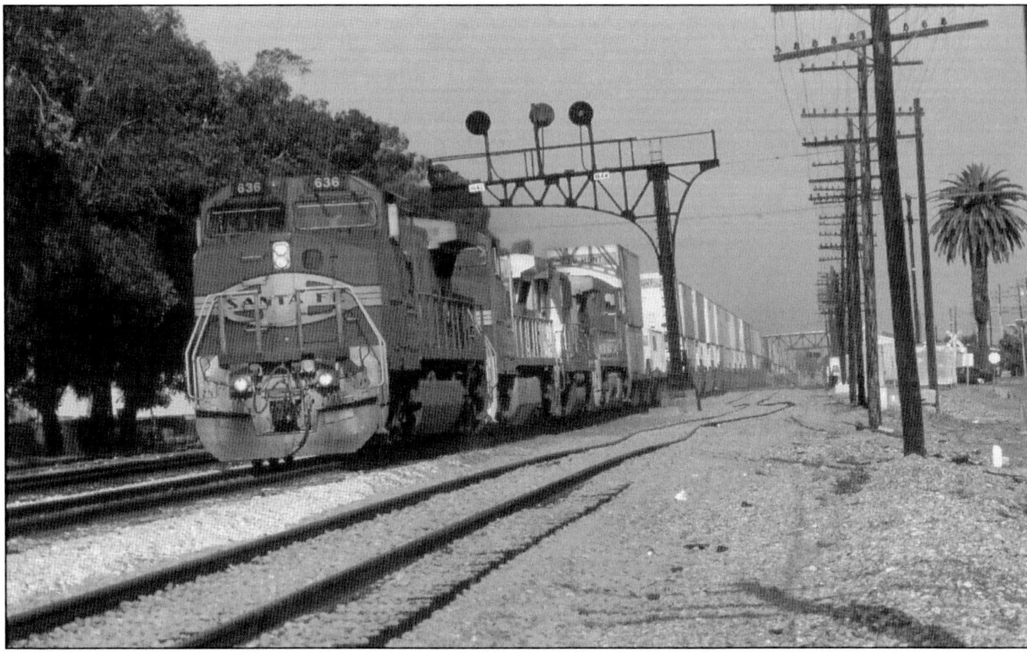

ATSF No. 638 leads two other big GE units west through Fullerton on March 1, 1995. This train consists entirely of stacked containers as far as the eye can see. The new pedestrian crossing at the Fullerton depot can be seen in the distance, along with the yet to be completed third main track in the foreground. (Photograph by and courtesy of the author.)

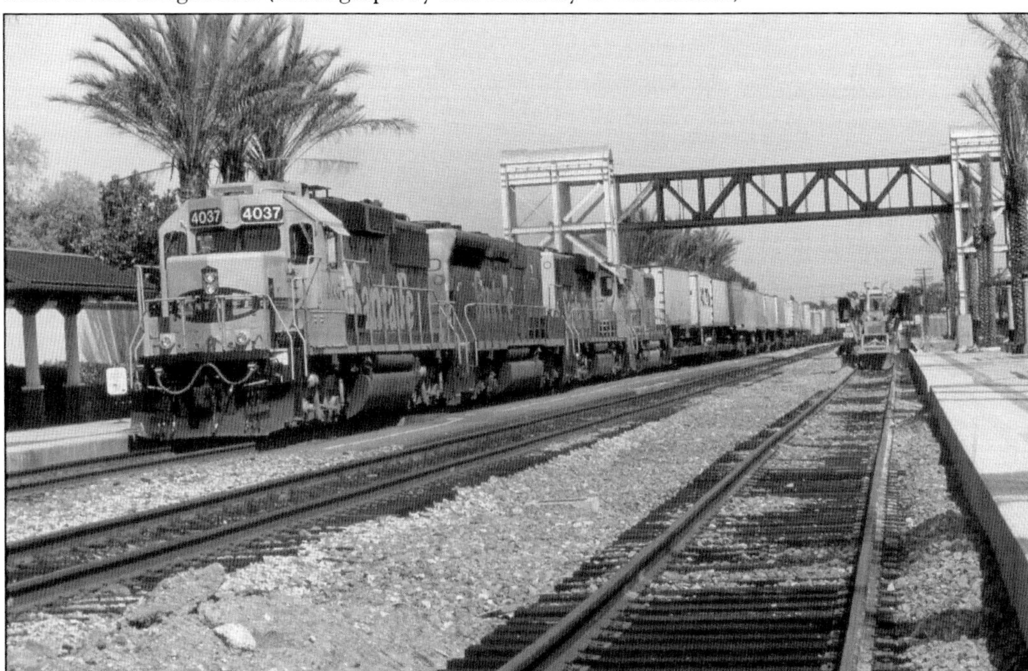

Extra 4037 west leads three other locomotives (including an SD 45 B unit) as it hustles through Fullerton with hot piggyback traffic. The ATSF No. 4037 (GP 60) was about six years old when this photograph was shot on March 1, 1995. (Photograph by and courtesy of the author.)

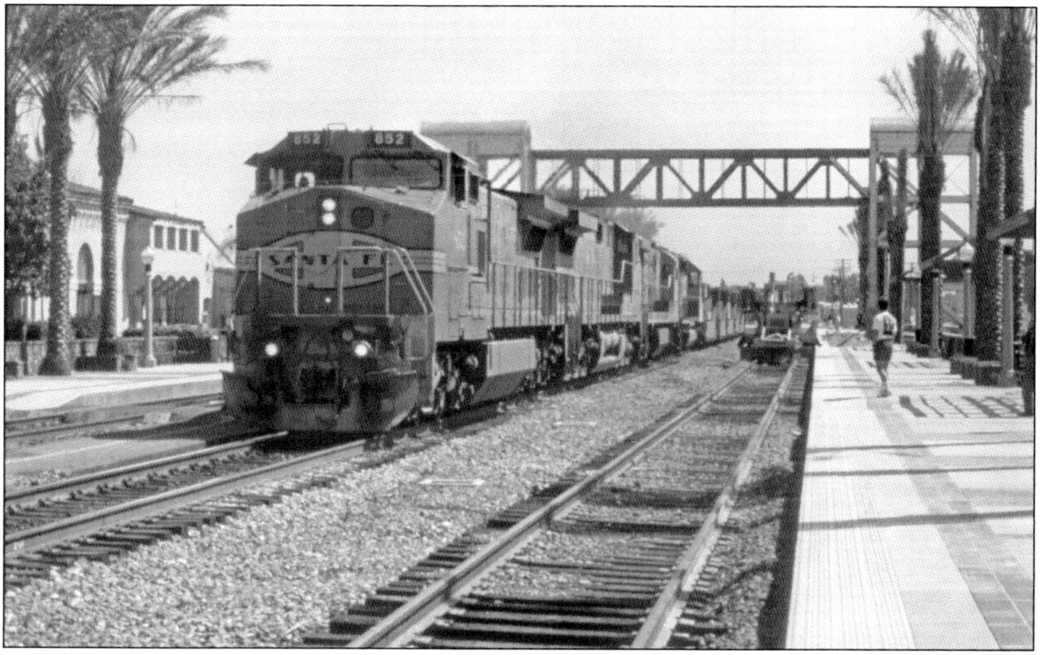

Santa Fe No. 852 leads three other locomotives as this train picks up speed heading toward Los Angeles on April 4, 1995. Fullerton has become the preferred location to watch trains in Orange County because of the frequency of BNSF, Amtrak, and Metrolink trains. (Photograph by and courtesy of the author.)

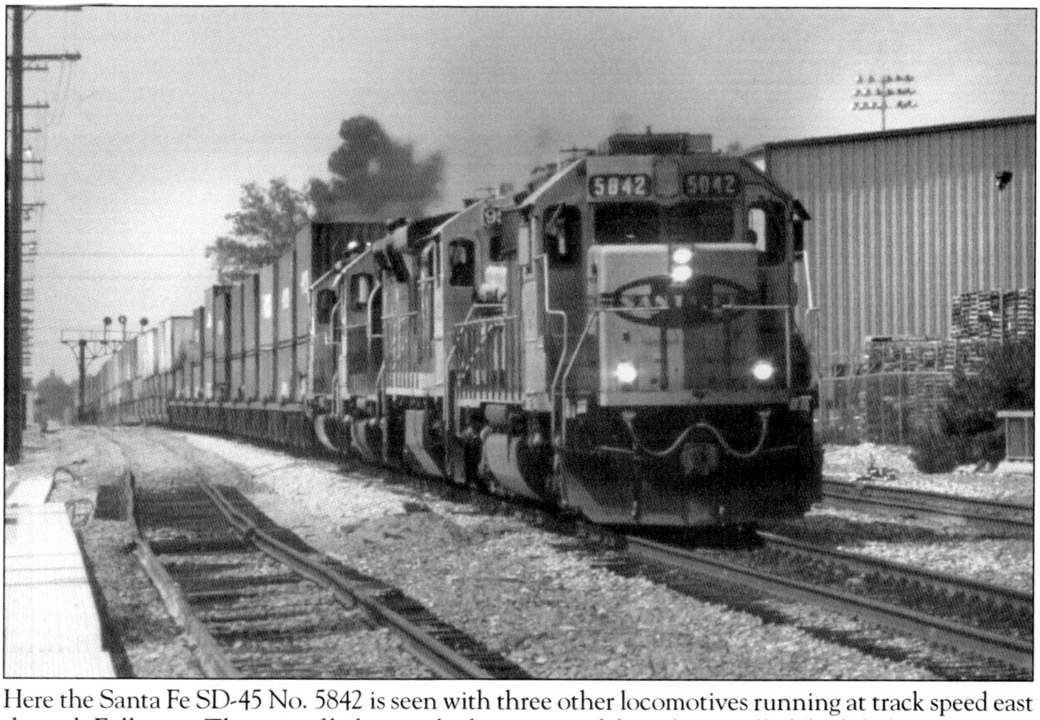

Here the Santa Fe SD-45 No. 5842 is seen with three other locomotives running at track speed east through Fullerton. The pair of lights on the lower part of the cab are called ditch lights. The third main track is still under construction on the left. (Photograph by and courtesy of the author.)

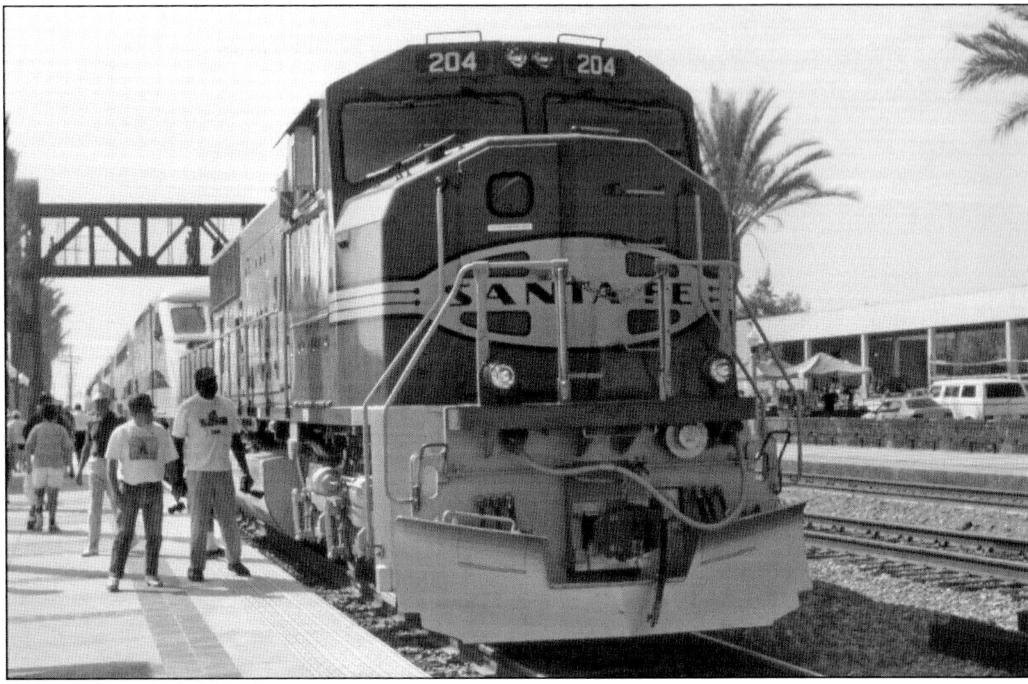

Santa Fe No. 204 stands on display along with Metrolink equipment on September 17, 1995, at Fullerton. This 4,300 horsepower SD-75 M, built by General Motors, was among the last locomotives purchased by the Atchison, Topeka, and Santa Fe Railway. It was painted in the iconic red-and-silver paint scheme. The merger with Burlington Northern would occur in 1996. (Photograph by and courtesy of the author.)

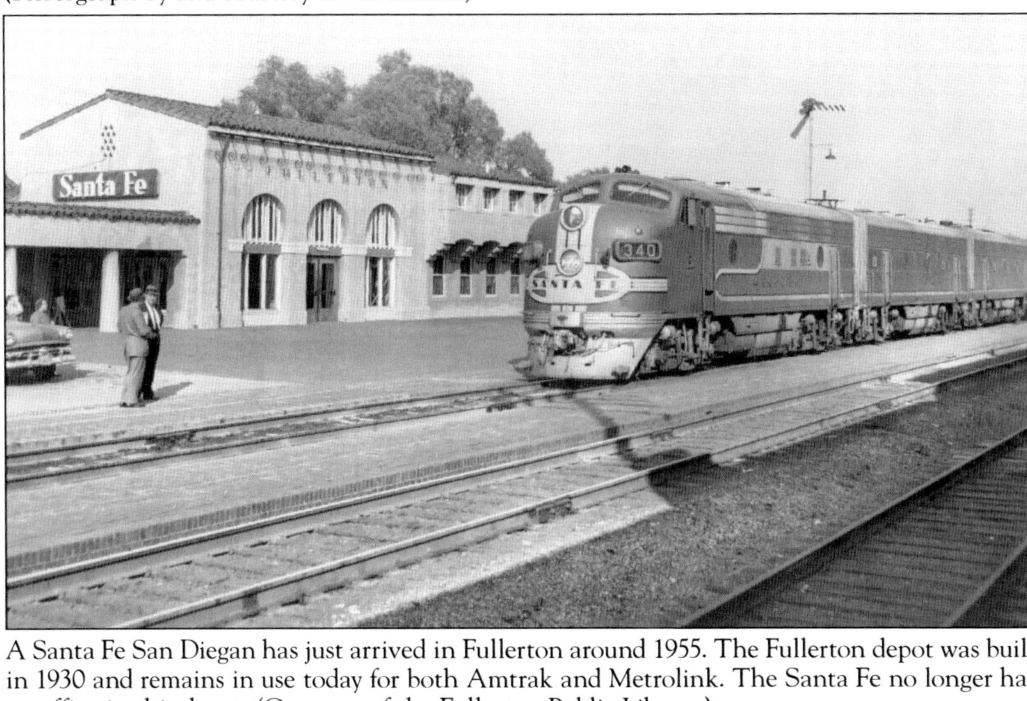

A Santa Fe San Diegan has just arrived in Fullerton around 1955. The Fullerton depot was built in 1930 and remains in use today for both Amtrak and Metrolink. The Santa Fe no longer has an office in this depot. (Courtesy of the Fullerton Public Library.)

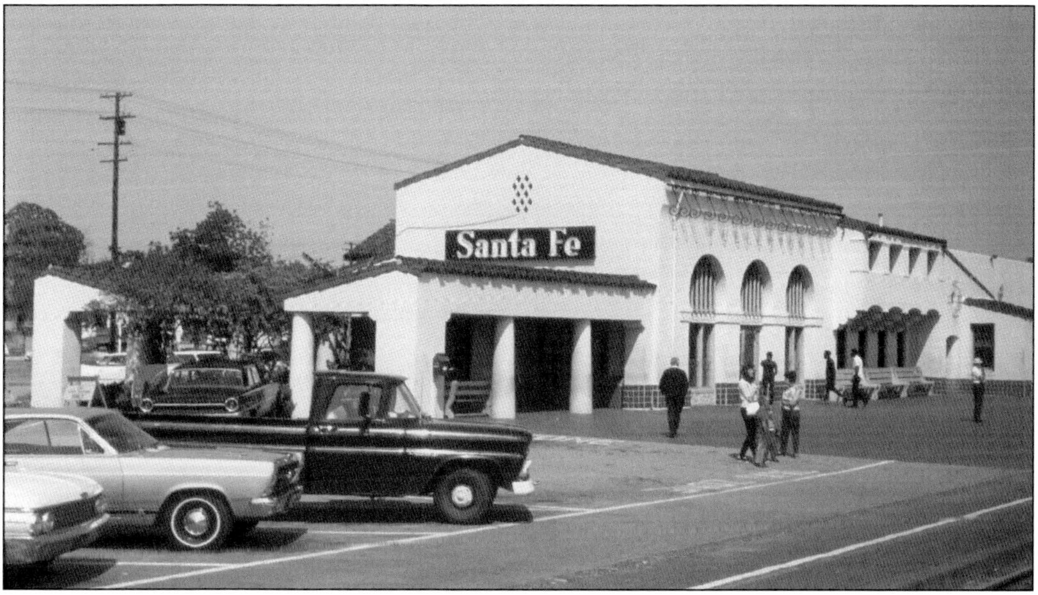

This is the Santa Fe's Fullerton depot as it appeared in 1967. The new railroad grade separation at Harbor Boulevard will use these parking spaces during construction. This depot was dedicated in 1930 and stands 100 feet east of the original depot's location. (Courtesy of the author.)

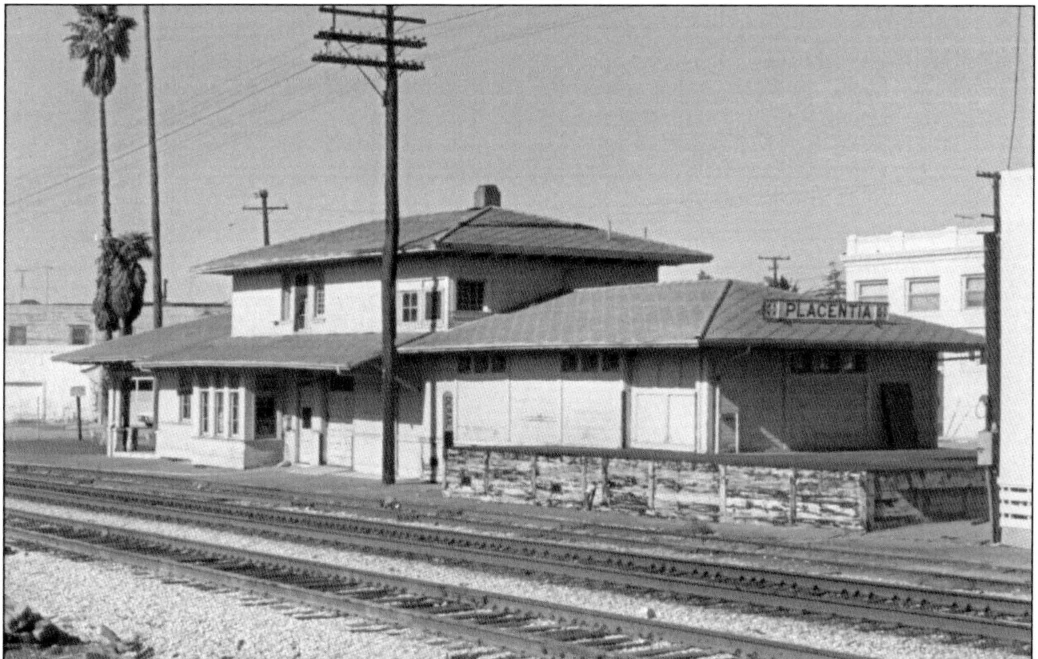

Here is the Placentia depot as it appeared on January 3, 1971. This depot was built in 1910 when the Placentia cut off was built by the Santa Fe to directly connect Fullerton and Atwood, thus closing a gap in what became the railroad's Third District. This depot was built to a standard plan used by the Santa Fe for various depots in the California Central Valley, including Lone Star, Reedley, Riverbank, Shafter, and Wasco, to name a few. Of these, only Lone Star and Shafter remain. (Courtesy of the author.)

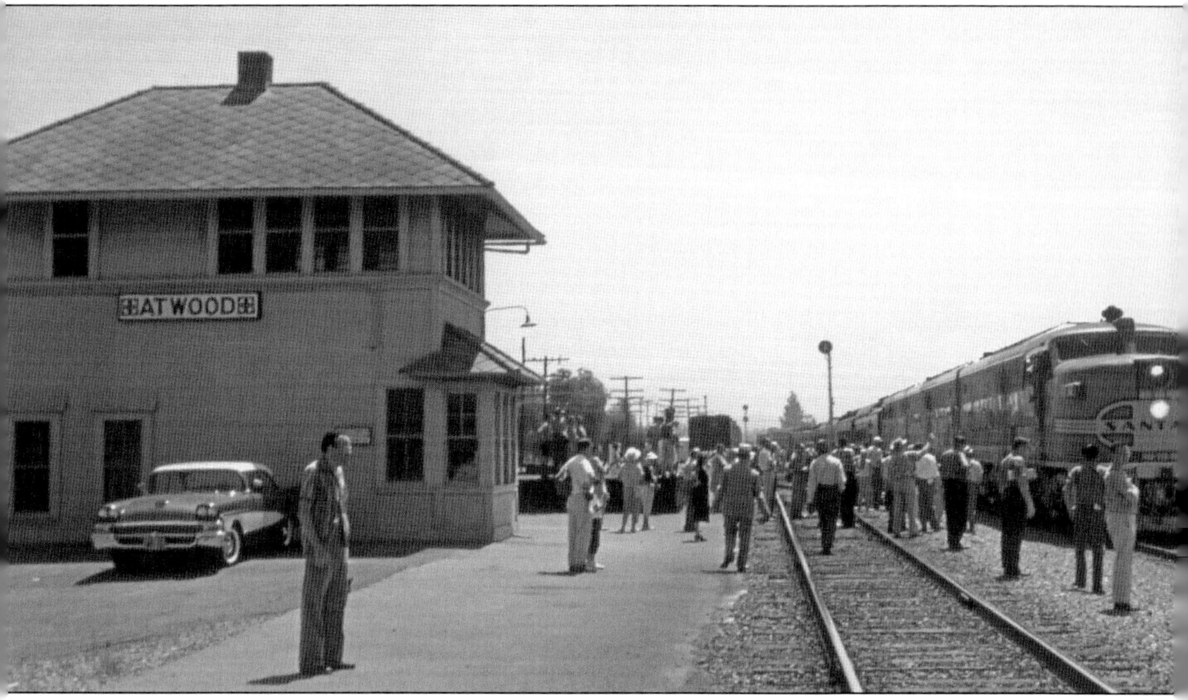

The Atwood depot's construction coincided with that of the Placentia cut off. Trains going down the Olive District diverted at this point from Santa Fe's Third District main line. The depot was closed in 1960 and was removed the following year. Prior to 1919, this location was known as Richfield, and the Olinda Spur traveled 4 miles north through oil fields and orange orchards; this spur was abandoned in 1945. On this day, sometime around 1959, an excursion train has stopped to take a look around at Atwood. (Courtesy of the author.)

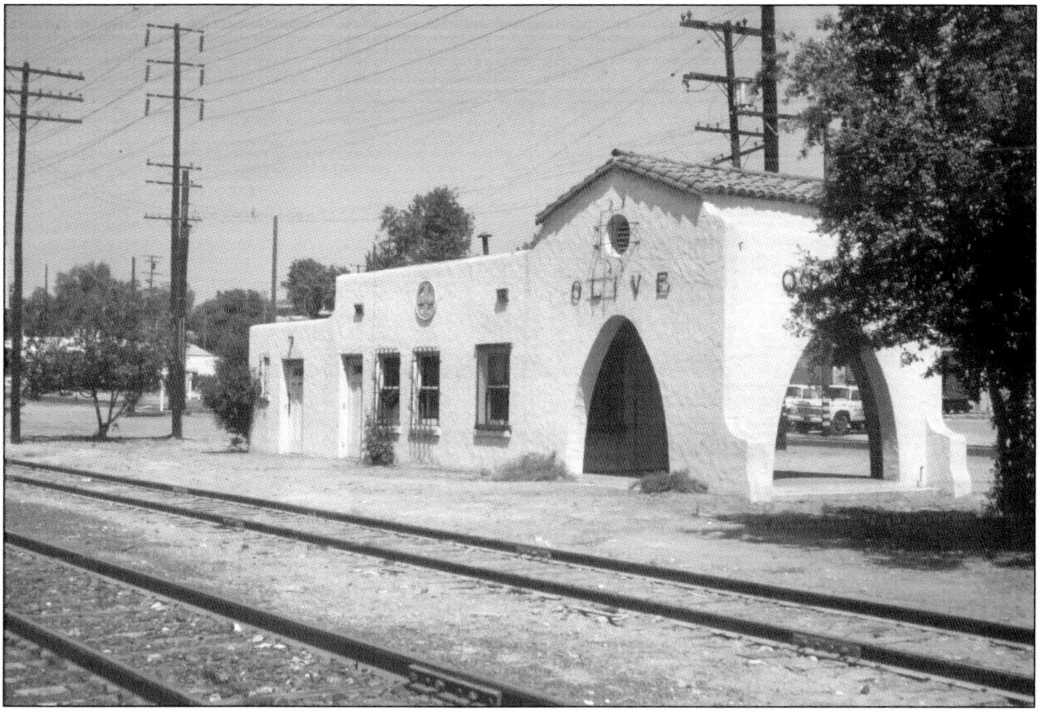

Santa Fe's depot in Olive was built in 1929 and was torn down in 1964. It stood on Santa Fe's Olive District between Atwood and Orange. (Courtesy of the author.)

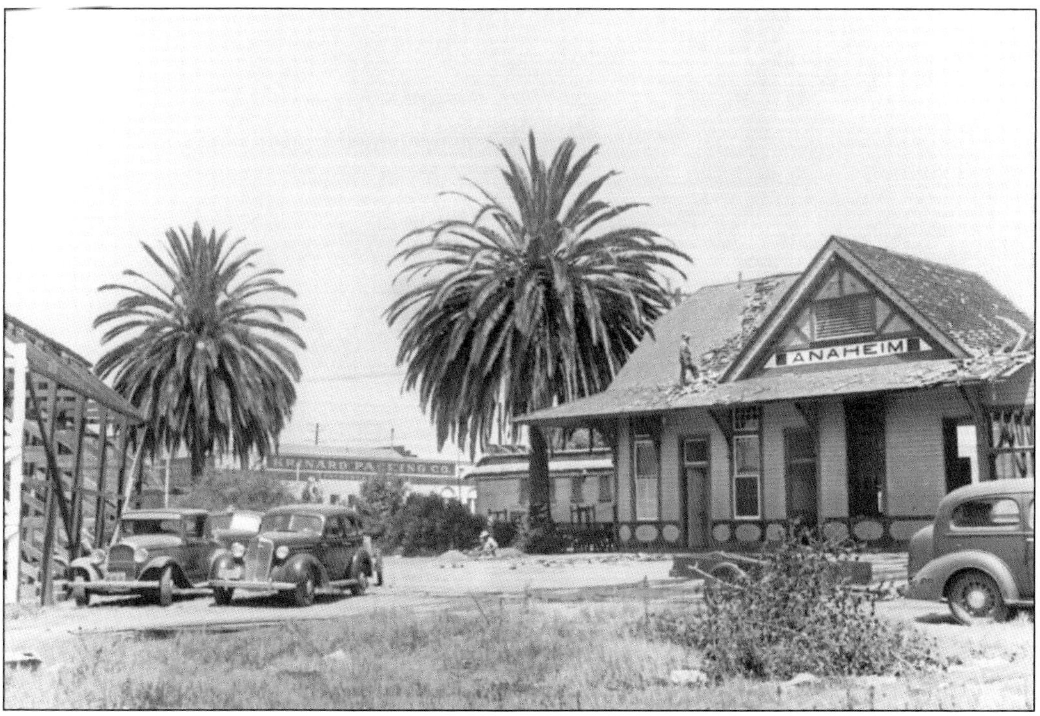

The original Santa Fe depot in Anaheim is in the process of being torn down. A new station would be built at this location that same year, 1941. (Courtesy of the Orange County Archives.)

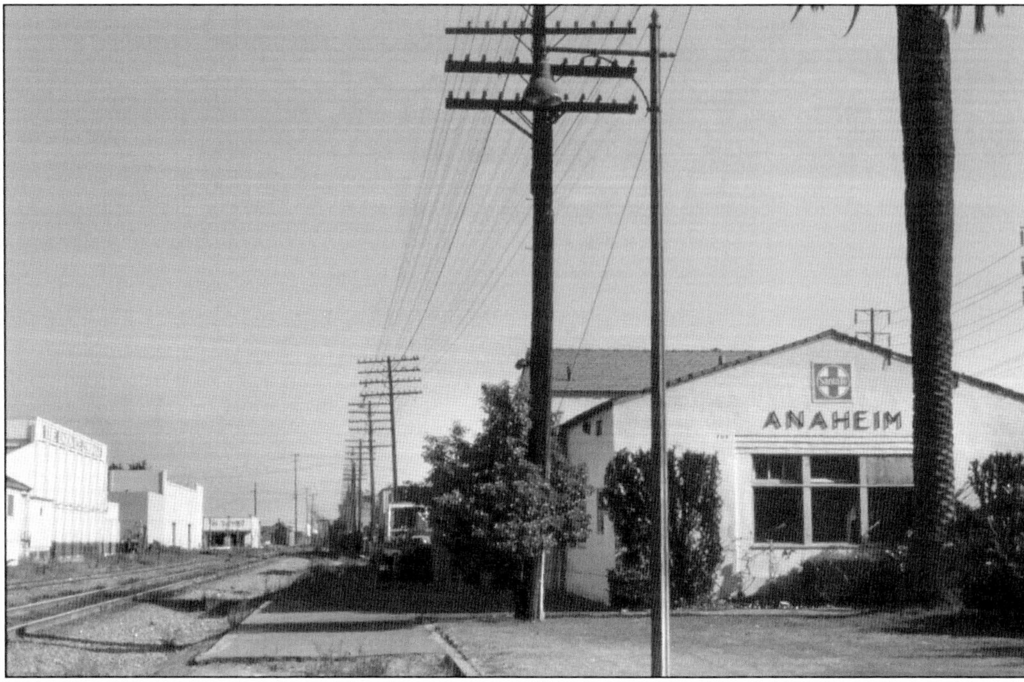

It is 1973, and neither passenger nor freight service is handled at this depot. This depot replaced the original Santa Fe depot in 1941. In an unusual twist, Union Pacific's Anaheim depot was relocated to this Lincoln Avenue site. The Santa Fe depot was demolished in June 1987. (Courtesy of the author.)

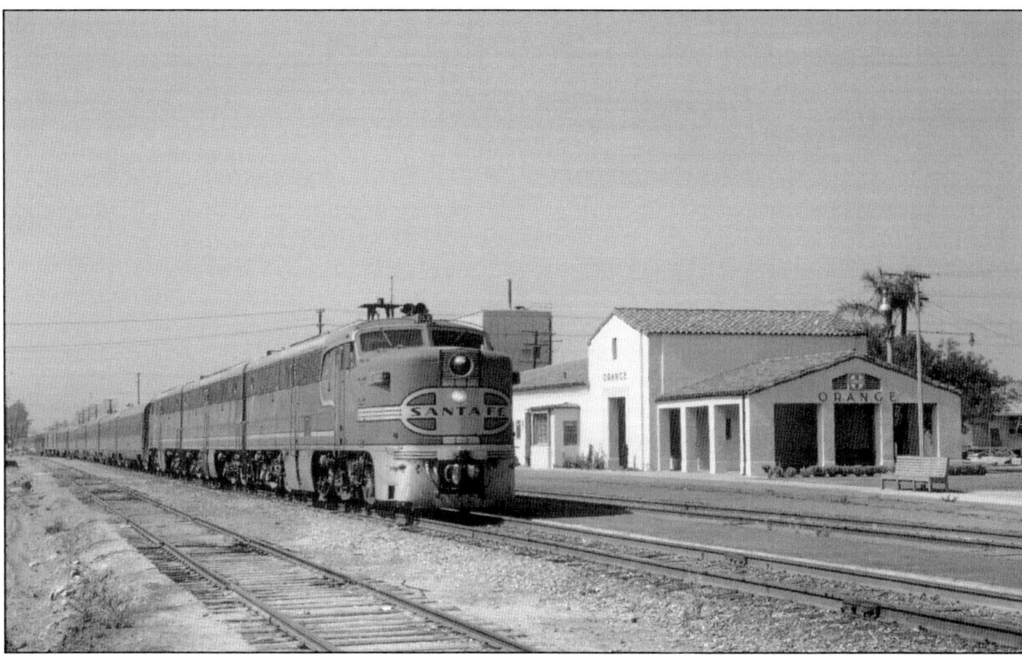

An eastbound San Diegan (by timetable) slips past the Orange Santa Fe depot on June 14, 1964, led by three PA units. The depot was purchased by the City of Orange and has been used by two different restaurants in recent years. (Photograph by and courtesy of Tom Gildersleeve.)

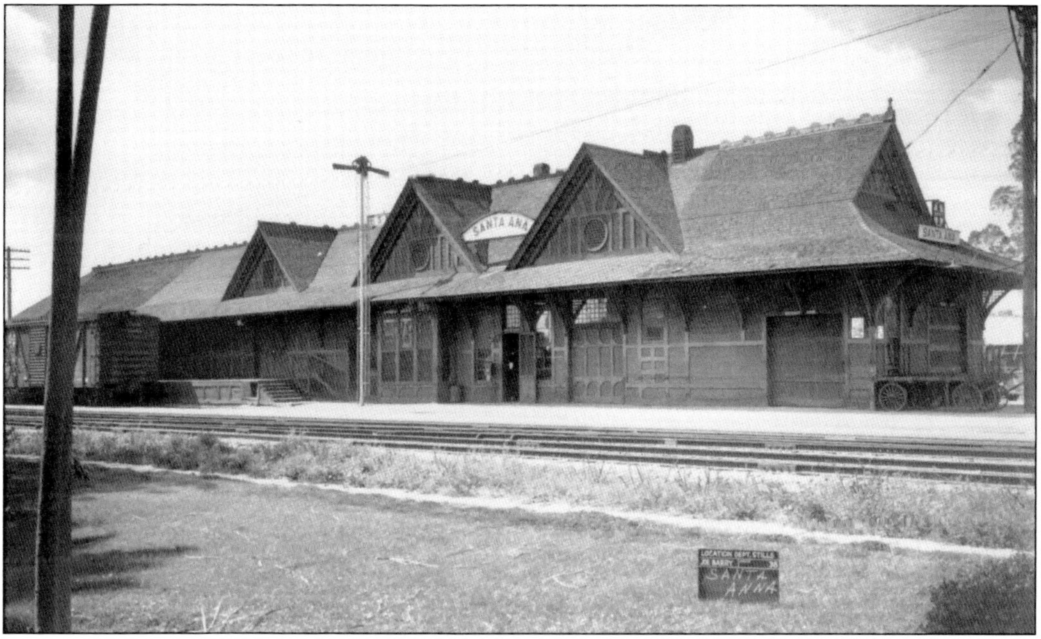

This is an unusual shot of Santa Ana's Santa Fe depot. This depot, built in 1887, was similar to others constructed on the line to San Diego but differed by having three decorative gables rather than the typical one. Please note the identifying marker in the right foreground for location department stills. (Courtesy of the author.)

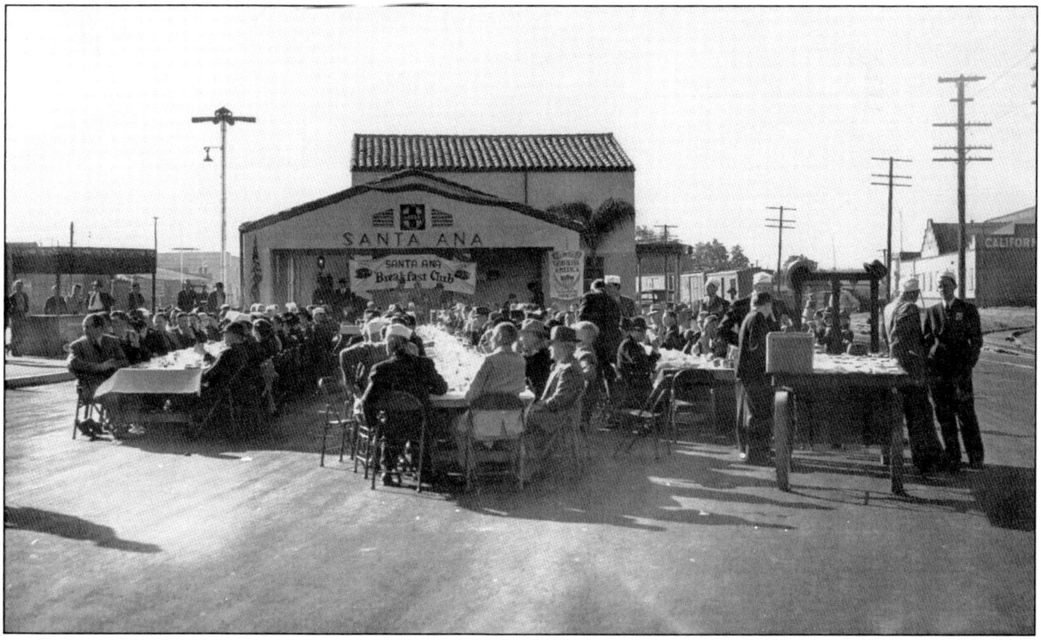

The happy occasion in May 1939 is the dedication of the new Santa Fe depot; this structure replaced the original depot built in 1887 at this location. The Santa Ana Breakfast Club has convened to mark the celebration. Note at this time that the depot had an open porch on its north end. Two additions were made in later years to provide office space to house freight business. (Courtesy of Tom Lutz.)

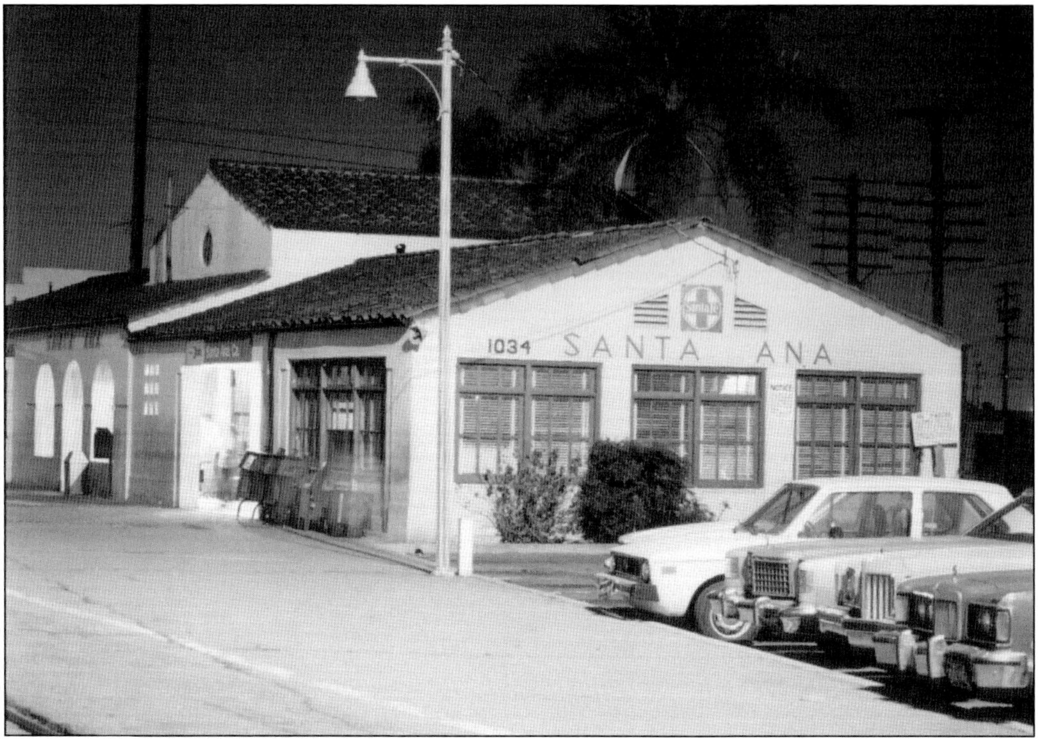

This is the Santa Ana Santa Fe depot during its final year of service. This nighttime shot was taken on March 4, 1985. By this date, the district freight office has moved out, and in just six months, Amtrak will relocate to the new Santa Ana depot under construction two blocks to the north. (Photograph by and courtesy of the author.)

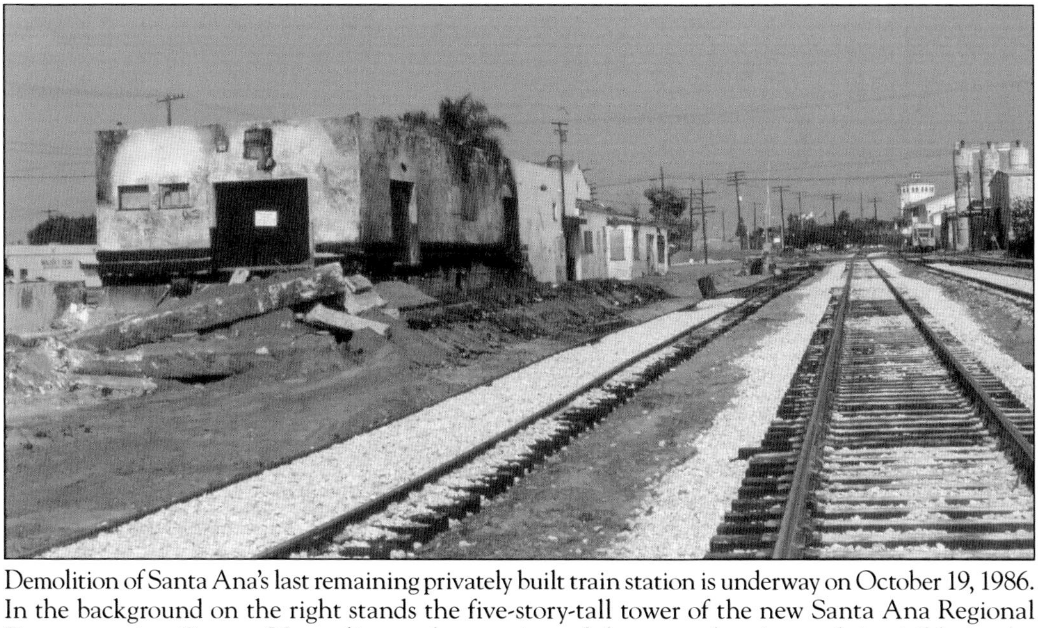

Demolition of Santa Ana's last remaining privately built train station is underway on October 19, 1986. In the background on the right stands the five-story-tall tower of the new Santa Ana Regional Transportation Center. Upgrading and extension of the second main track is visible in the foreground. (Photograph by and courtesy of the author.)

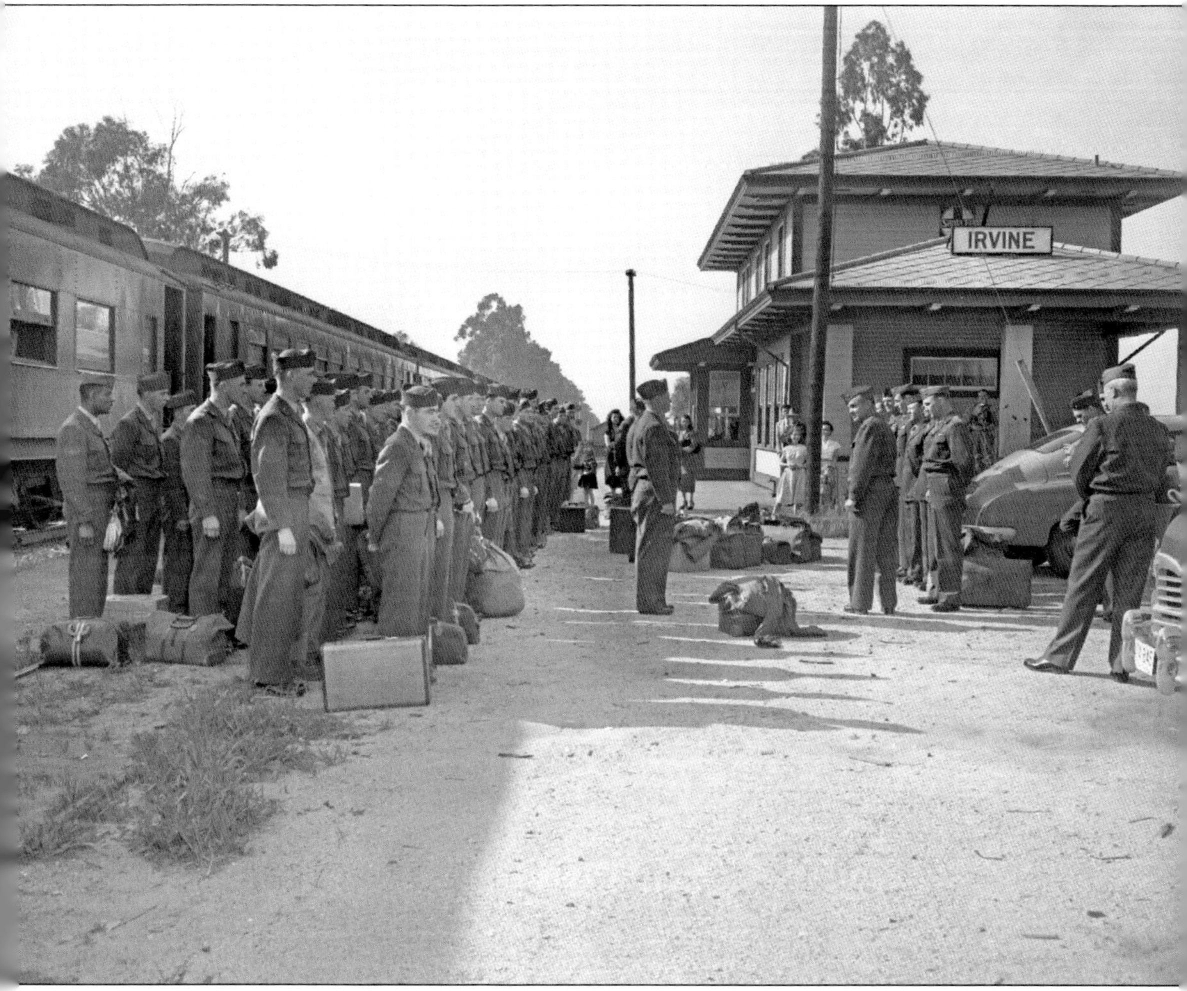

In a scene repeated many times since World War II, U.S. Marines are preparing to board a Santa Fe troop train and deploy overseas. It is 1951, and the war in Korea is underway. The Santa Fe depot was located just west of Sand Canyon Avenue. (Courtesy of the Old Courthouse Museum, Orange County Parks.)

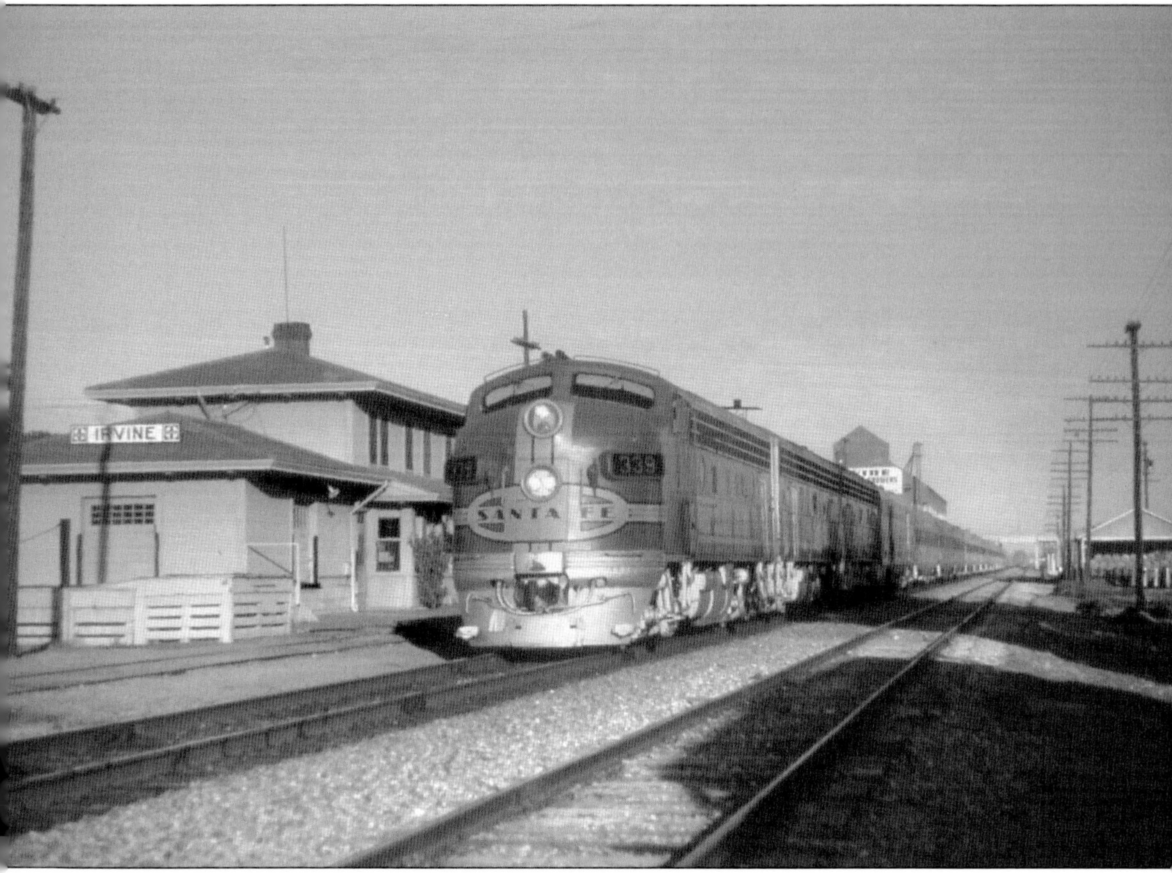

A late afternoon northbound Santa Fe San Diegan races past the Irvine Santa Fe depot on July 15, 1964. This location is just west of Sand Canyon Road and was part of the original town of Irvine; the depot was built in 1910. The depot was closed in 1968 and demolished two years later. This location was renamed Valencia by the Santa Fe when the Irvine Post Office was relocated to the University of California, Irvine, in 1965. (Photograph by and courtesy of Tom Gildersleeve.)

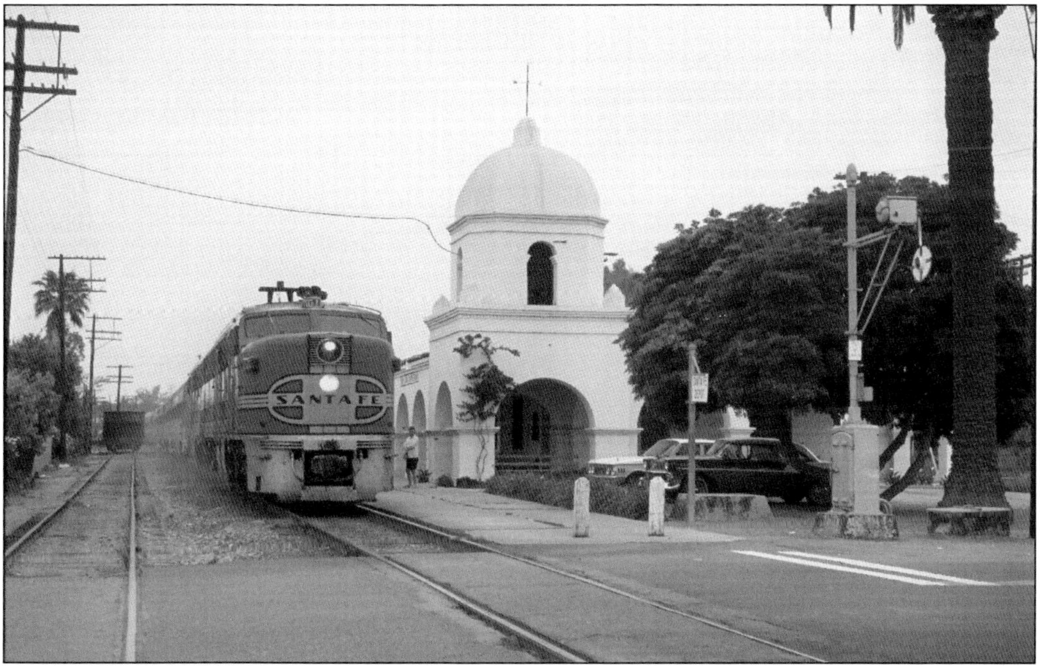

A San Diegan passing by the old depot that was built 70 years earlier interrupts the quiet of San Juan Capistrano on May 23, 1964. (Photograph by and courtesy of Tom Gildersleeve.)

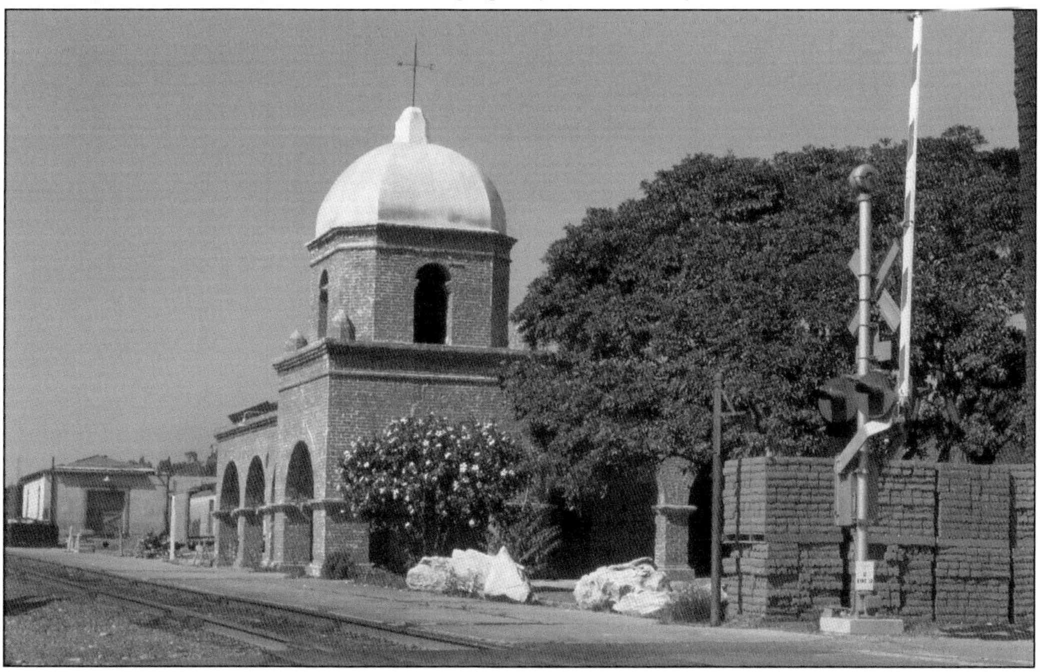

In August 1974, the old San Juan Capistrano depot is undergoing renovation to become a restaurant. The whitewash has been removed to reveal the red brick of this structure. It is the oldest existing train depot in Orange County and was built in 1894. Prior to 1905, the location was called Capistrano. This depot was in operation until 1968 but has remained an active passenger stop for both Amtrak and Metrolink. (Photograph by and courtesy of Cliff Prather.)

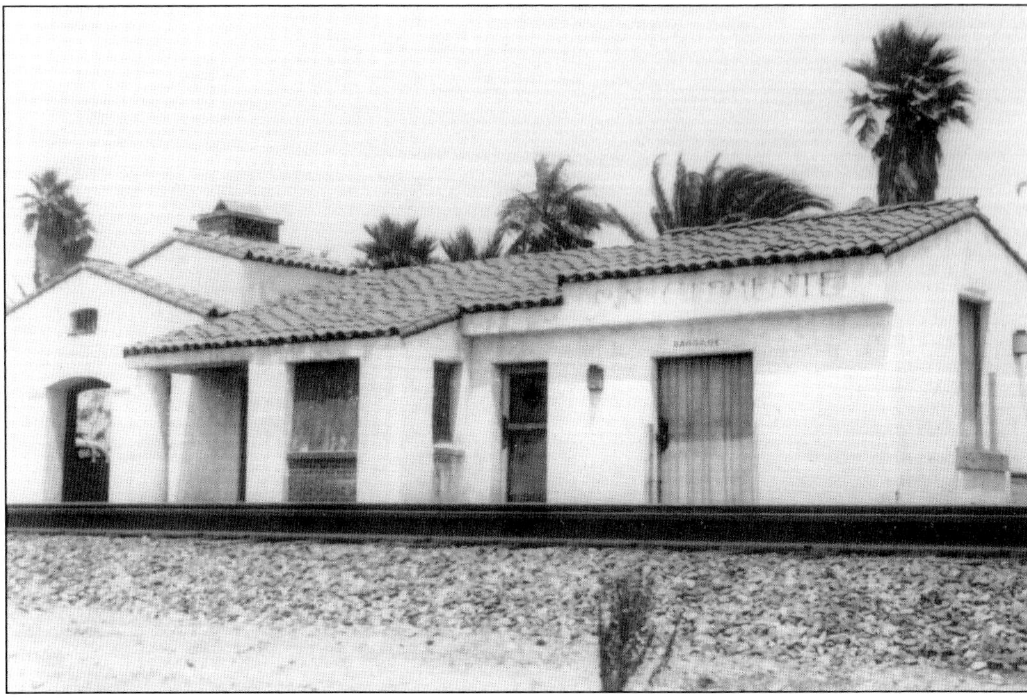

The little Santa Fe depot in San Clemente was built in 1931, closed in 1940, and removed in 1964. San Clemente would later have a cinder block shelter depot at the pier and later a new Metrolink station. (Courtesy of the author.)

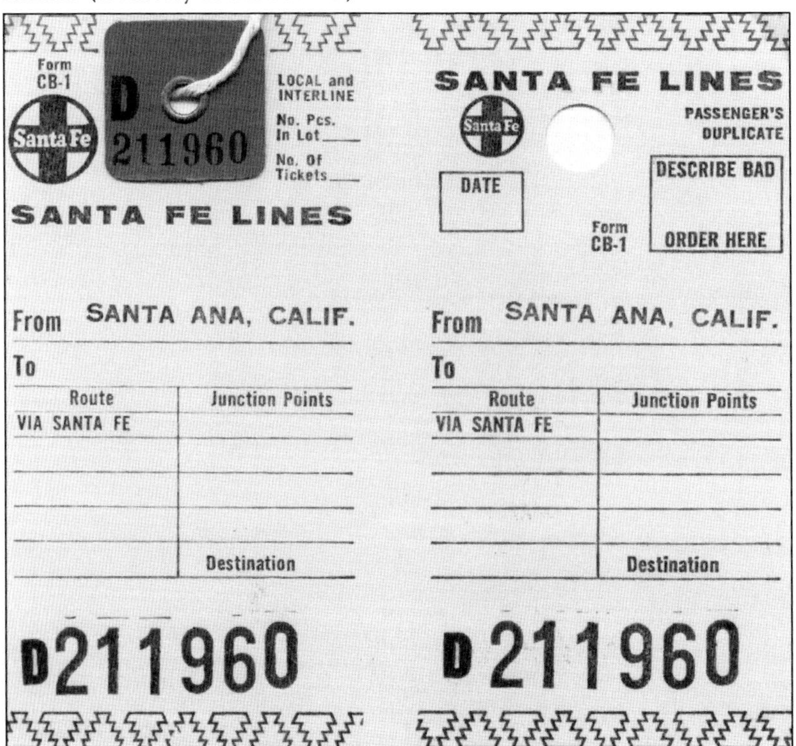

Pictured is a baggage tag from the Santa Fe era for baggage checked on trains from Santa Ana. (Courtesy of the author.)

Four

The Union Pacific Railroad

The Union Pacific (UP) was the last major railroad to reach Orange County. In 1922–1923, the UP pushed forward in Orange County with an eye to capturing part of the agriculture and freight business. UP's branch extended from Whittier to La Habra and then stretched to Fullerton and eventually terminated in Anaheim. The UP built substantial Spanish-style depots in each city it served. Although there were plans to extend a rail line to Santa Ana and other areas, the plans did not proceed due to the changing business environment, competition, and opposition by property owners.

The UP eventually did extend its reach through the county via acquisitions. In 1995, the UP took over the SP and the SP's remaining PE lines. As the mix of uses and business demands have changed, the UP's lines in Orange County have continued to be scaled back, with many rail sidings pulled up or in disuse. Meanwhile, the UP has grown to become the nation's largest railroad. This has been achieved with UP's takeover of several rail lines since the early 1980s, including the Western Pacific, Missouri Pacific, Denver and Rio Grande Western, the Missouri, Kansas and Texas, Chicago and North Western, and the SP.

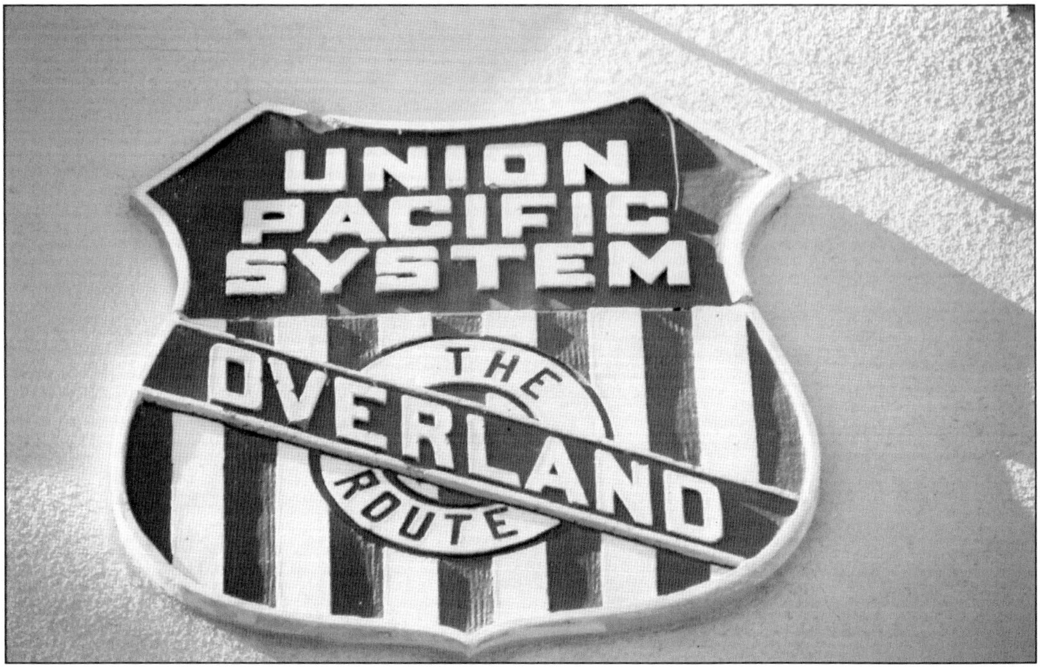

This is the red, white, and blue logo of the UP as it appears on the east facade of the La Habra depot. (Photograph by and courtesy of the author.)

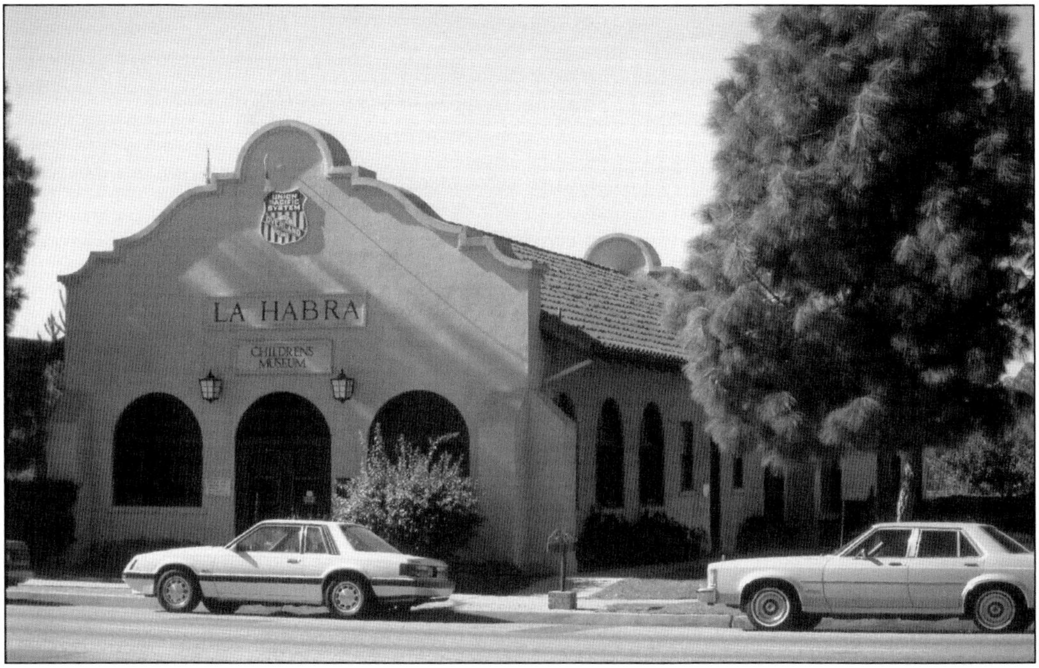

The Children's Museum of La Habra makes its home in the former UP depot. The UP arrived in Orange County in 1922–1923 and extended a branch line from Whittier to La Habra, Fullerton, and Anaheim. There were plans to extend this line farther south into Santa Ana, but it was later determined that there was not a need for a fourth railroad in that city. (Photograph by and courtesy of the author.)

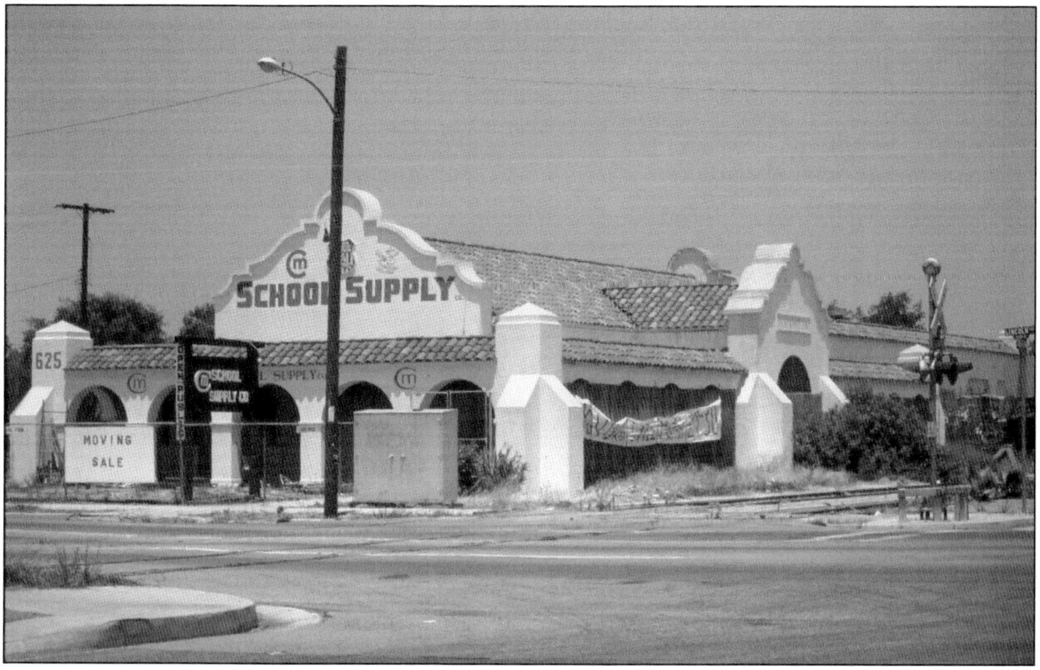

When the railroads no longer needed their train stations, the structures were sometimes leased to other businesses, torn down, or relocated. In this view, Anaheim's UP depot on East Lincoln Avenue can be seen in July 1987 before it was relocated across the street. The tenant at that time, however, needed to find another home. (Photograph by and courtesy of the author.)

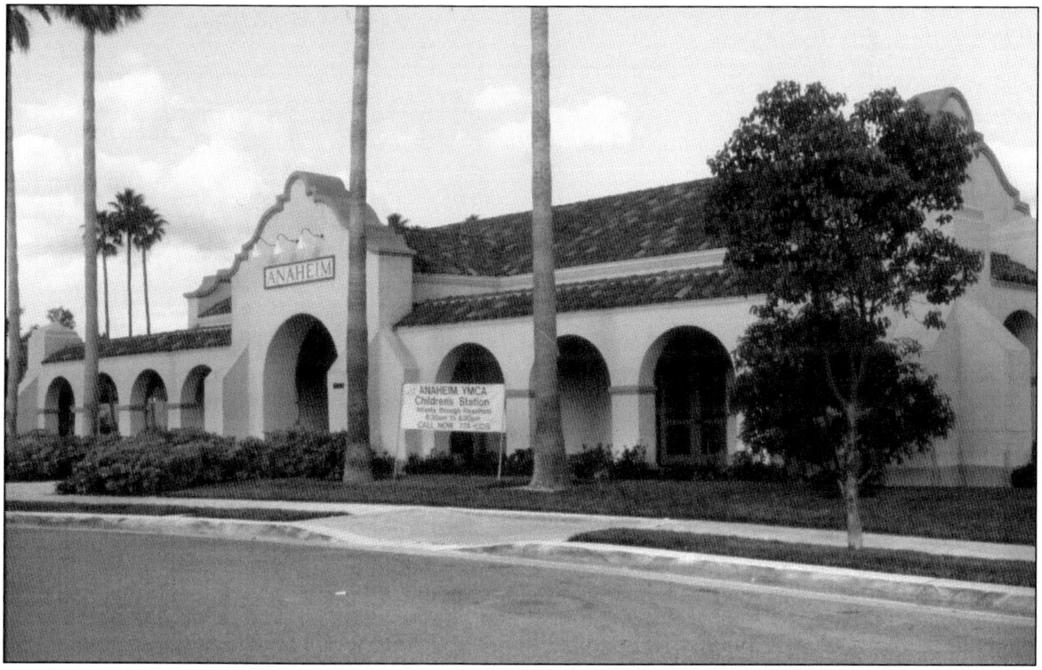

Anaheim's UP depot has been relocated to this new site on the south side of Lincoln Avenue at 100 South Atchison Street. UP opened three depots in Orange County, and all three still exist, but none remain in railroad use. (Photograph by and courtesy of the author.)

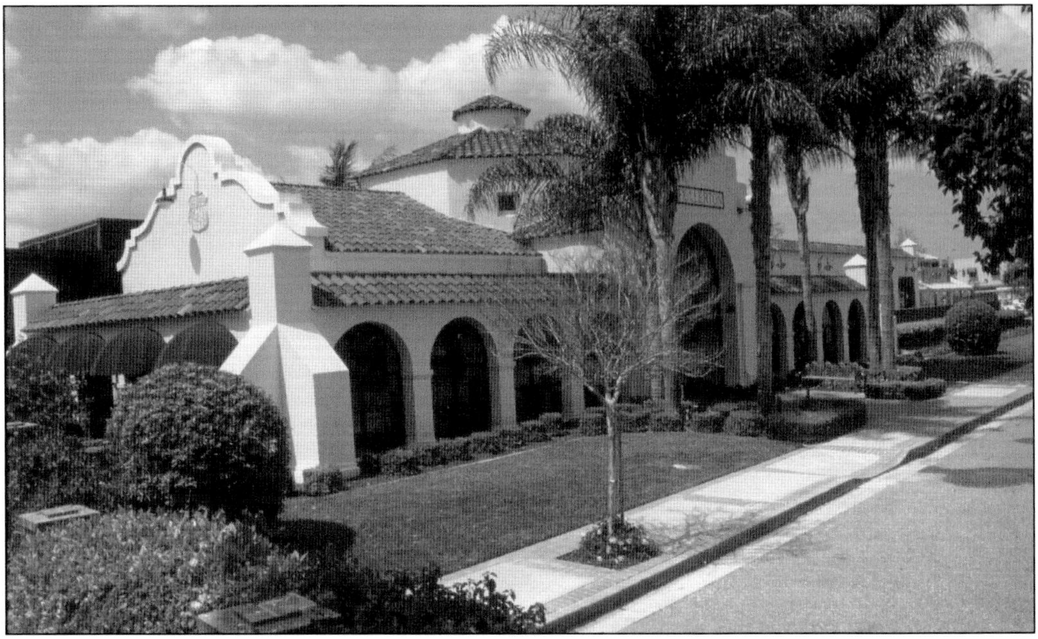

It was a sunny afternoon when this photograph was taken of the relocated UP depot in Fullerton on April 4, 1994. Following the structure's relocation, the depot was converted into the popular old Spaghetti Factory restaurant. The arched area was enclosed as part of the conversion project. The UP's "Overland" logo is on the south side of the depot. (Photograph by and courtesy of the author.)

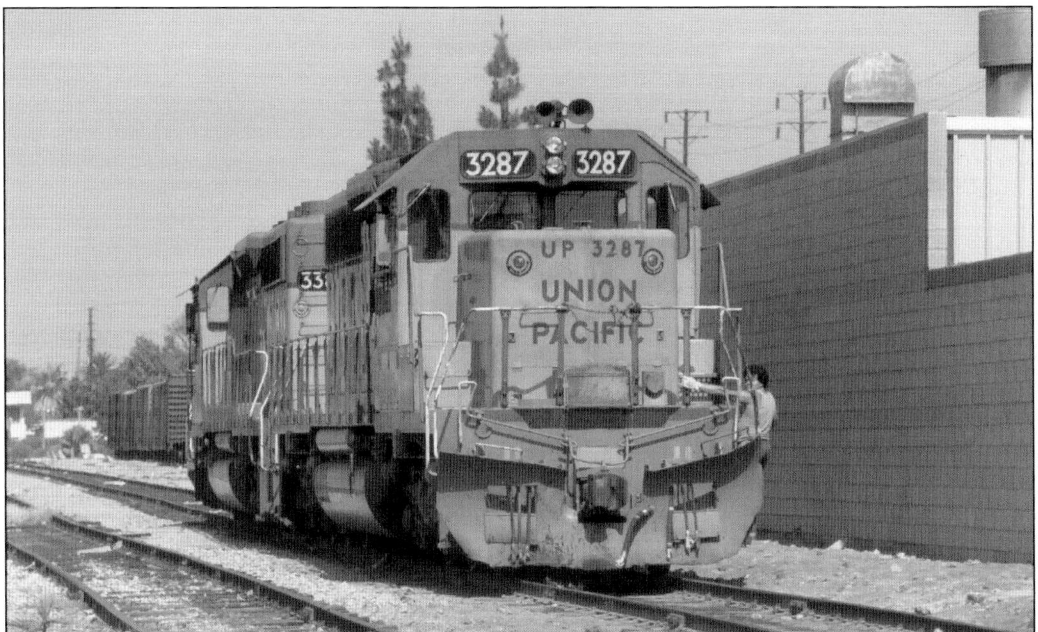

In January 1987, a pair of UP SD 40 locomotives can be seen on the tracks in Fullerton. By this date, the UP depot has been relocated to the east and north, near the Santa Fe depot. (Photograph by and courtesy of the author.)

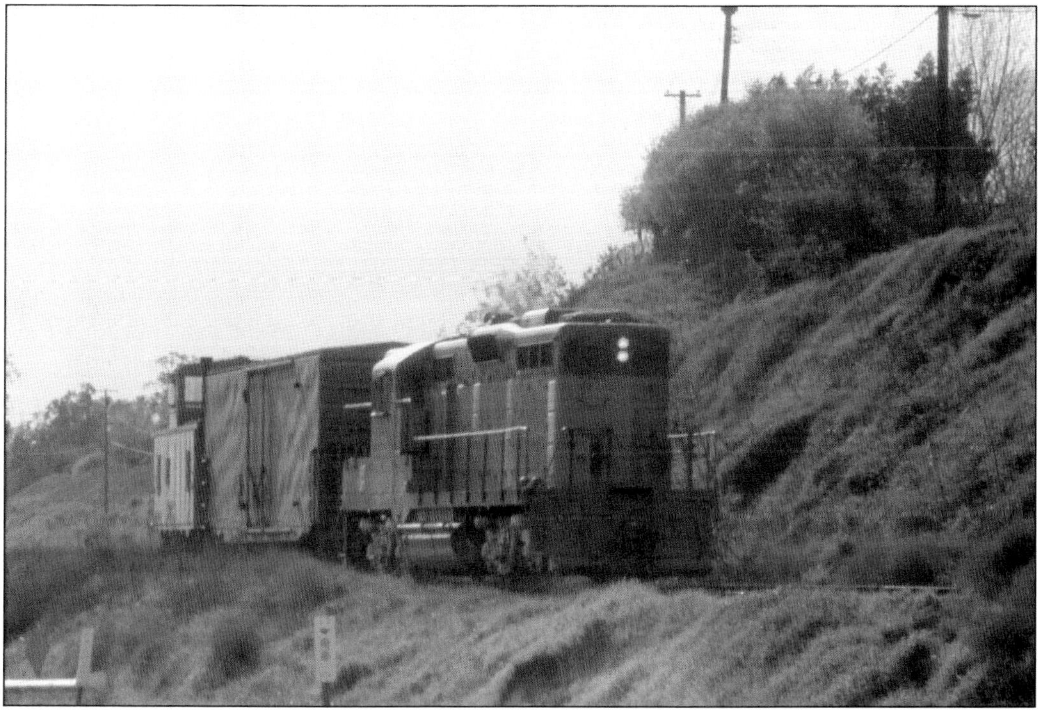

A typical Fullerton local is shown between Fullerton and La Habra on February 20, 1971. (Photograph by and courtesy of Cliff Prather.)

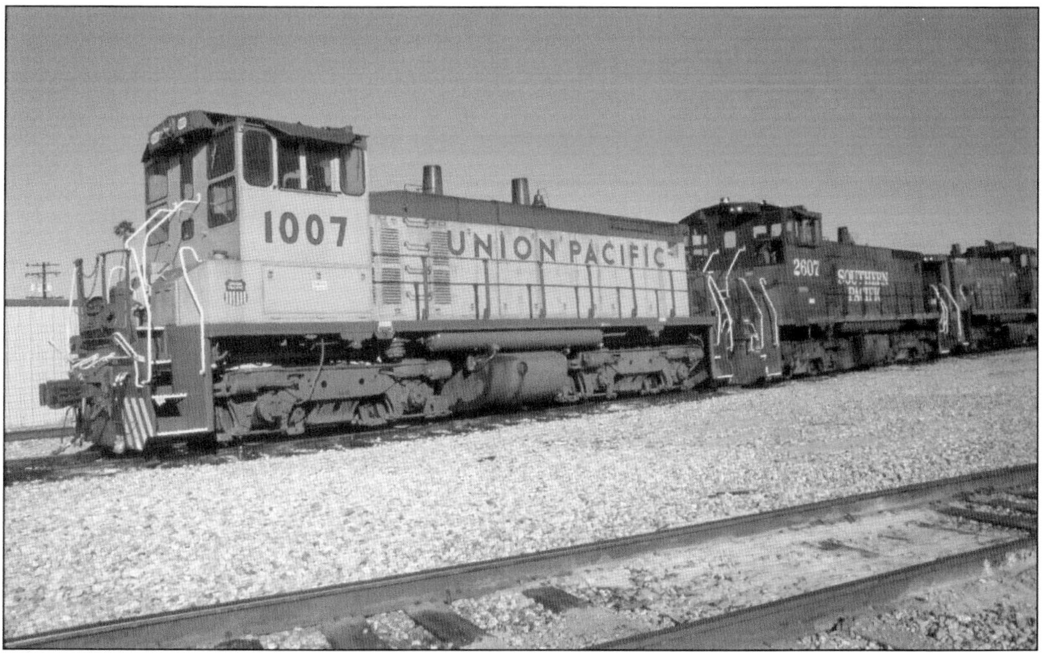

During most of Orange County's history, the dominant railroads have been the Santa Fe and the SP. The landscape today has changed, as the UP absorbed SP in 1995, and the Santa Fe merged with the Burlington Northern to create the Burlington Northern Santa Fe (BNSF). (Photograph by and courtesy of the author.)

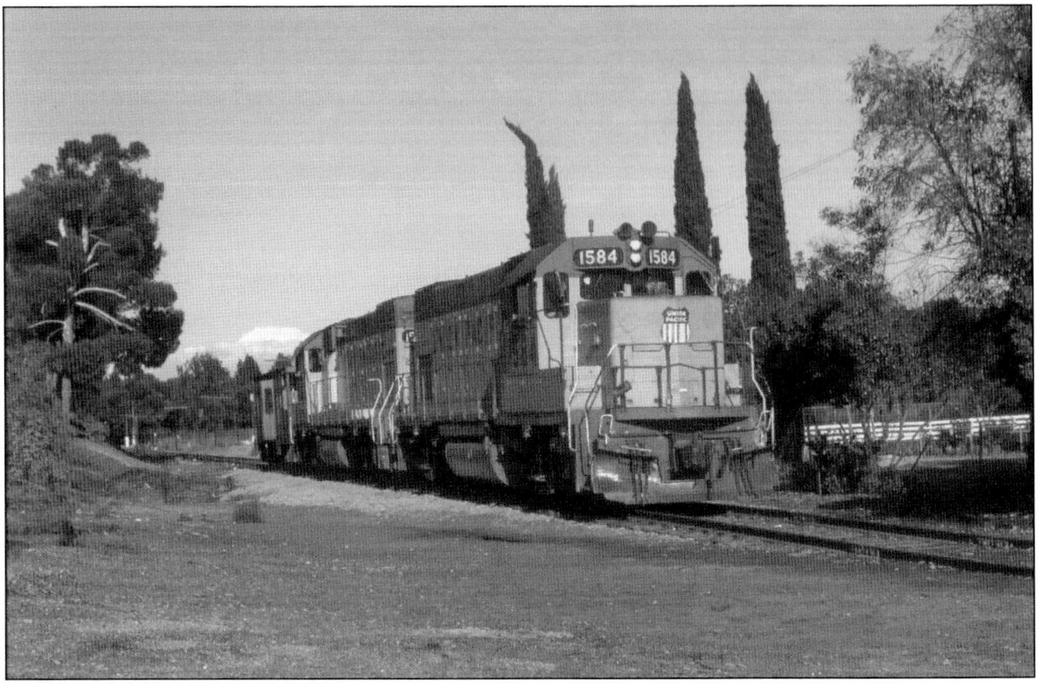

This is a light UP Fullerton local with two locomotives and a caboose on a sunny December 18, 1992. UP's Orange County competitors always handled more traffic than the UP. (Photograph by and courtesy of Cliff Prather.)

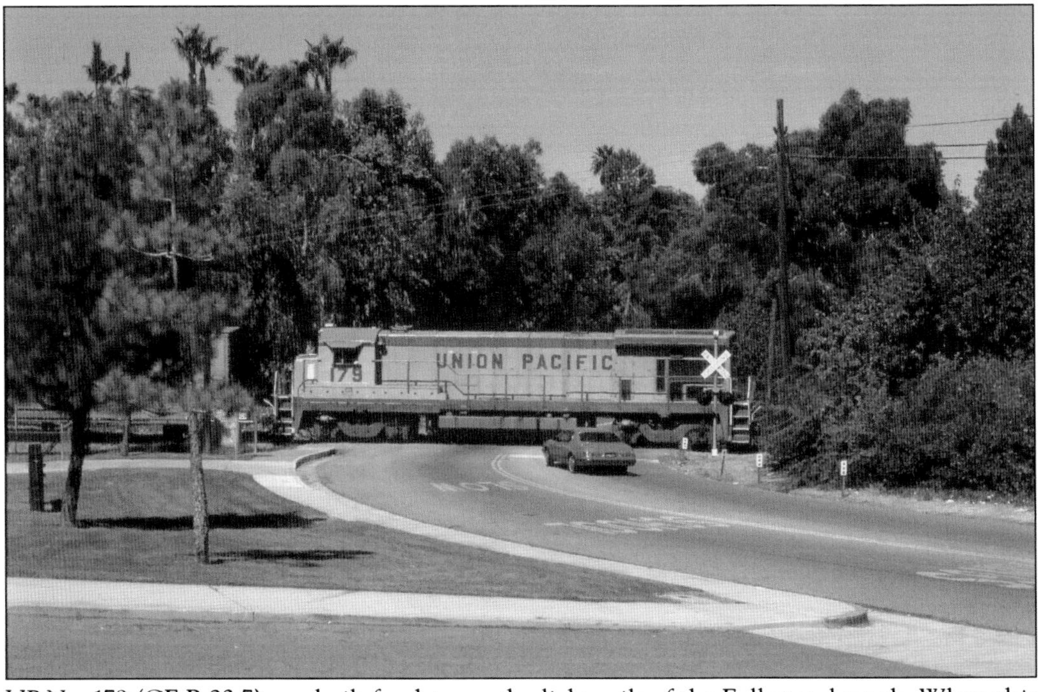

UP No. 179 (GE B-23-7) was built for duty on the light rails of the Fullerton branch. When this photograph was taken in the Sunny Hills on August 22, 1987, the No. 179 was about six years old. (Photograph by and courtesy of Cliff Prather.)

Five

The Pacific Electric Railway

The Pacific Electric (PE) was an undertaking of Henry Huntington. Railroading ran in the family, since Henry Huntington's uncle Collis P. Huntington was one of the "Big Four" that led the development of the Central Pacific transcontinental railroad (the UP met the Central Pacific at Promontory Point in Utah in 1869). Henry led the development of the Pacific Electric Railway (PE) across Southern California. From downtown Los Angeles, the PE lines extended to the San Fernando Valley, Santa Monica, Torrance, Long Beach, Pasadena, San Bernardino and Riverside.

The PE's Southern District included three main lines from Los Angeles County: first was Whittier to Yorba Linda and Fullerton; second was Watts to Santa Ana; and third was Long Beach to Huntington Beach and Newport Beach. Passenger and freight services were offered on all three lines. Passenger service ended on the Yorba Linda–Fullerton line in 1938; passenger service on the Santa Ana and the Newport Beach lines ended in 1950 and marked the end of passenger trolley service in Orange County. Various PE lines remained in service for freight business. Those tracks that were not abandoned were absorbed by the SP, and limited amounts of this track remain in service in north Orange County. All traces of the coastal lines have been erased except for memories and a few photographs.

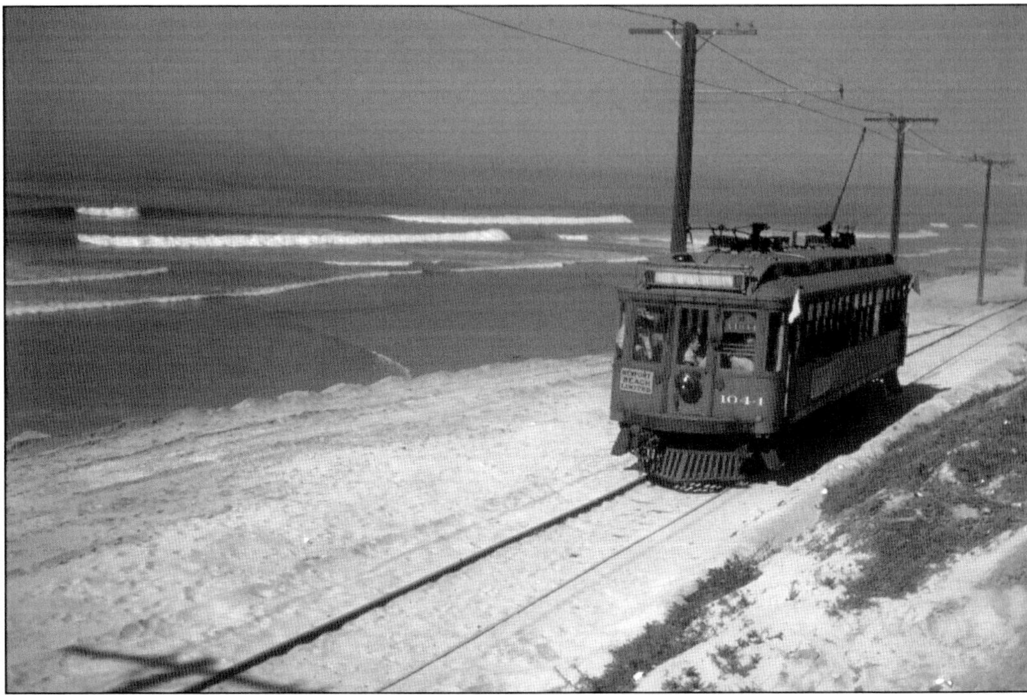

A PE car runs along the surf in Huntington Beach on a southbound trip to Newport Beach. It is hard to believe these trains were so close to the shore. (Courtesy of the author.)

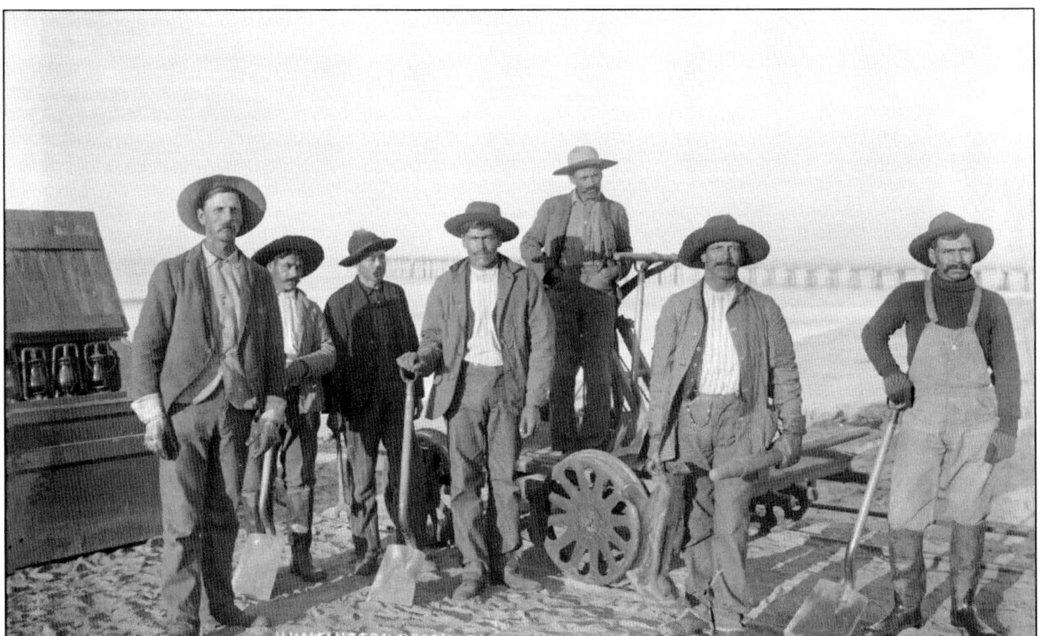

This rare photograph shows a PE foreman with his maintenance of way crew. This crew is assigned to the Newport-Balboa line that ran northward along the coast to Long Beach and beyond. This photograph dates from around 1910. The Huntington Beach Pier is visible in the background. (Courtesy of the Orange County Archives.)

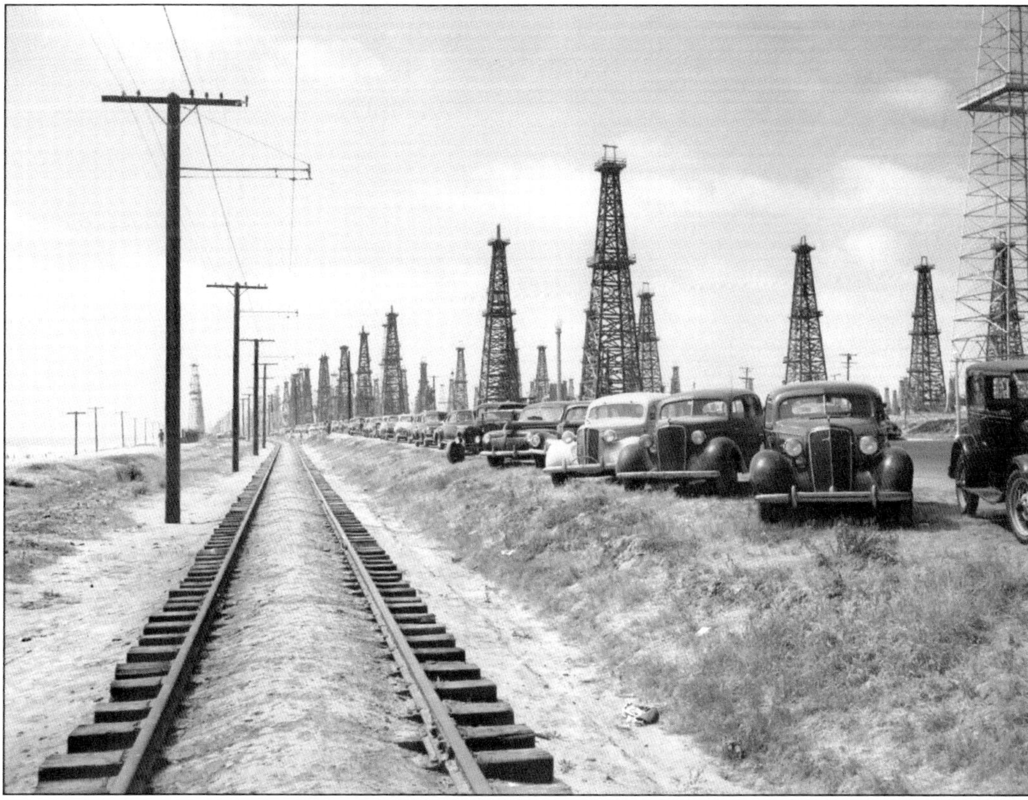

The former two-track line has been whittled back to just a single track. The oil derricks characterized the Huntington Beach skyline in 1946. Parked along the tracks as far as one can see is the PE's Victorian competition. (Courtesy of the Orange County Archives.)

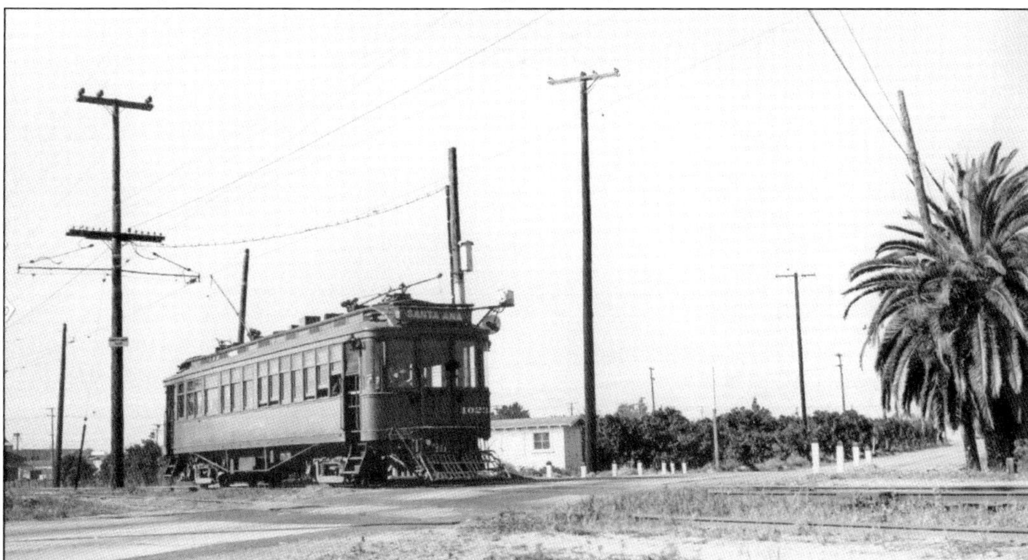

No. 1023 is hightailing it through Garden Grove on its trip to Santa Ana. Note the rural nature of this area in the 1920s. (Courtesy of the author.)

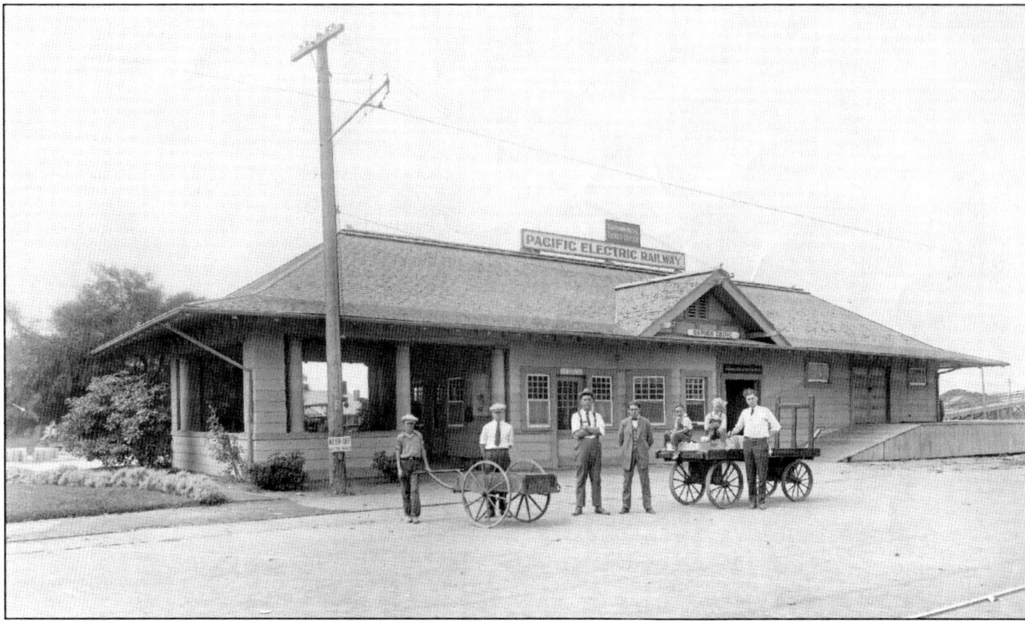

This is the PE depot in Garden Grove. Note the electric catenary for the sidetrack in front of the station. (Courtesy of the Garden Grove Historical Society.)

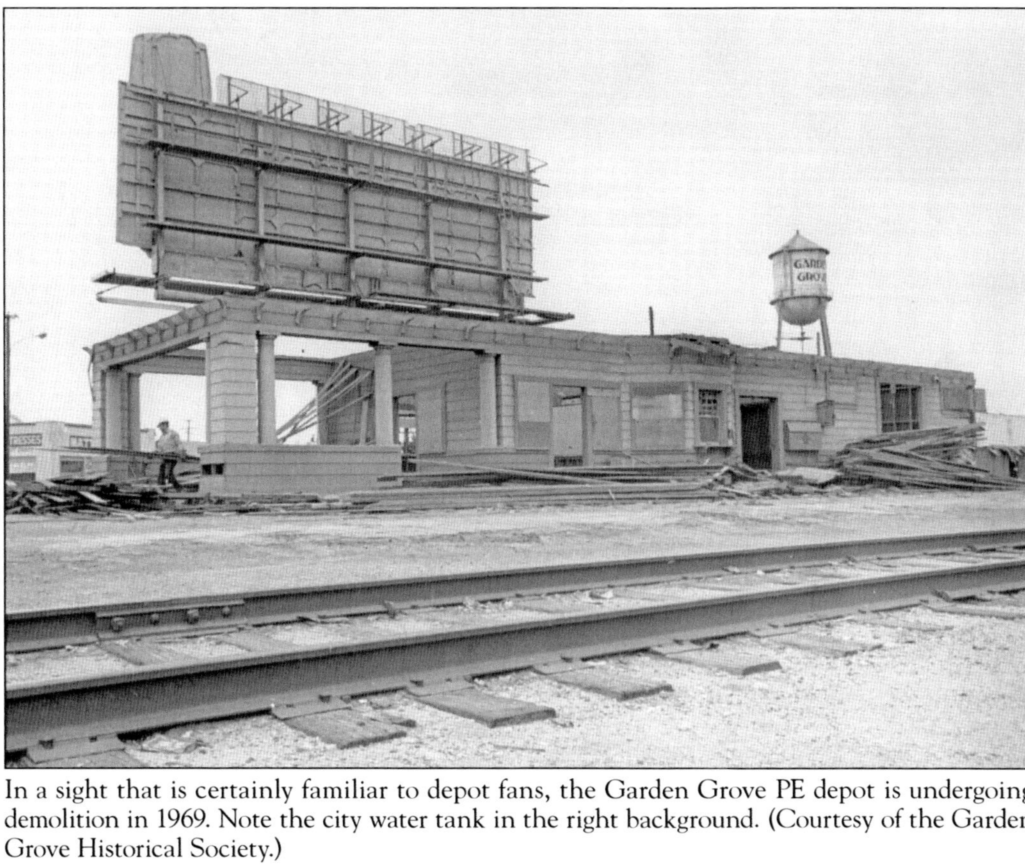

In a sight that is certainly familiar to depot fans, the Garden Grove PE depot is undergoing demolition in 1969. Note the city water tank in the right background. (Courtesy of the Garden Grove Historical Society.)

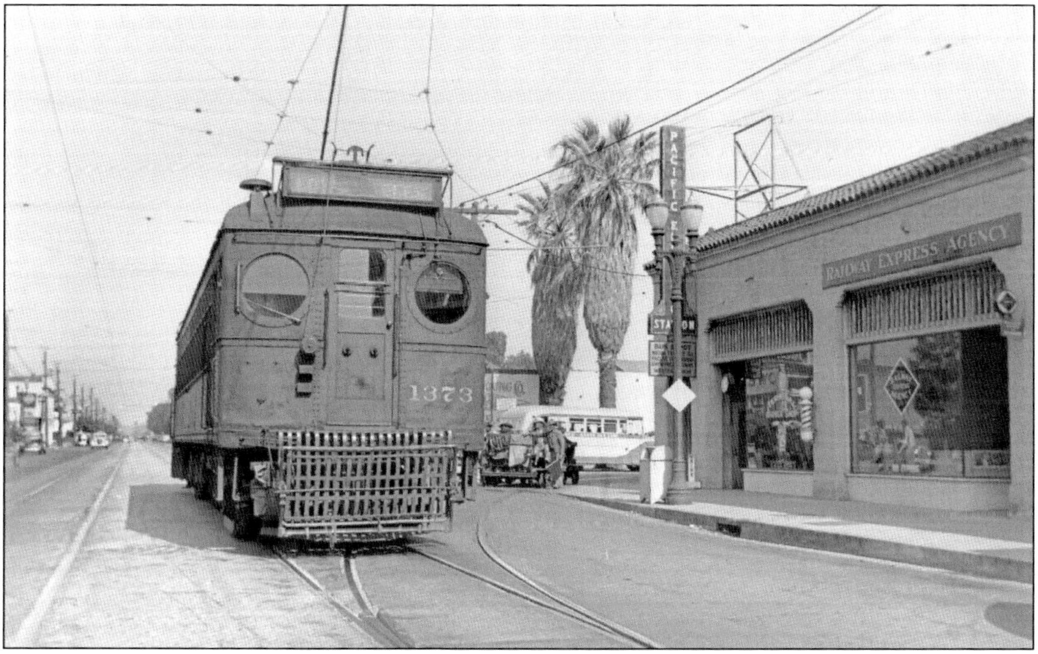

Although the PE arrived in Santa Ana in 1905, the company used the SP depot on Fourth Street as its terminal. In 1926, this L-shaped combination passenger and freight depot was built at 424 East Fourth Street. At this location, the PE's line to Huntington Beach diverged to the south. Others using this depot included Motor Transit, Pacific Greyhound, and UP stages. Note the maintenance of way crew waiting patiently for the eastbound trolley to pass. (Photograph by Ralph Melching; courtesy of the author.)

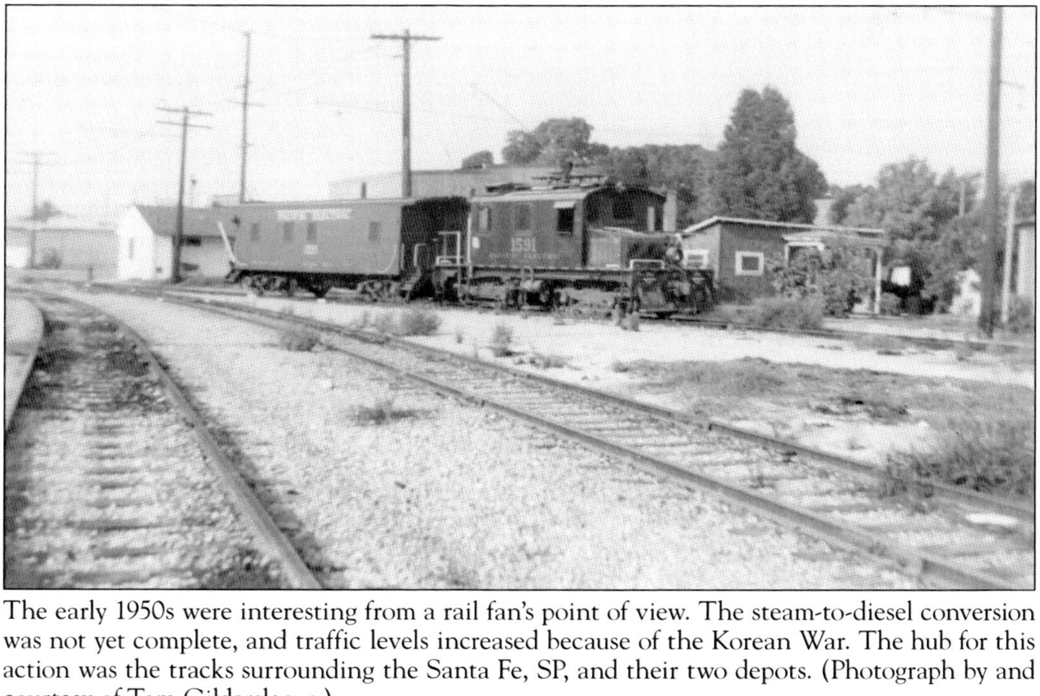

The early 1950s were interesting from a rail fan's point of view. The steam-to-diesel conversion was not yet complete, and traffic levels increased because of the Korean War. The hub for this action was the tracks surrounding the Santa Fe, SP, and their two depots. (Photograph by and courtesy of Tom Gildersleeve.)

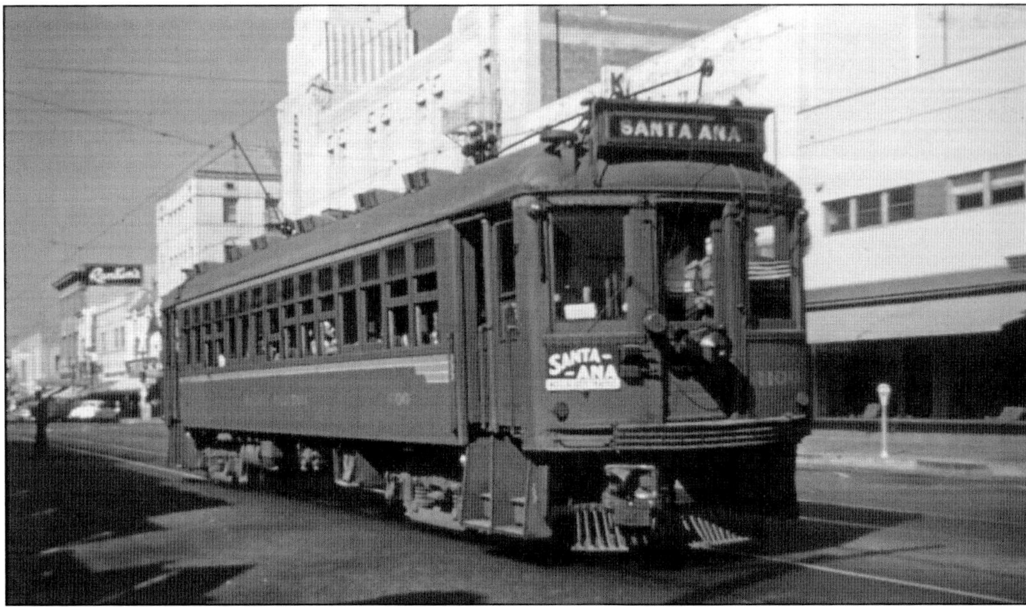

On a quiet day, PE No. 1100 is moving east on Fourth Street in Santa Ana around 1948. Visible in this shot are several downtown department stores, including J. C. Penney, Montgomery Ward, and Rankins. (Courtesy of the author.)

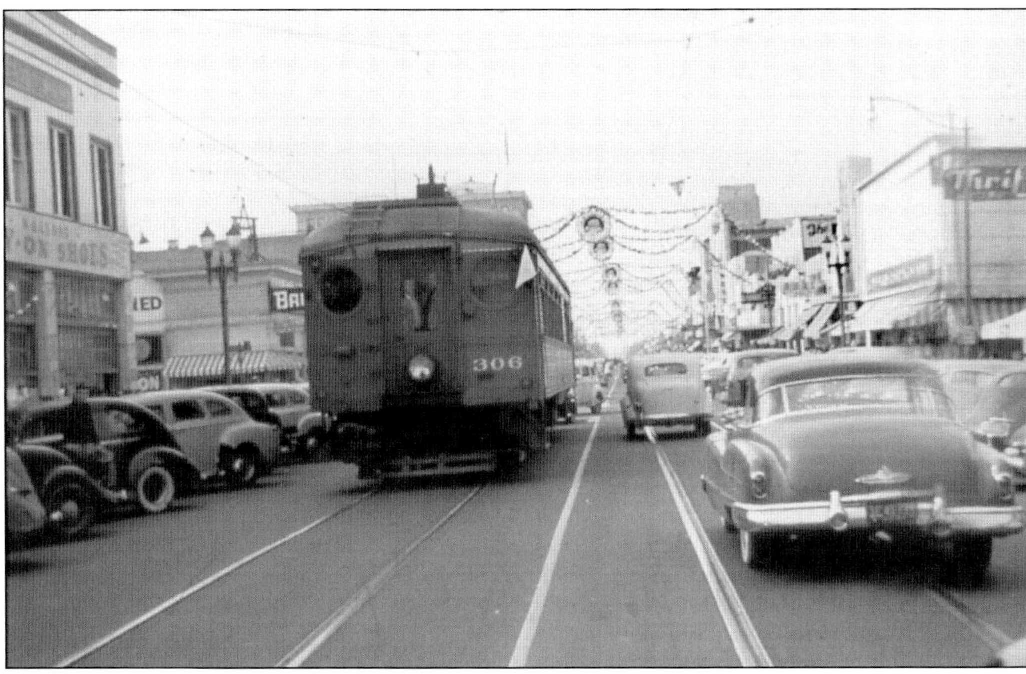

After more than 45 years, regular PE passenger service will come to an end in July 1950. This appears to be a special excursion for rail fans. It is easy to see how the competition for the PE has changed as shoppers thronged to downtown Santa Ana before Christmas 1950. This view is looking west from Fourth and Spurgeon Streets. (Courtesy of the author.)

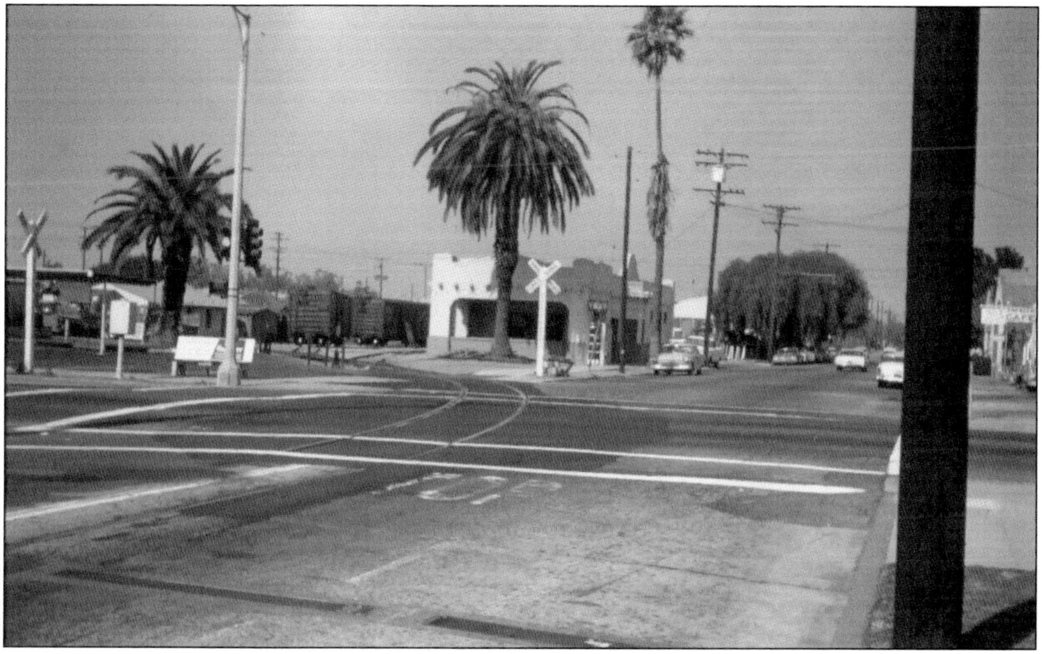

The Orange PE depot is shown here on February 10, 1964, at the northwest corner of Chapman Avenue and Lemon Street. The curving rails used to run down Lemon Street on the route to Santa Ana. When the PE folded, SP operated the former PE trackage in Orange from a point called Marlboro, north of Katella Avenue. (Courtesy of the author.)

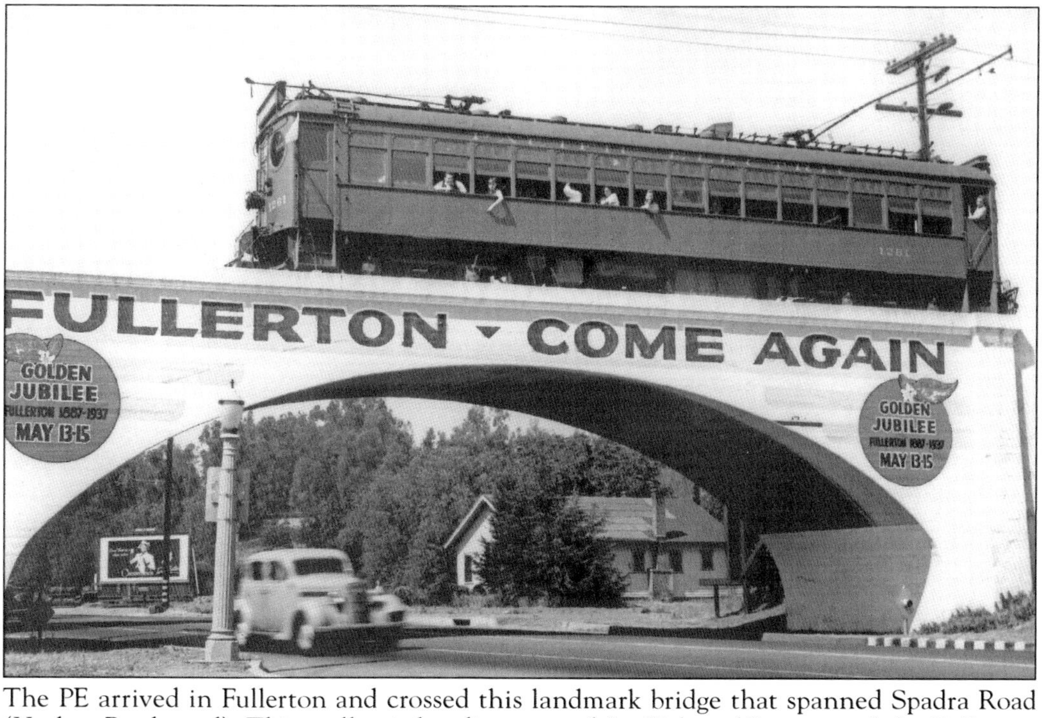

The PE arrived in Fullerton and crossed this landmark bridge that spanned Spadra Road (Harbor Boulevard). This trolley is heading toward La Habra. (Courtesy of the Fullerton Public Library.)

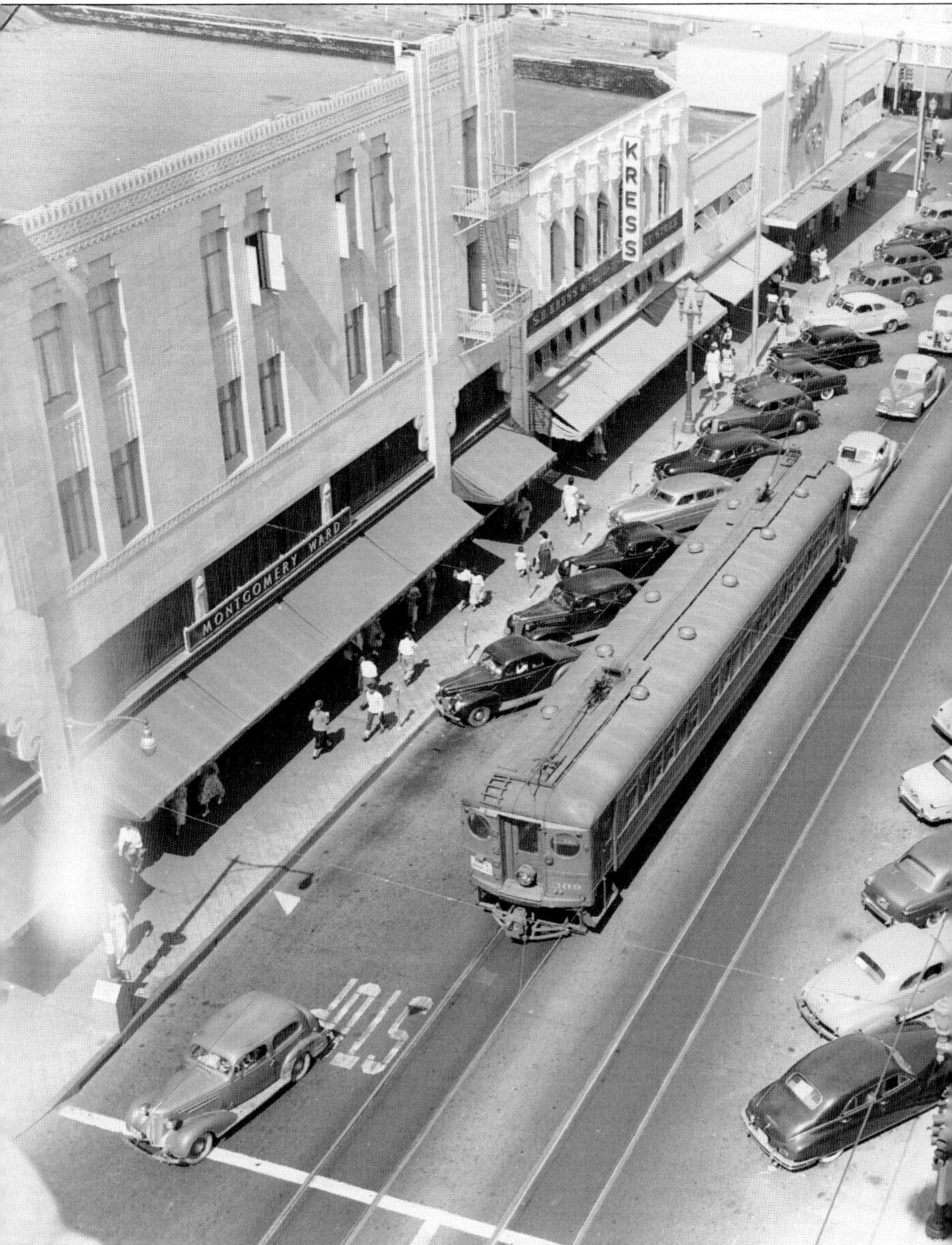
KRESS
MONTGOMERY WARD
STOP

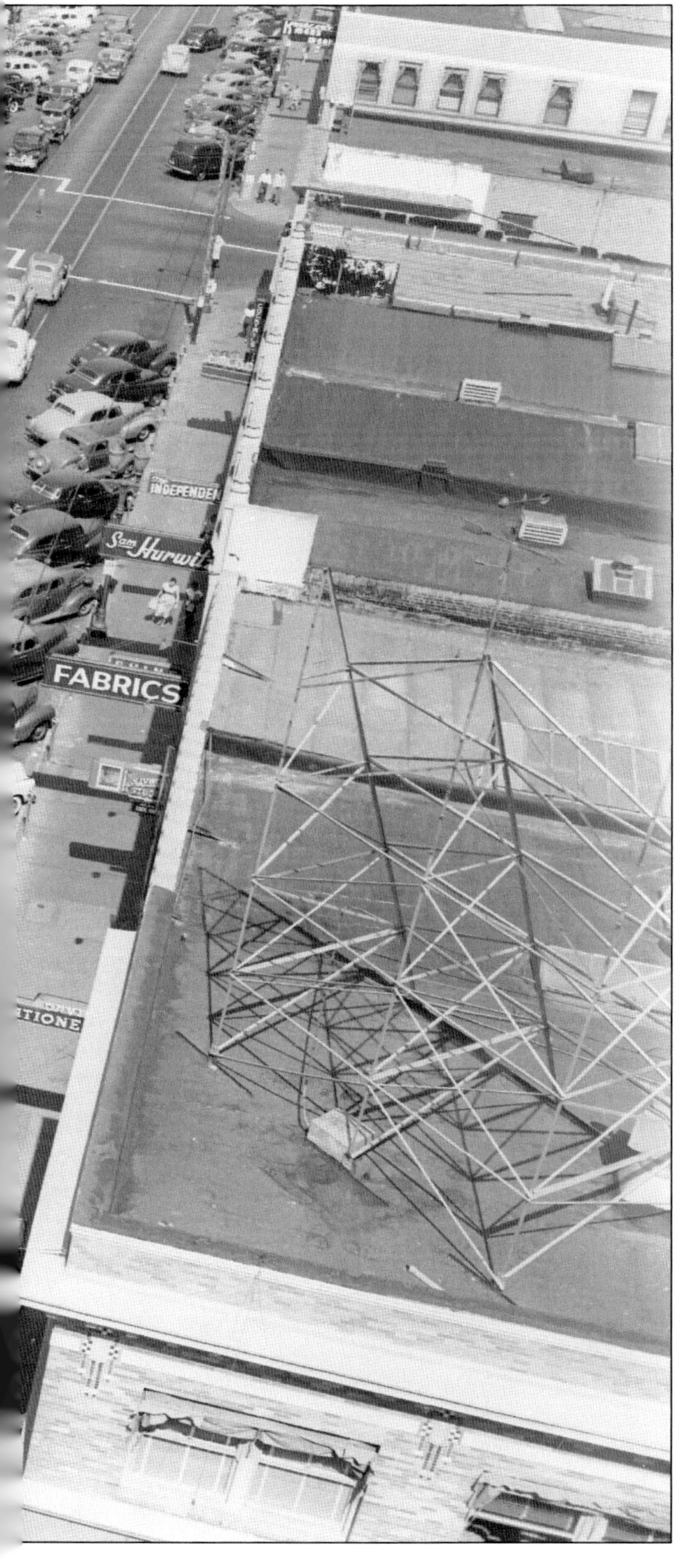

PE car No. 309 is shown heading west on Fourth Street at Main Street. This was the last day of regular PE passenger service in Santa Ana on July 2, 1950. The PE contributed greatly to the growth and prominence of Santa Ana. On the left side of this picture, one can see retailers Montgomery Ward, Kress Five and Dime, and J. C. Penney; W. T. Grant is at the northeast corner of Fourth and Bush Streets. (Courtesy of the Orange County Archives.)

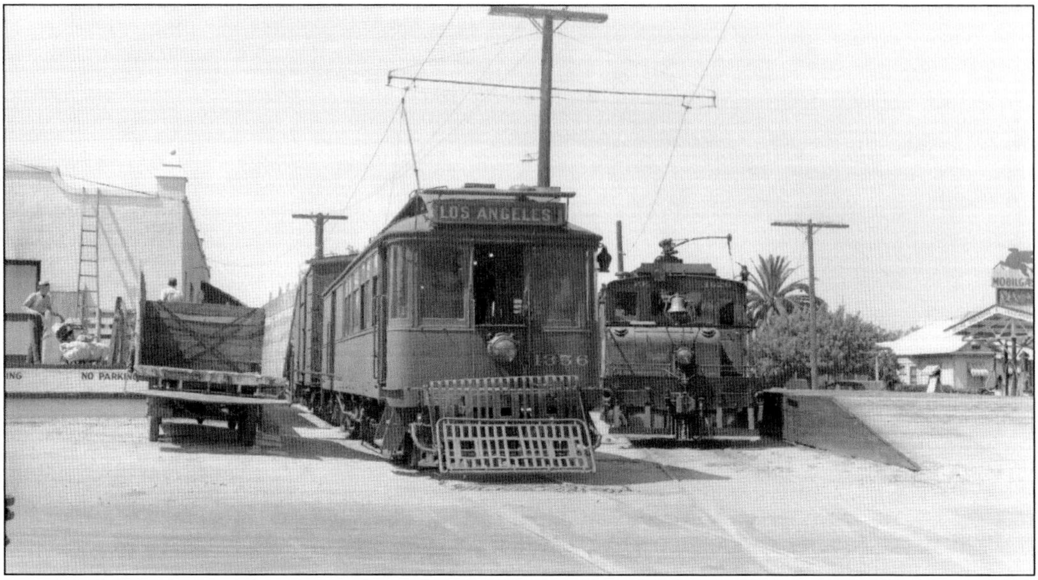

Most people know of the PE Redcars that spanned much of Southern California. The PE also had an extensive network of freight service to complement the less-than-carload service business. This view shows the south end of the PE's depot in Fullerton. Car No. 1356 has backed up to some freight cars spotted at the loading dock. Meanwhile, freight engine No. 1620 rests on the adjoining track. This depot remains standing on Commonwealth Avenue just north of the Santa Fe and UP depots. (Courtesy of the author.)

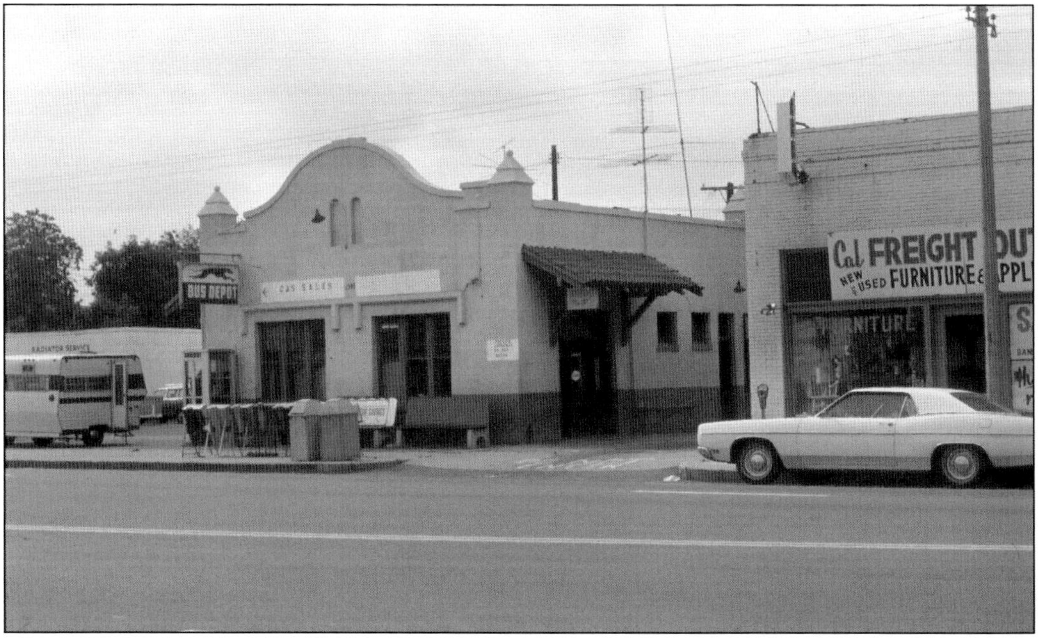

The Fullerton PE depot was located on East Commonwealth Avenue. Fullerton still retains all three of its train depots (Santa Fe, PE, and UP). The latter two serve only meals, and only the Santa Fe serves passenger trains—Amtrak and Metrolink. When this photograph was taken, the depot served Greyhound and the Southern California Rapid Transit District (SCRTD) bus line from Los Angeles. (Photograph by and courtesy of Cliff Prather.)

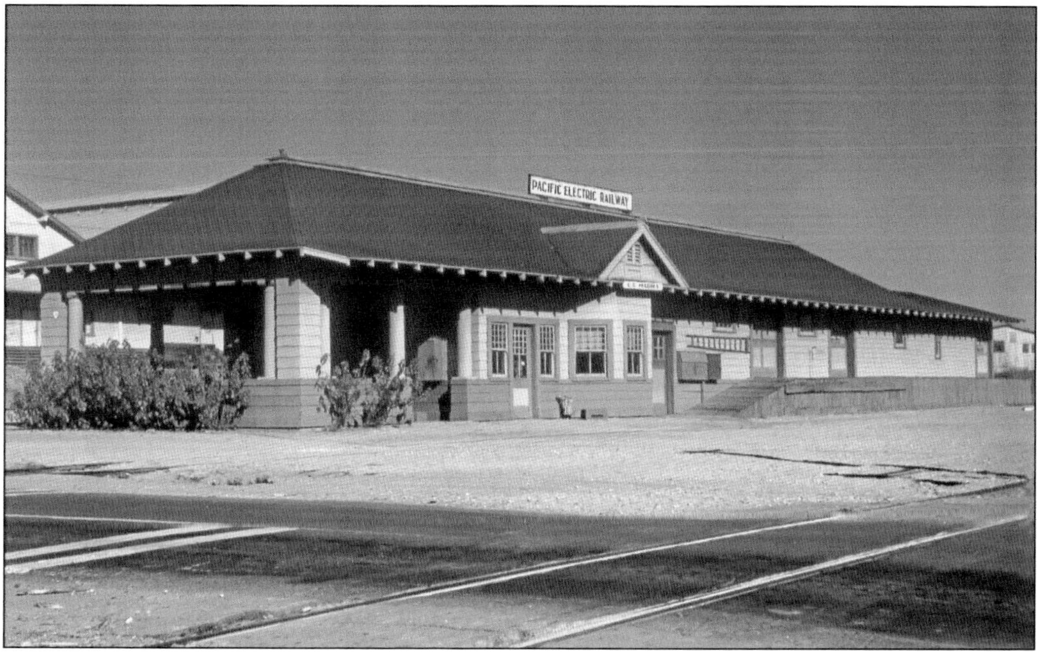

This is the La Habra PE depot as seen in November 1956. Many PE depots were painted in standard, two gray colors. (Courtesy of the author.)

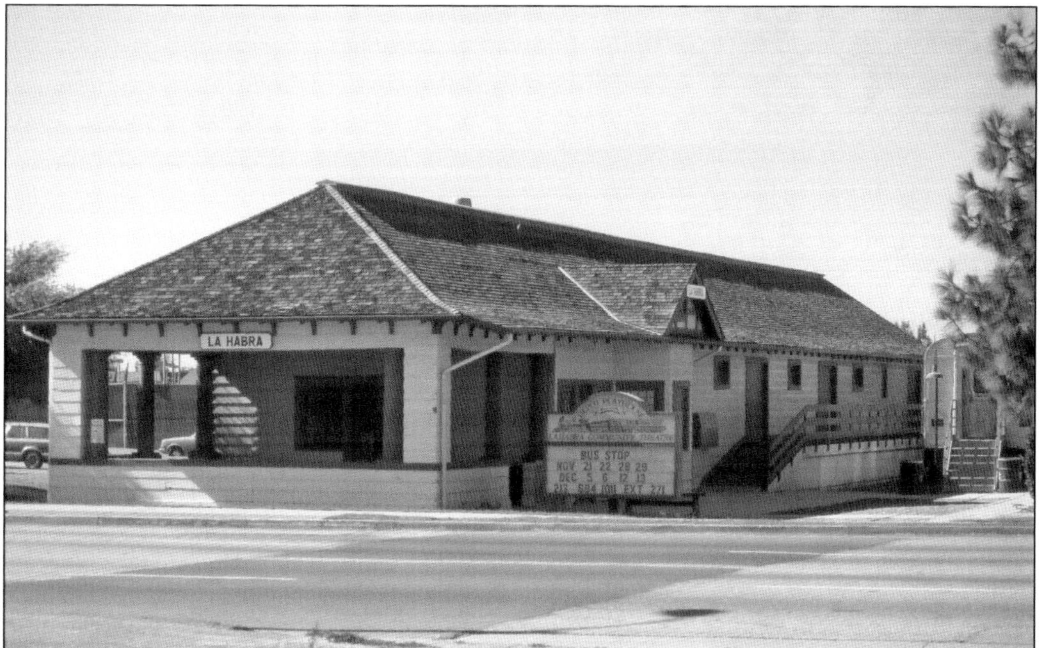

La Habra PE Depot has been relocated to a new site along the UP tracks and south of the UP depot, as shown in this view from November 11, 1986. The PE depots at Brea, Garden Grove, and Yorba Linda were built in the same style as La Habra. (Photograph by and courtesy of the author.)

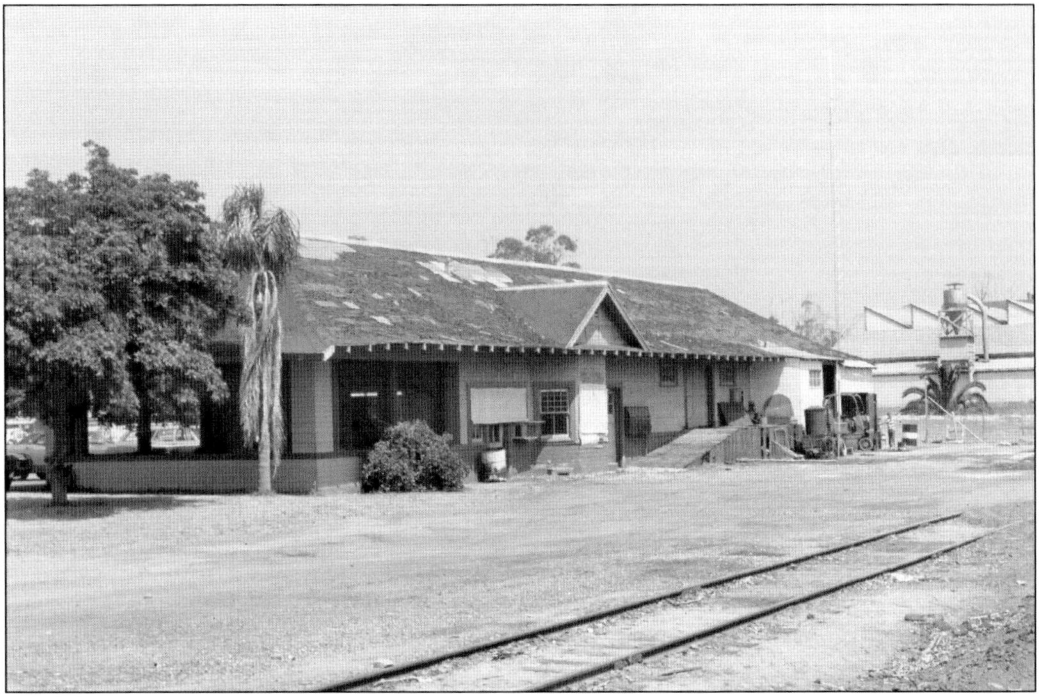

The PE had three lines entering north, central, and south Orange County. This photograph shows the PE depot at the end of the northern line in Yorba Linda on January 12, 1971. Similar depots were built in Brea, Garden Grove, and La Habra. (Photograph by and courtesy of Cliff Prather.)

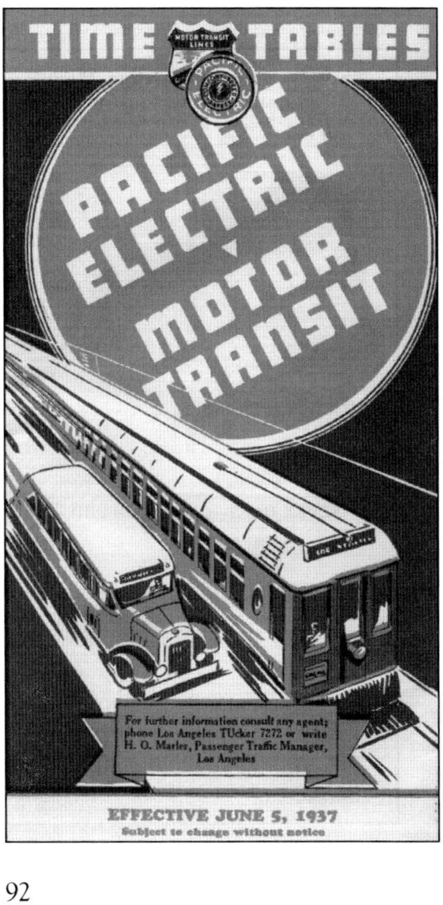

This is the PE system timetable in June 1937. The 10 years prior were years of retrenchment for PE trolleys; PE Motor Transit was increasingly the preferred way to keep business. The upcoming World War II years would be peak years for the system that would unravel in the 1950s. (Courtesy of the author.)

Six

Accidents Will Happen

Derailments and accidents occur on the rails from time to time. Although safety is paramount (expect a train on any track in any direction at any time), accidents will happen. The results can be catastrophic and spectacular when tons of steel collide with a car, truck, or another train. These photographs are a sample from the history of Orange County. Each photograph underscores that a healthy respect for trains is warranted any time one is near the tracks.

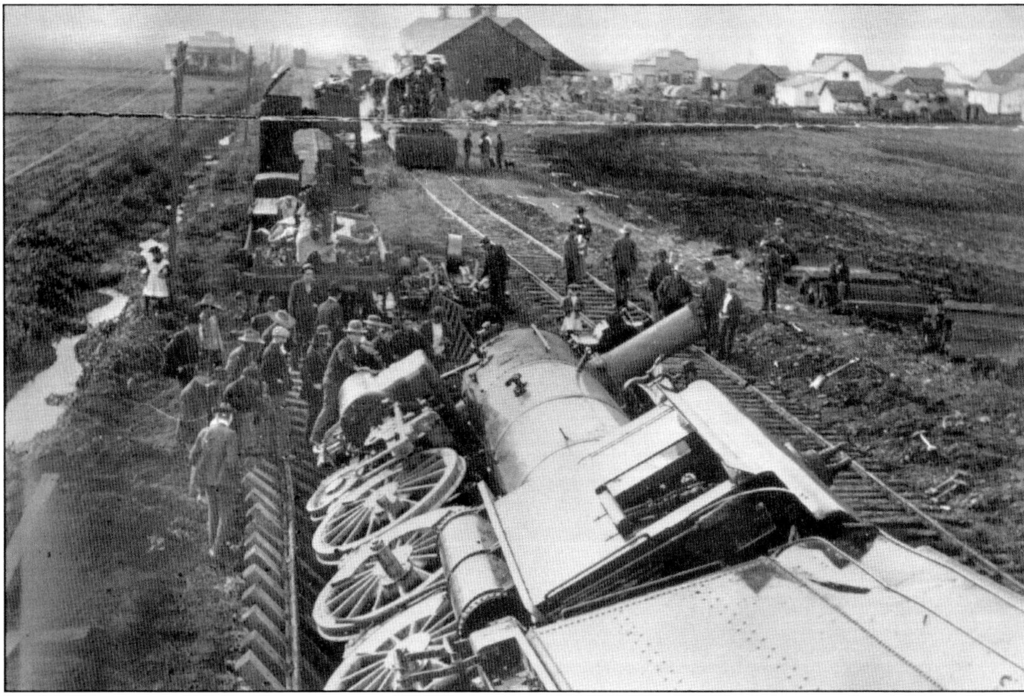

This SP locomotive found the roadbed to be a little too soft. Hopefully there would not be a repeat of a train sunk in the peat bed of southwest Orange County. This accident occurred on January 13, 1905. (Courtesy of the Orange County Archives.)

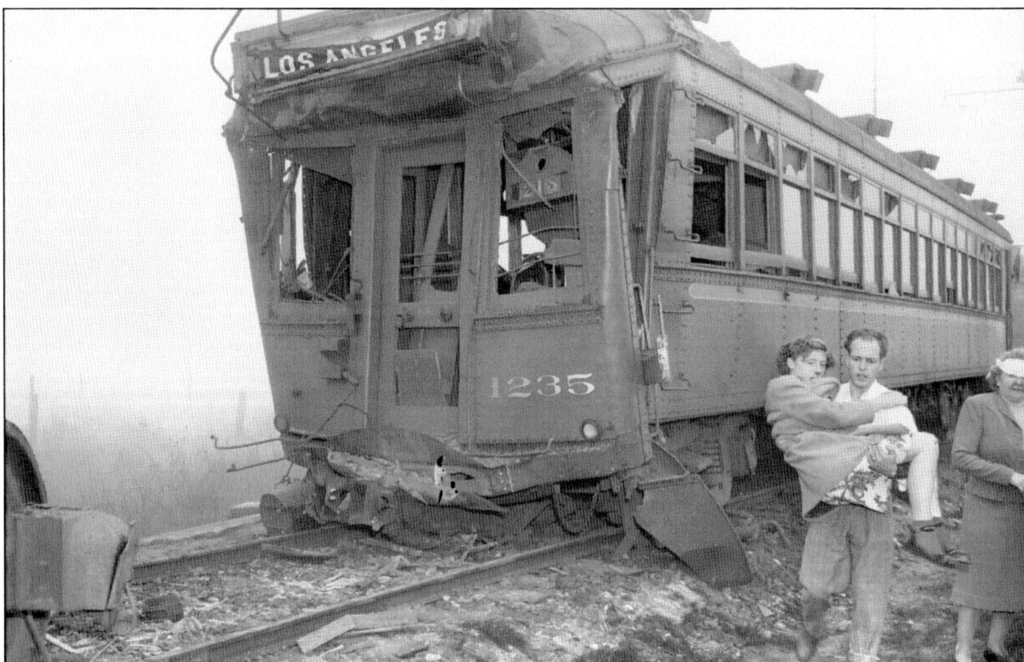

A serious crash involving PE car No. 1235 happened on the northbound Santa Ana line on November 29, 1946. (Courtesy of the Orange County Archives.)

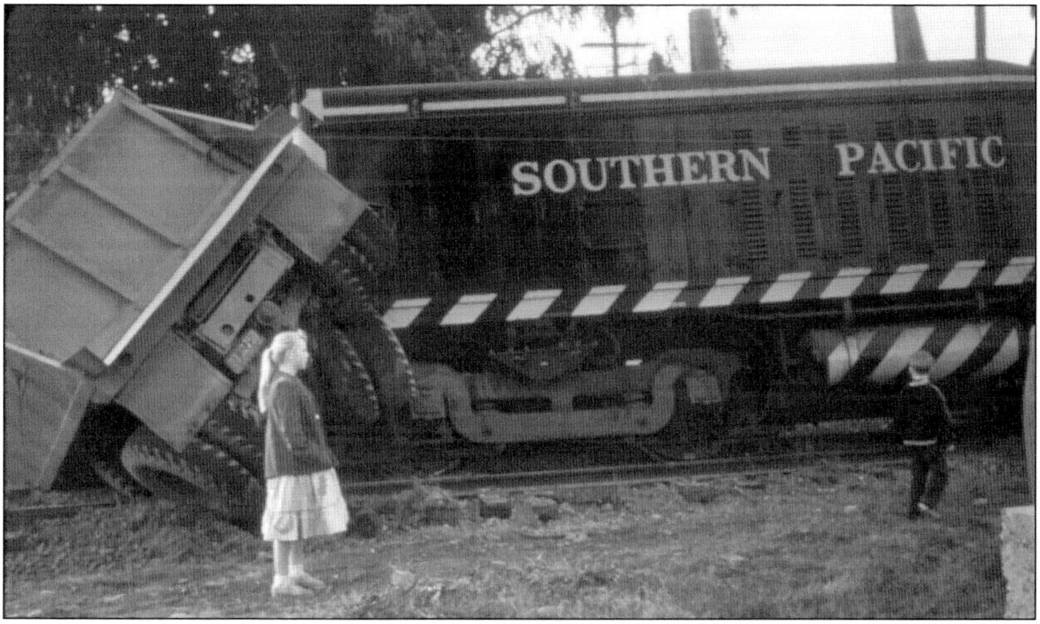

Two young children get an up-close look at the end result of a collision between an SP locomotive and a dump truck in 1956 near Chapman Avenue and McPherson Street. It seems security at the accident scene is a little looser than would be the case these days. (Photograph by Weldon Field; courtesy of the Orange History Center, Orange Public Library.)

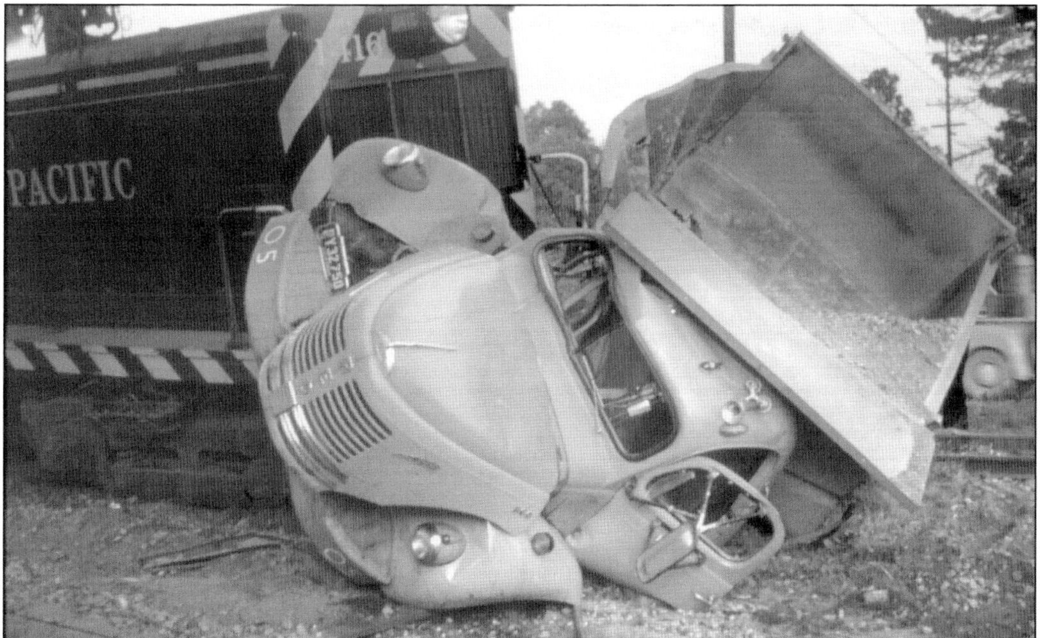

This is another view of the 1956 crash in Orange near Chapman Avenue and McPherson Street. While the result is quite a spectacle, clearly the locomotive will live to haul another day; the dump truck is a total loss. (Photograph by Weldon Field; courtesy of the Orange History Center, Orange Public Library.)

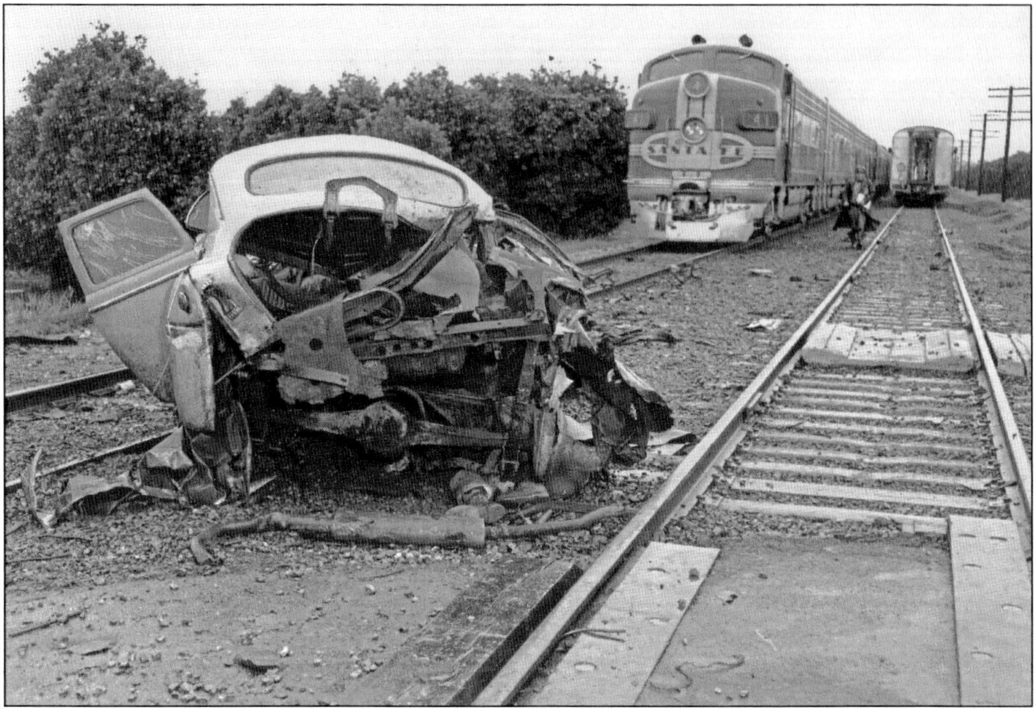

Cars and trains do not mix well at grade crossings. This photograph shows the end results of a crash involving at a southbound San Diegan at Grand Avenue in Santa Ana. The northbound train finds the crossing blocked with wreckage, while the train that struck the car has stopped in the distance. (Photograph by Mell Patrick; courtesy of the author.)

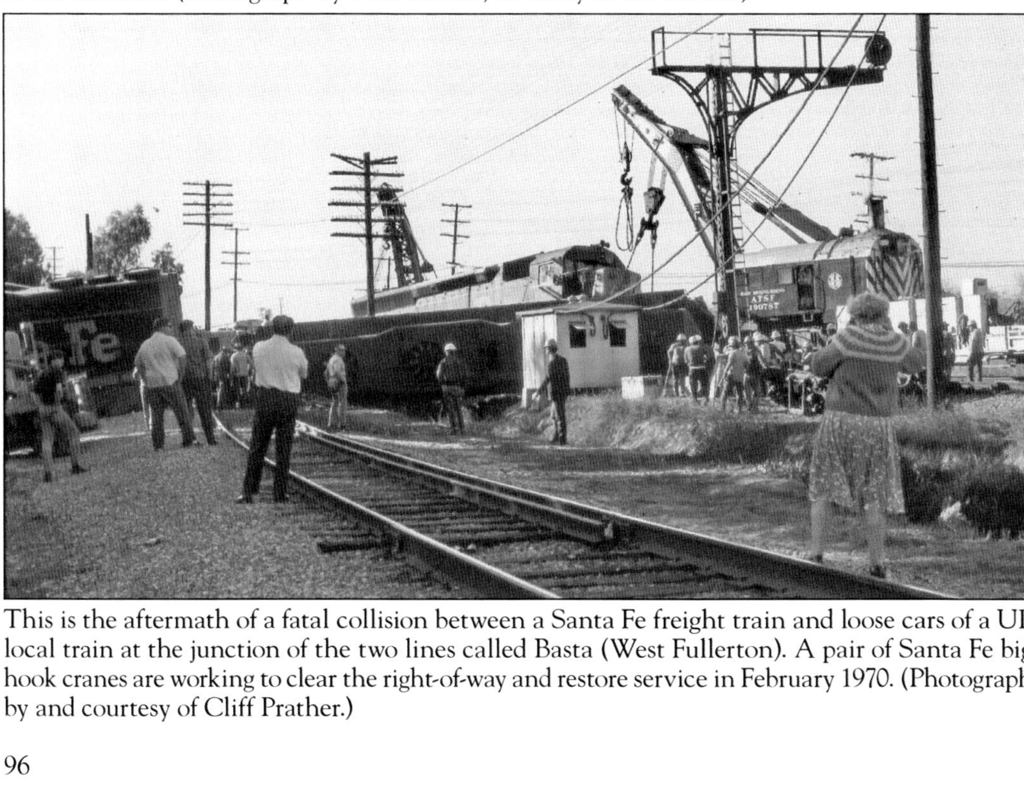

This is the aftermath of a fatal collision between a Santa Fe freight train and loose cars of a UP local train at the junction of the two lines called Basta (West Fullerton). A pair of Santa Fe big hook cranes are working to clear the right-of-way and restore service in February 1970. (Photograph by and courtesy of Cliff Prather.)

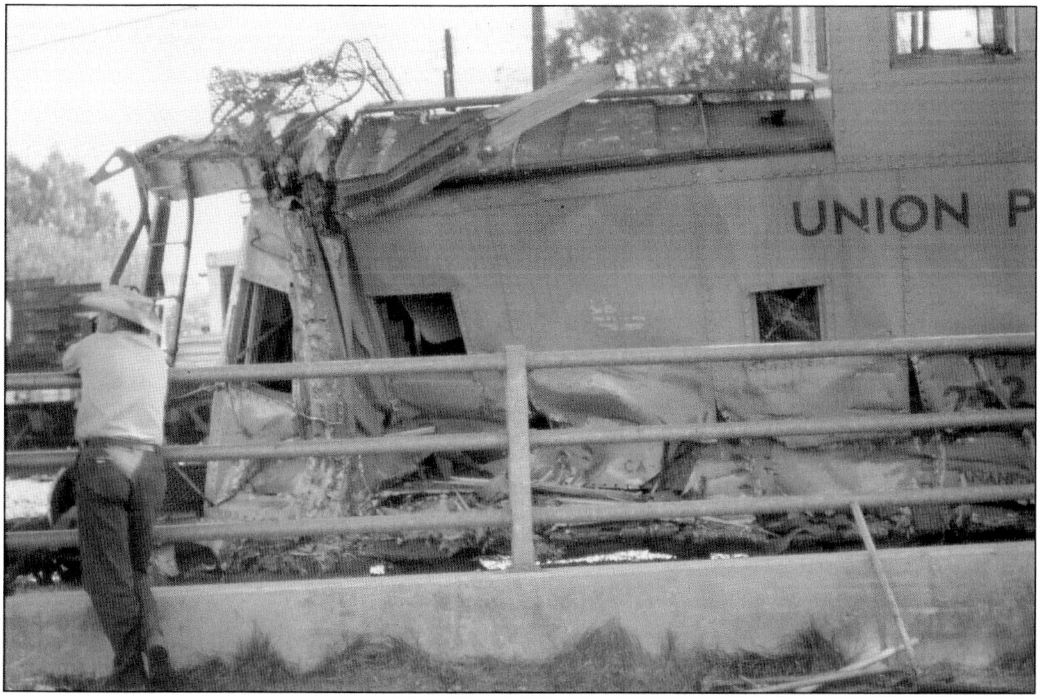

A UP local was switching at the Hunt Wesson factory in Fullerton. While the work was underway, the caboose in this photograph and some other freight cars rolled into the crossing of the UP and Santa Fe at Basta (West Fullerton). An oncoming westbound Santa Fe freight slammed into the errant caboose and cars, and left the UP train conductor dead. This crossing has since been removed. (Photograph by and courtesy of Cliff Prather.)

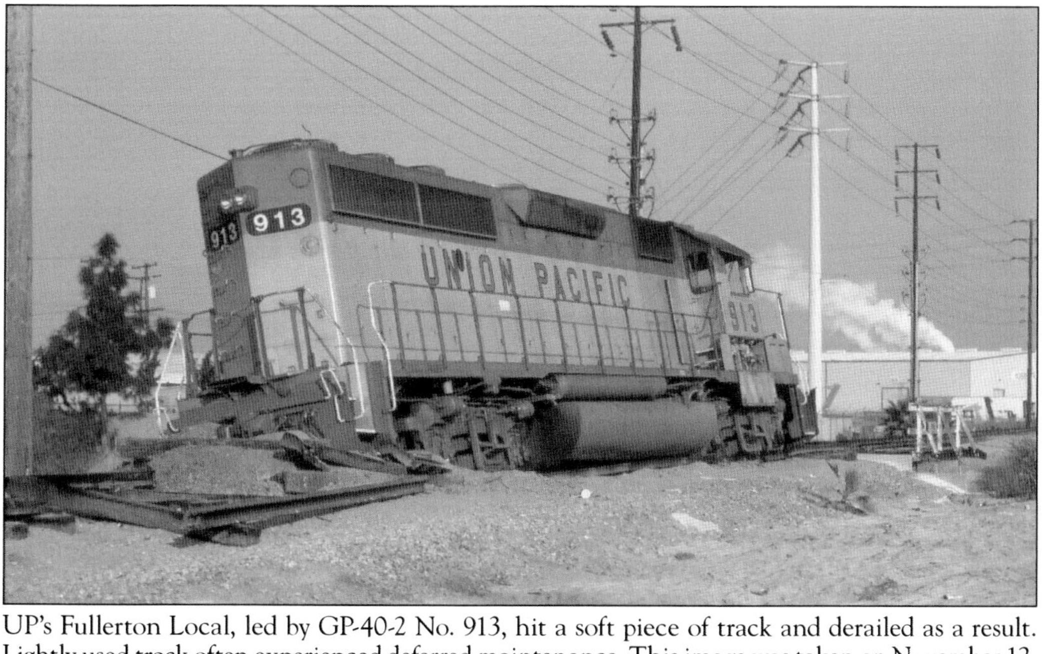

UP's Fullerton Local, led by GP-40-2 No. 913, hit a soft piece of track and derailed as a result. Lightly used track often experienced deferred maintenance. This image was taken on November 12, 1988. (Photograph by and courtesy of Cliff Prather.)

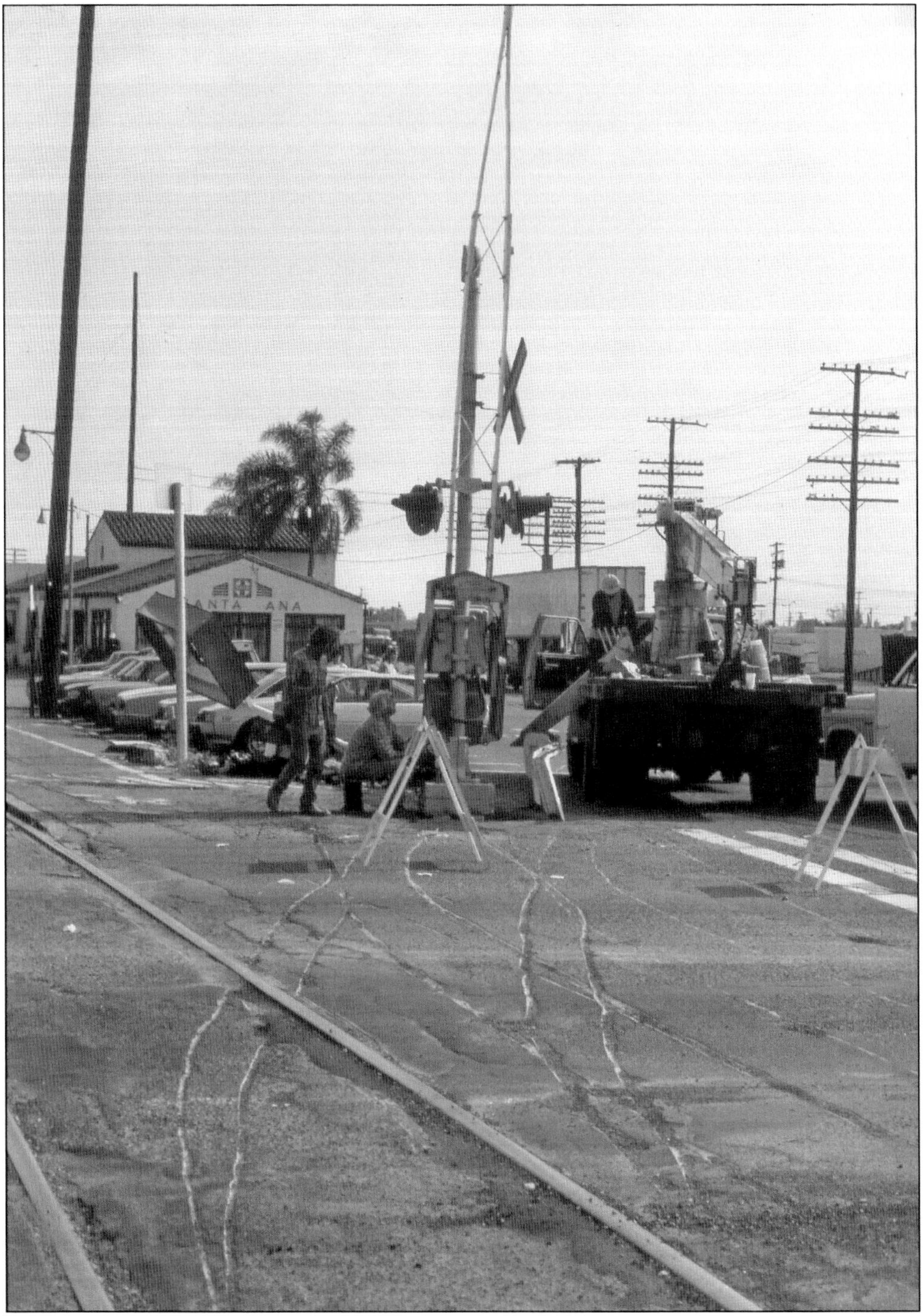

On April 5, 1985, cars from a southbound Santa Fe freight train derailed and crashed into the sign advertising the Santa Fe depot on Fourth Street in Santa Ana. The next day, Santa Fe crews are cleaning up the mess. The street was scarred by the flanged wheels of the derailed cars as they careened off the tracks. Fortunately, there were no injuries. (Photograph by and courtesy of the author.)

Seven

Amtrak, Metrolink, and the Age of Mergers

Major developments have shaped the national and local railroad picture. In May 1971, Amtrak assumed most American intercity passenger train operation. In the early 1990s, the Southern California Railroad Authority was established, and Metrolink began providing regional commuter passenger train service. And finally, merger fever impacted all of Orange County's freight carriers; the Santa Fe merged to form the Burlington Northern Santa Fe, and UP absorbed the SP. While the names have changed one thing is clear—there are more trains running in Orange County today than at any previous time.

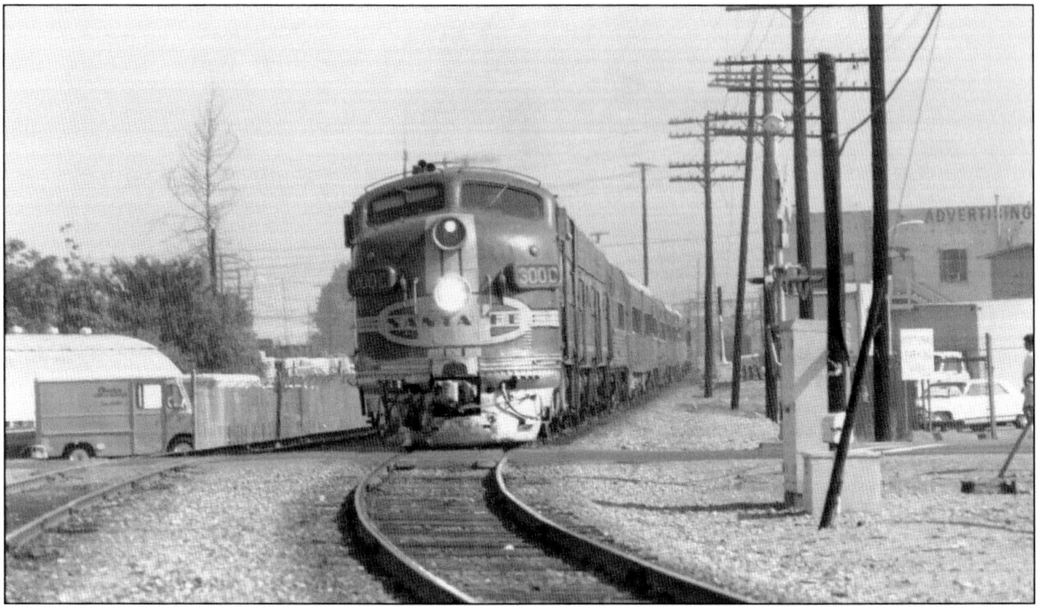

On June 23, 1973, Cliff Prather turned his camera on Amtrak train No. 770. The train has just left the Santa Ana station and is heading into the big turn south of Chestnut Avenue. In Amtrak's early years, the appearance of some trains changed very little. (Photograph by and courtesy of Cliff Prather.)

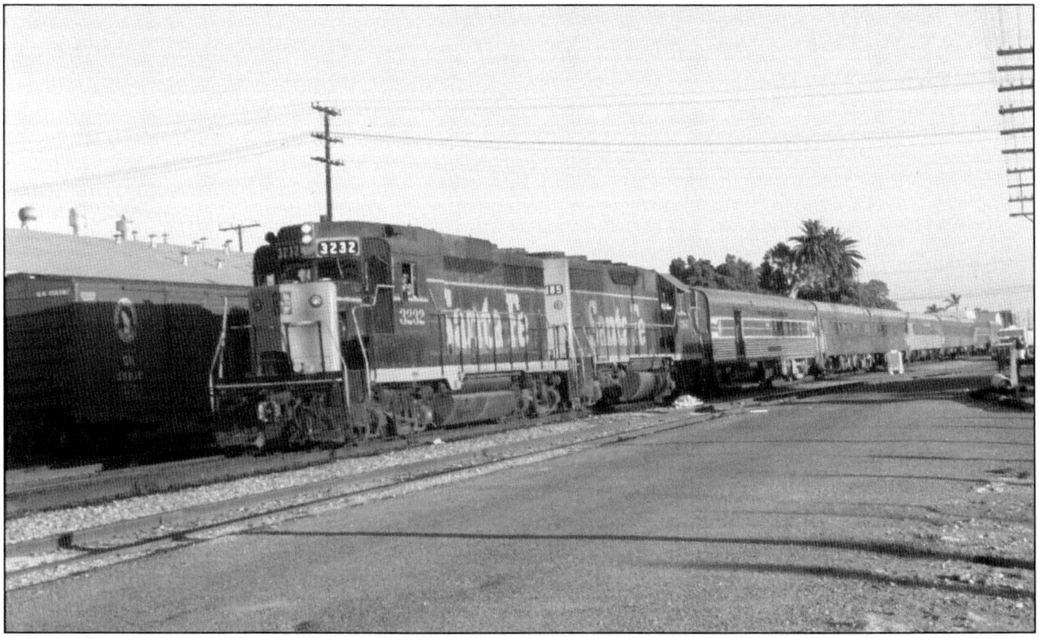

In the late afternoon of July 30, 1972, today's Amtrak San Diegan is powered by a Santa Fe freight locomotive as it heads toward Los Angeles in Orange. No. 3232 is a GP 30 locomotive and is assisted by GP 35 No. 3385. Blue and yellow were the standard colors for Santa Fe diesel freight units in the 1960s and 1970s; red and silver were the standard colors for passenger locomotives. In the late 1980s, Santa Fe boldly reconnected with the image of its past and readopted the red and silver colors for its new diesel locomotives. (Photograph by and courtesy of Cliff Prather.)

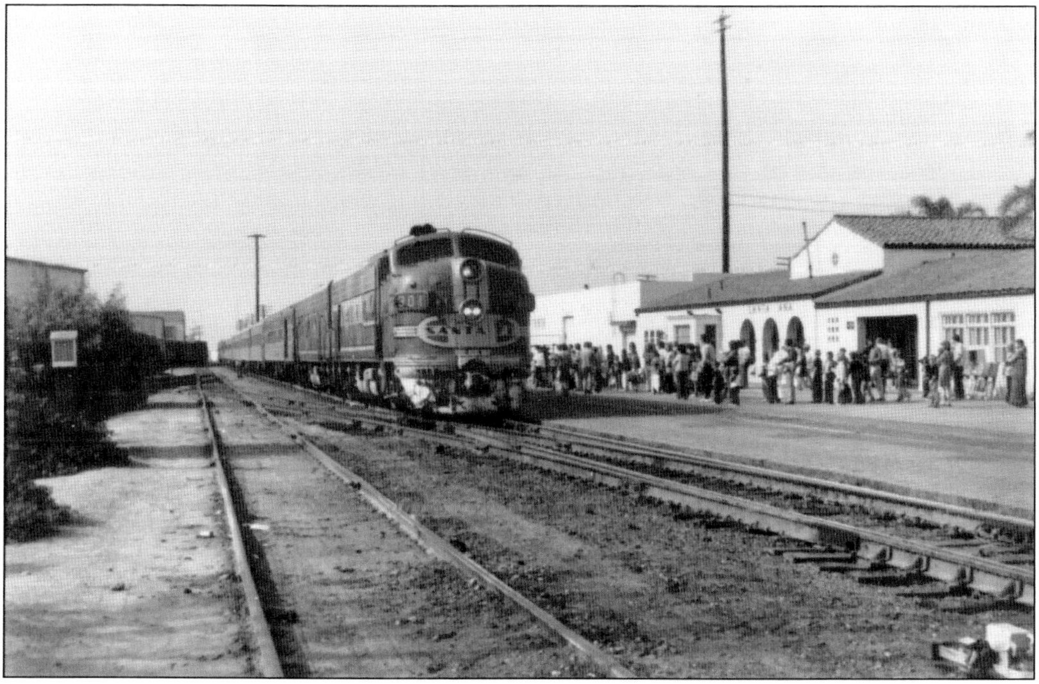

On June 16, 1973, Amtrak's train No. 771 is greeted by a large crowd waiting to board the train. This view appears little different than in the Santa Fe years; the Amtrak *Santa Ana* sign has not yet been tacked onto the venerable old depot. (Photograph by and courtesy of Cliff Prather.)

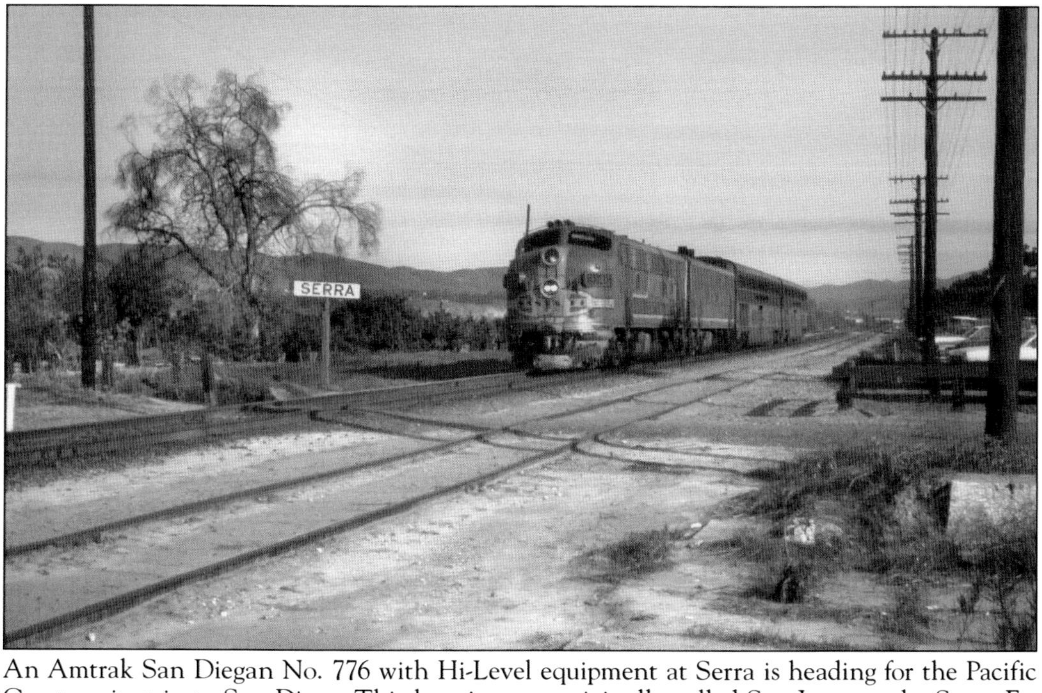

An Amtrak San Diegan No. 776 with Hi-Level equipment at Serra is heading for the Pacific Coast on its trip to San Diego. This location was originally called San Juan on the Santa Fe, and a depot similar to the ones at Carlsbad and Encinitas once stood at this location. (Courtesy of the author.)

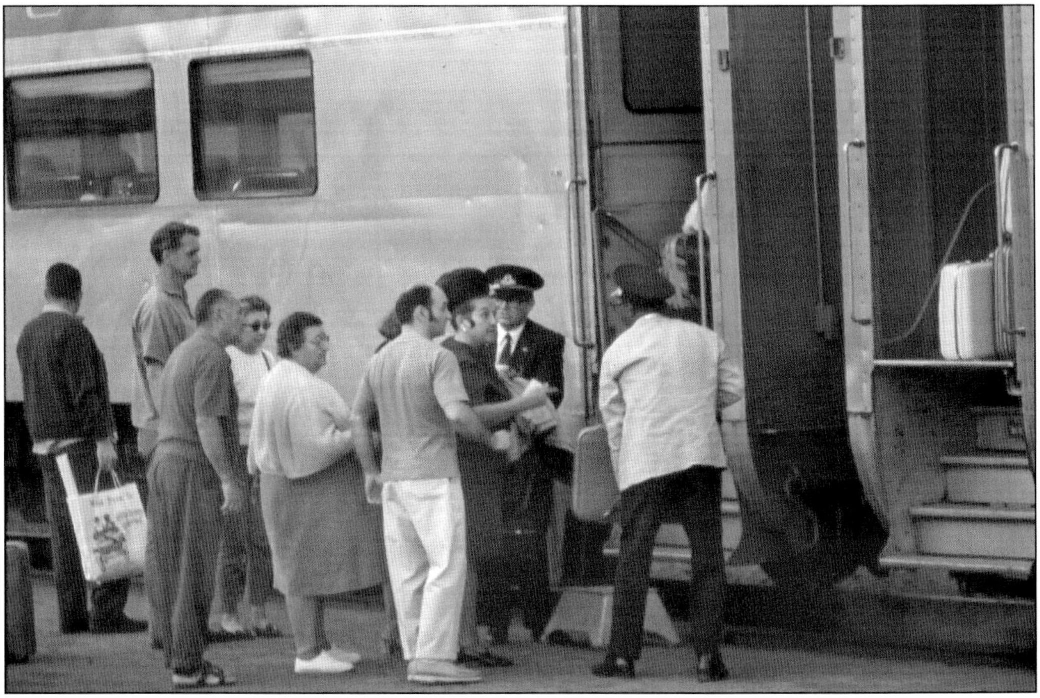

Seen here is train time at the Santa Ana Amtrak station in March 1972. Amtrak has yet to repaint this former SP coach, and the conductor still wears a Santa Fe cap although Amtrak took over service on May 1, 1971. (Photograph by and courtesy of Cliff Prather.)

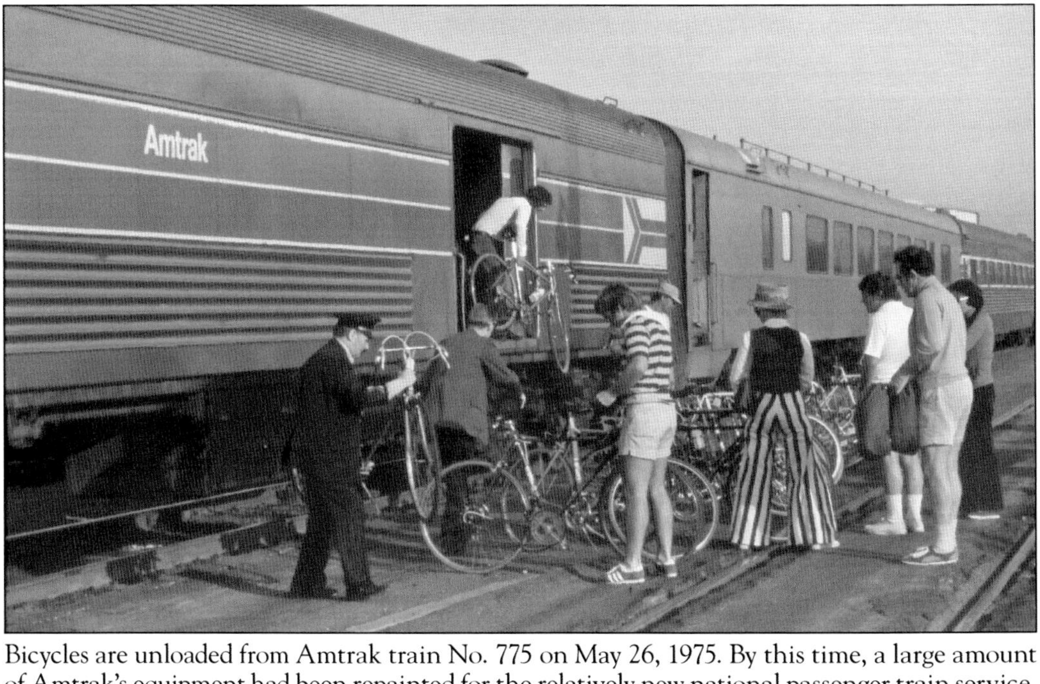

Bicycles are unloaded from Amtrak train No. 775 on May 26, 1975. By this time, a large amount of Amtrak's equipment had been repainted for the relatively new national passenger train service. Who is the funny guy with the striped pants? Well, it was the 1970s. (Photograph by and courtesy of Cliff Prather.)

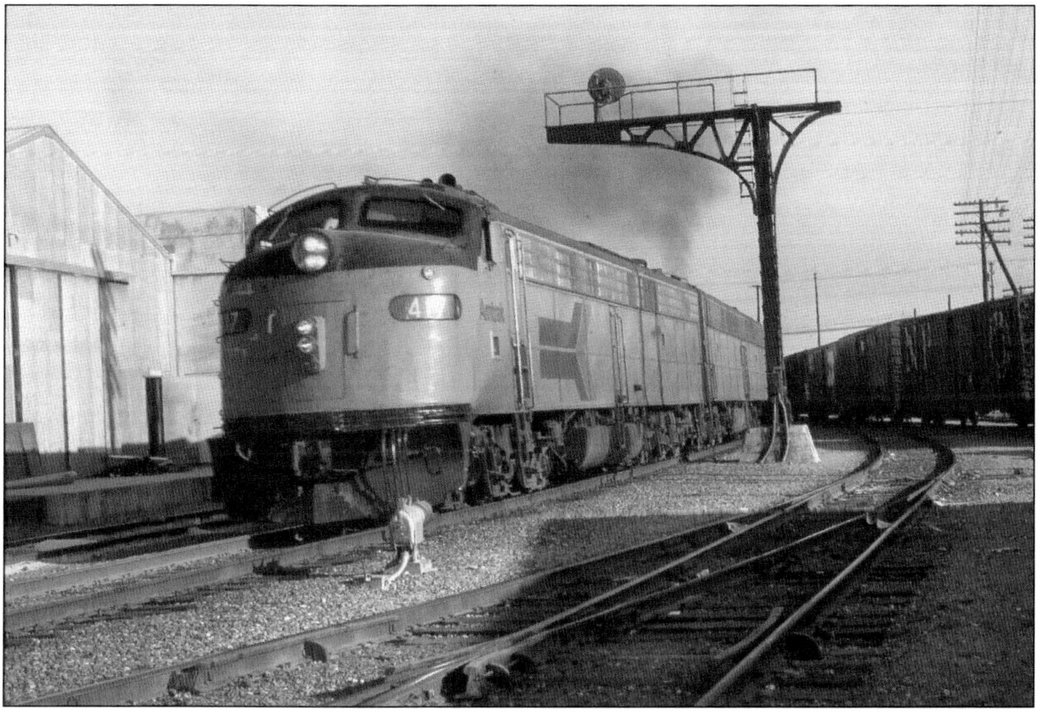

Amtrak train No. 775 gets a running start away from the Santa Ana depot. In about one hour, the train will reach the bumper post at Los Angles Union Passenger Terminal. Note the dwarf signal in the foreground; this was the end of two main tracks. Amtrak was three months past its fifth birthday when this photograph was made on July 31, 1975. (Photograph by and courtesy of Cliff Prather.)

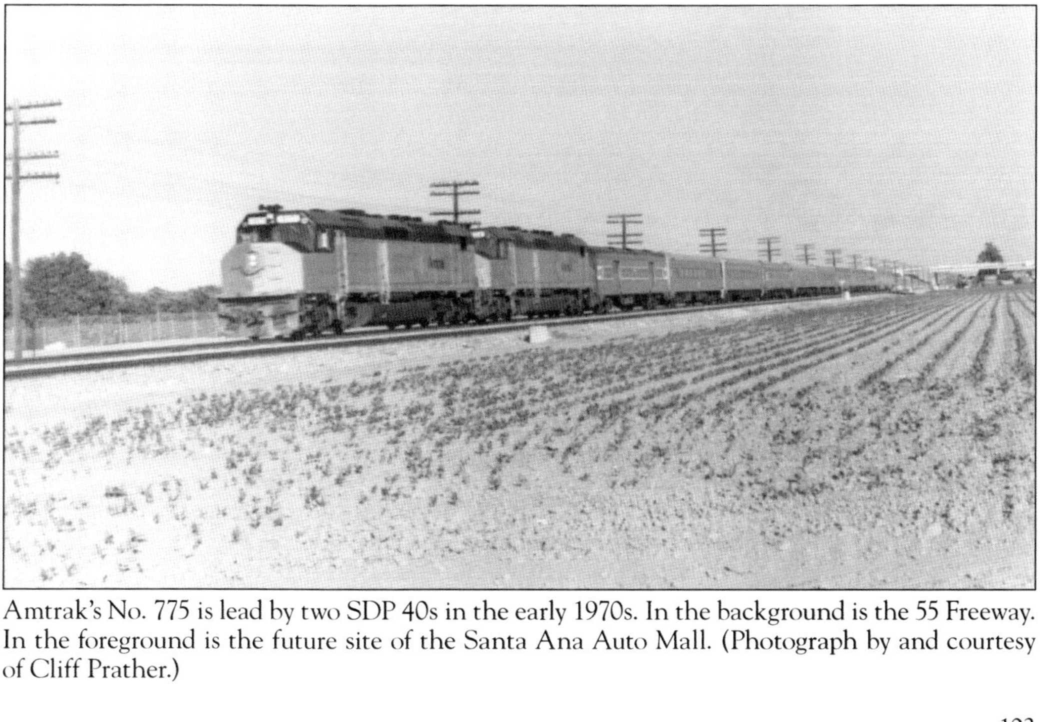

Amtrak's No. 775 is lead by two SDP 40s in the early 1970s. In the background is the 55 Freeway. In the foreground is the future site of the Santa Ana Auto Mall. (Photograph by and courtesy of Cliff Prather.)

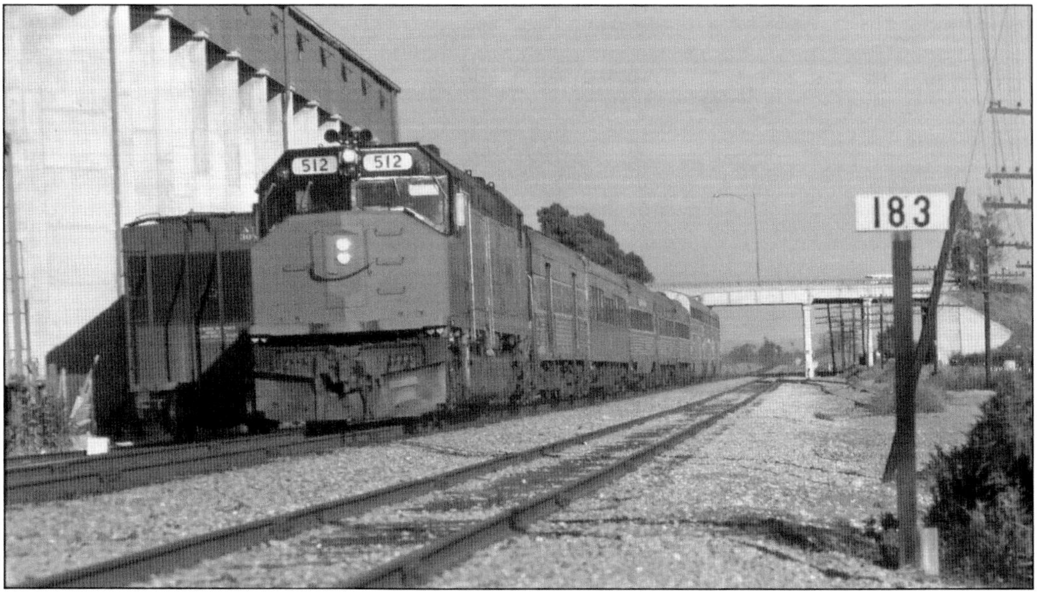

At Sand Canyon Road in Irvine, Amtrak train No. 775 is seen. The locomotive in the lead is an SDP 40 and was built specifically for Amtrak. Since the relocation of the Irvine station, the Santa Fe now calls this location Valencia. The large bean warehouse on the right has been converted into a hotel. (Photograph by and courtesy of Cliff Prather.)

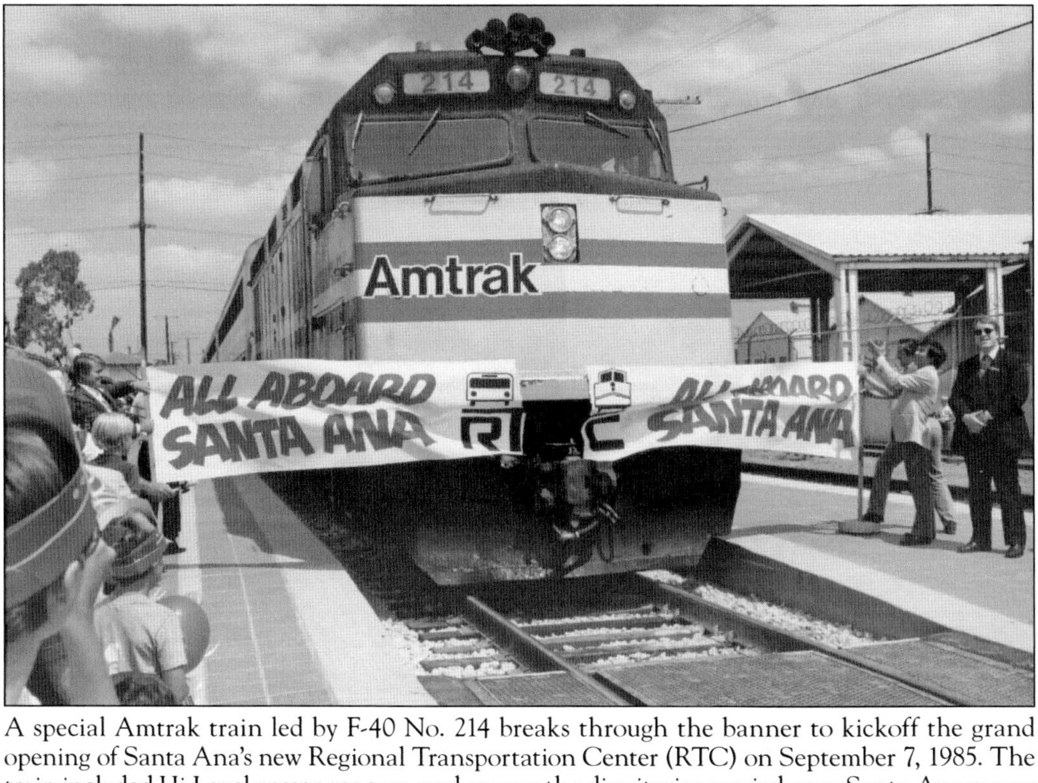

A special Amtrak train led by F-40 No. 214 breaks through the banner to kickoff the grand opening of Santa Ana's new Regional Transportation Center (RTC) on September 7, 1985. The train included Hi-Level passenger cars, and among the dignitaries carried were Santa Ana mayor Dan Griset and Los Angeles mayor Tom Bradley. (Courtesy of the author.)

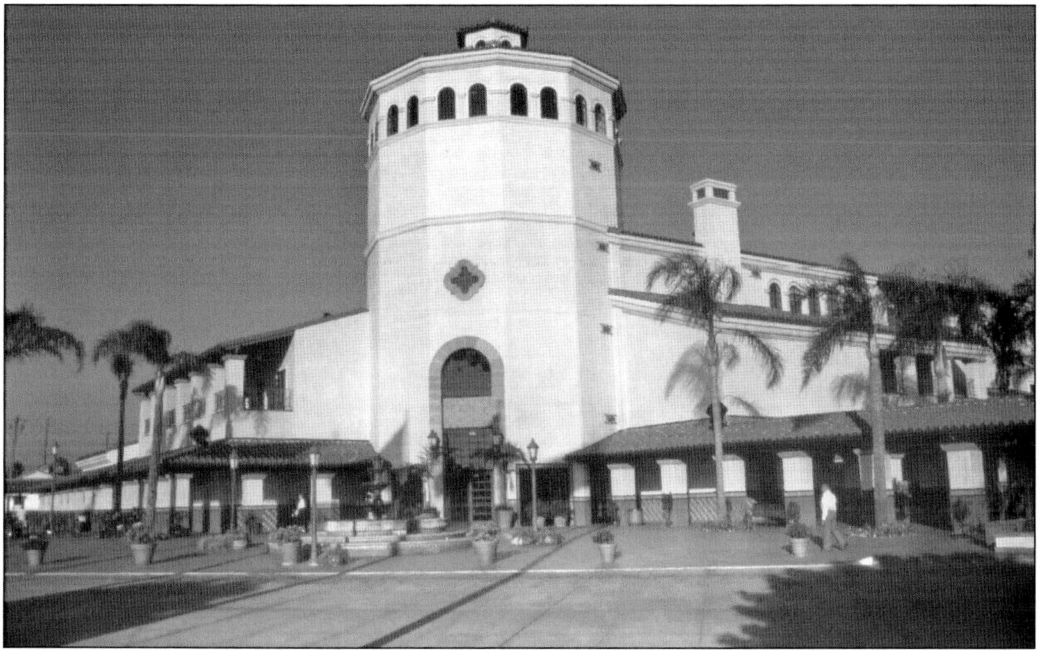

The Santa Ana RTC opened at 1000 East Santa Ana Boulevard in September 1985. Upon opening, the center served Amtrak, the Orange County Transportation Authority, and intercity buses. Metrolink rail service began in 1994. (Photograph by and courtesy of the author.)

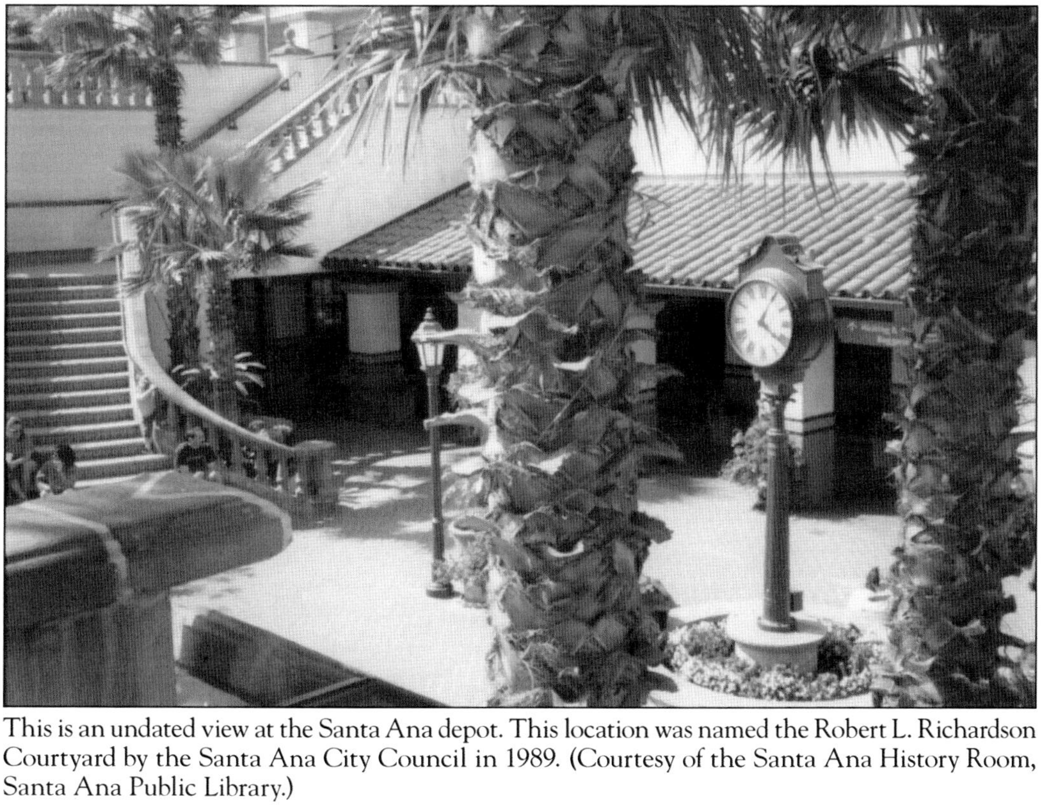

This is an undated view at the Santa Ana depot. This location was named the Robert L. Richardson Courtyard by the Santa Ana City Council in 1989. (Courtesy of the Santa Ana History Room, Santa Ana Public Library.)

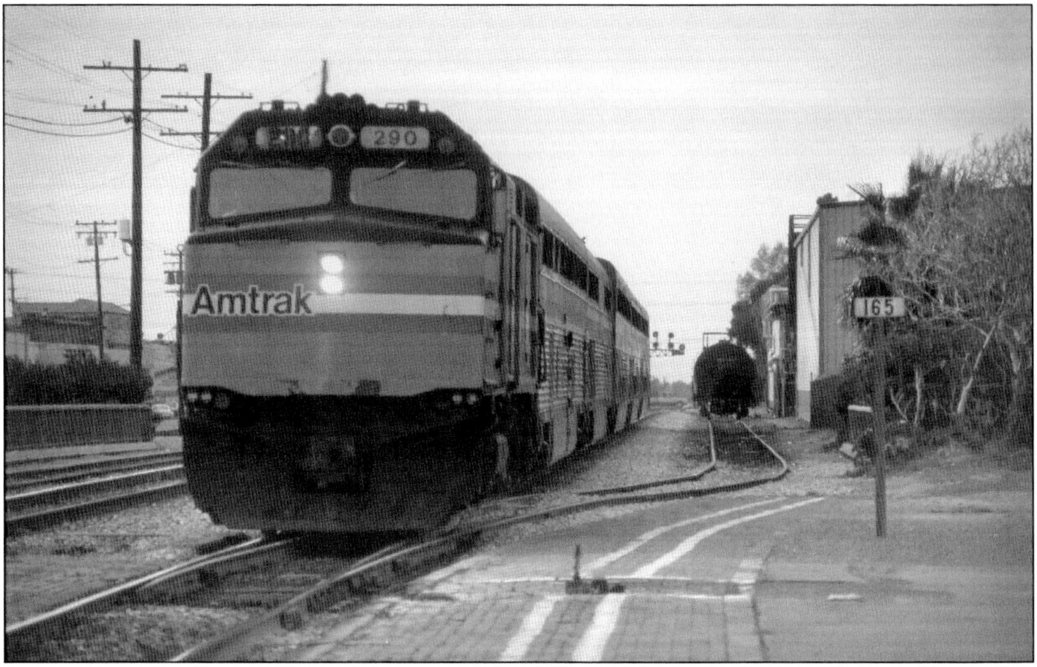

Amtrak train No. 36, the *Desert Wind*, slowly approaches the Fullerton train station. This train connected with Amtrak's *Pioneer* and the *San Francisco Zephyr* in Salt Lake City. This photograph was taken on November 16, 1986. (Photograph by and courtesy of the author.)

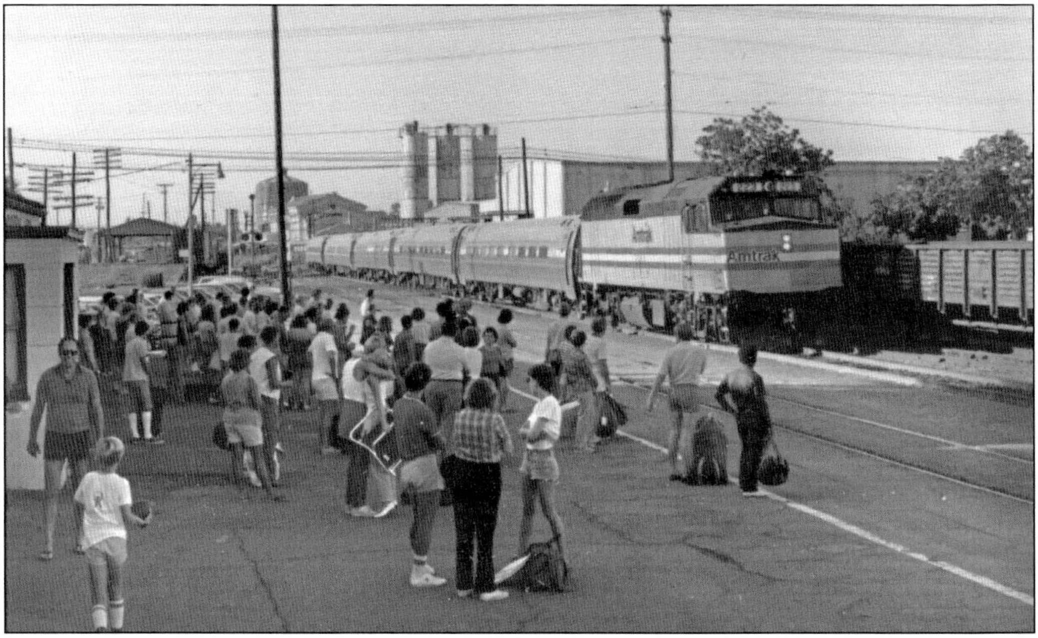

Seen here is a common scene from the 1970s and 1980s at the old Santa Fe depot in Santa Ana as a San Diegan arrives. A large group of passengers is waiting patiently behind the safety stripe as Amtrak No. 223 (F-40) leads five Amfleet coaches on the sprint to San Diego. The old depot's days are numbered—in the background the new depot can be seen under construction. (Photograph by and courtesy of the author.)

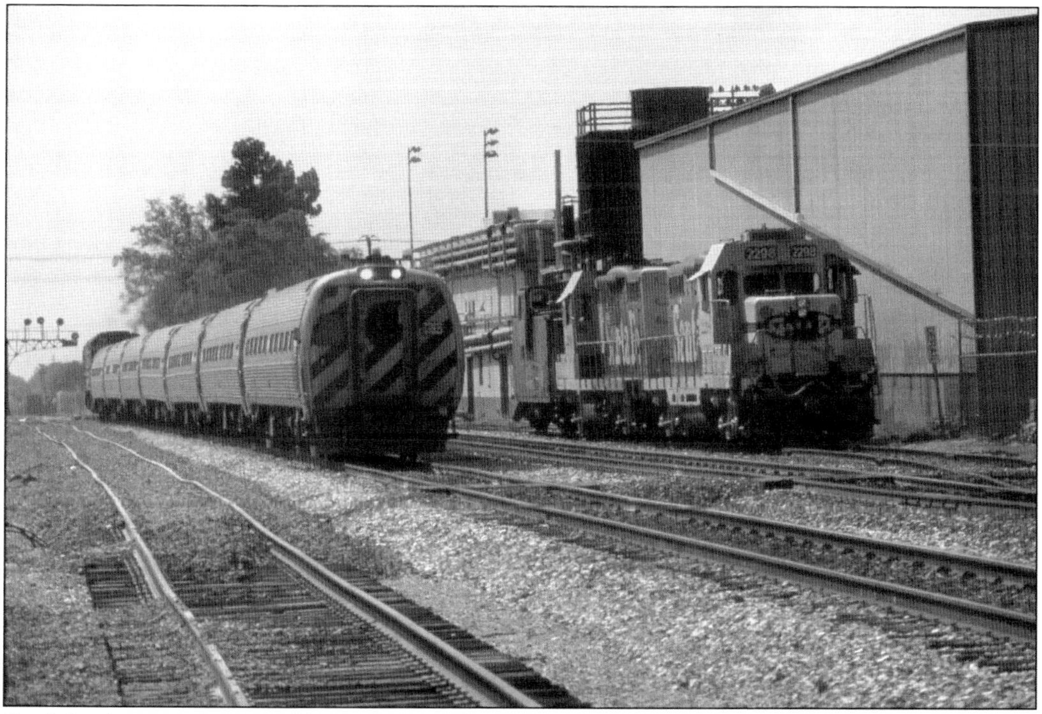

On March 1, 1995, a southbound Amtrak San Diegan is led by control car No. 9632 and is approaching Fullerton. The introduction of cab cars on this line enabled the engineers to operate the train in any direction, and no switching of the trains was necessary at either Los Angeles or San Diego, which reduced labor costs. A pair of GP 7s assigned to Fullerton is parked on a sidetrack. (Photograph by and courtesy of the author.)

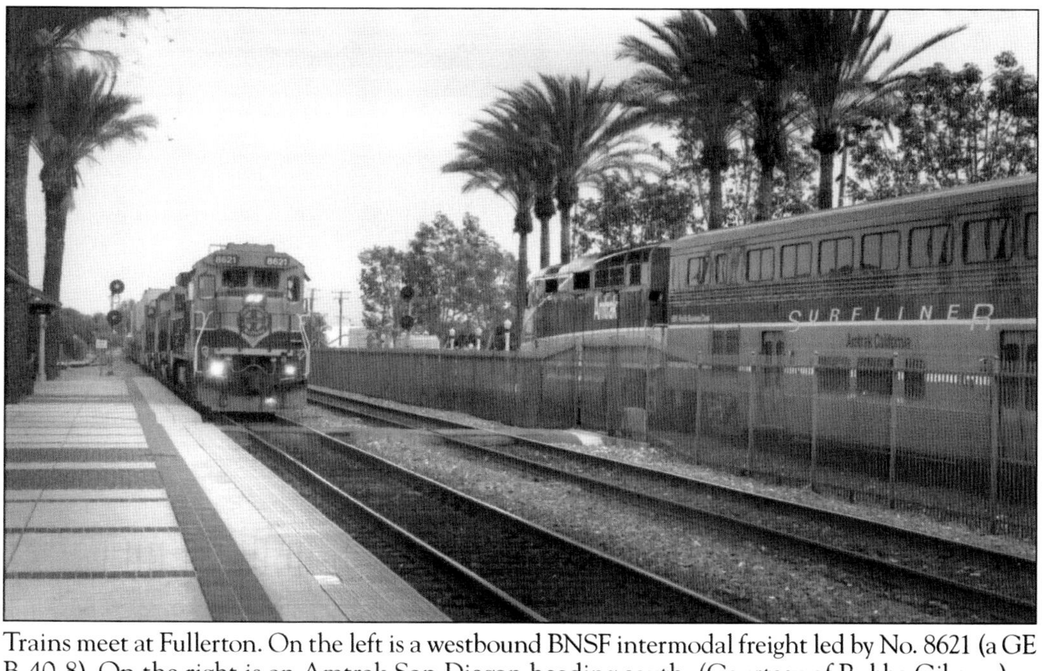

Trains meet at Fullerton. On the left is a westbound BNSF intermodal freight led by No. 8621 (a GE B-40-8). On the right is an Amtrak San Diegan heading south. (Courtesy of Robbe Gibson.)

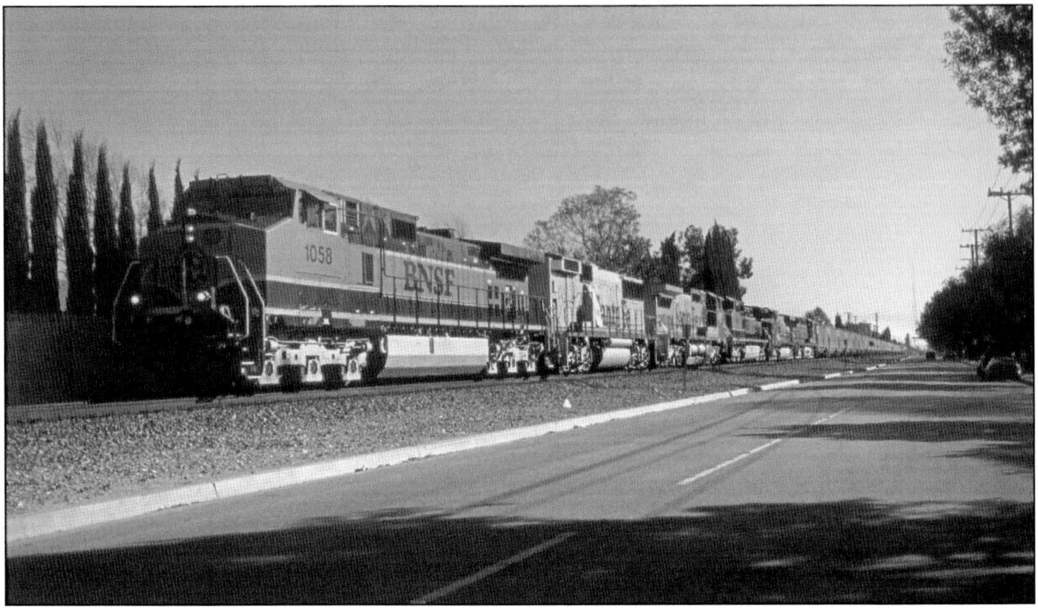

In March 1995, six big units (all GEs except for the GP-60B) are leading a manifest train north along Lincoln Avenue in north Santa Ana in March 1995. While the BNSF has trackage rights here, the line from Atwood to Orange and Fullerton to Oceanside is now owned by Metrolink. By this date, this was one of only two short stretches of the Santa Fe lines in Orange County yet to be double tracked. (Photograph by and courtesy of the author.)

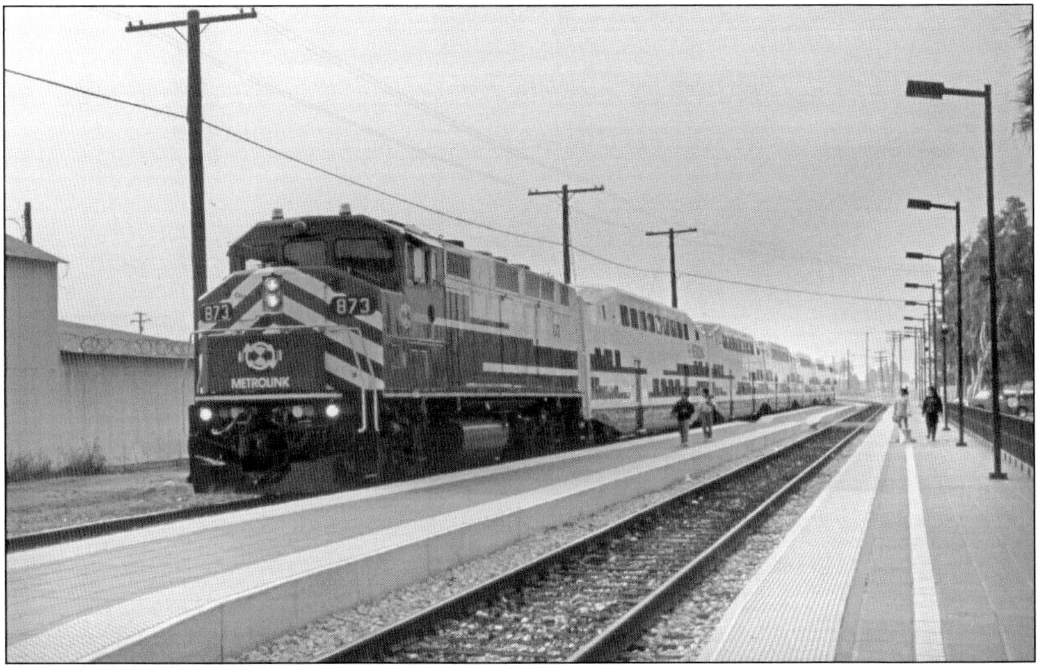

It is March 1994, and Metrolink service has arrived in Orange County. No. 873 is an F-59 and is one of up to 25 that Metrolink owned. This locomotive, shown at the Santa Ana depot in the "pull mode," is in its as-delivered, periwinkle blue–and-white paint scheme. (Photograph by and courtesy of the author.)

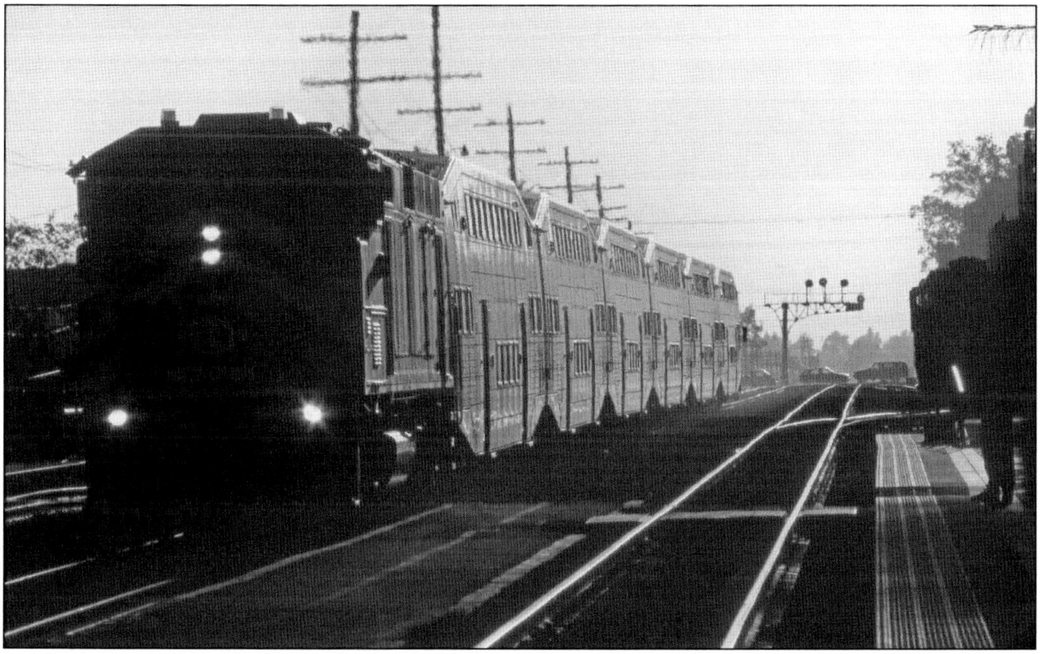

Metrolink trains are frequent visitors to Orange County. Lines now include the Oceanside-to–Los Angeles line (the Orange County Line), the 91 line (Los Angeles to Riverside via Fullerton), and the Inland Empire–to–Orange County line. This April 4, 1995, view shows an Orange County line train arriving at Fullerton led by an F-59ph. (Photograph by and courtesy of the author.)

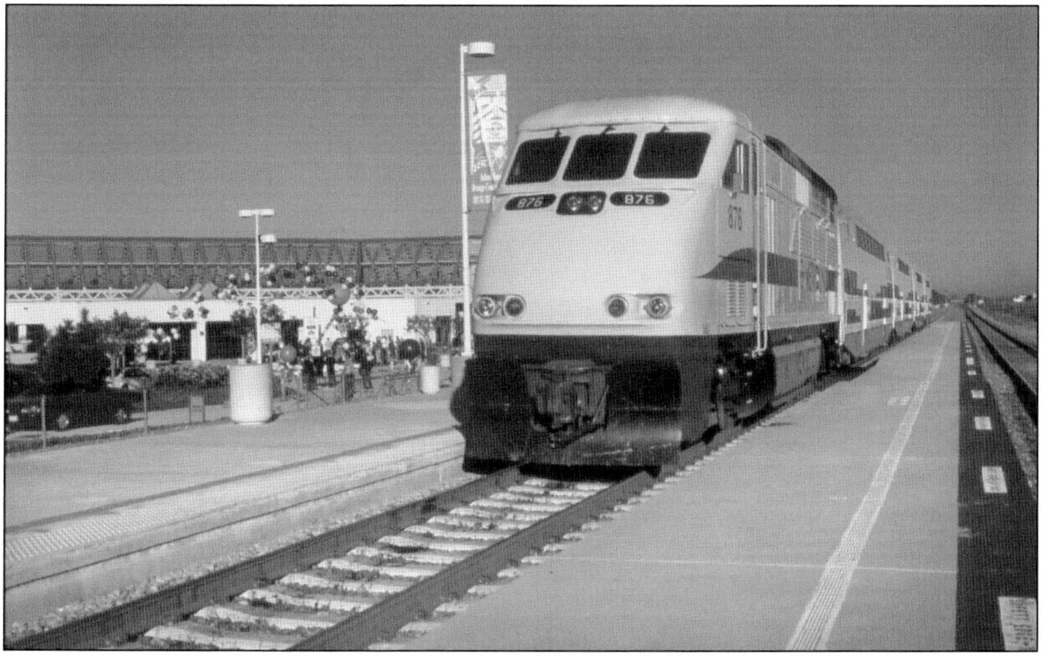

A Metrolink train is led by F-59 No. 876 and is at the Irvine Transportation Center on October 2, 1995. Metrolink service began in 1992 and was introduced to Orange County in 1994. Ridership and frequency of service have increased steadily as the popularity of Metrolink has grown. (Photograph by and courtesy of the author.)

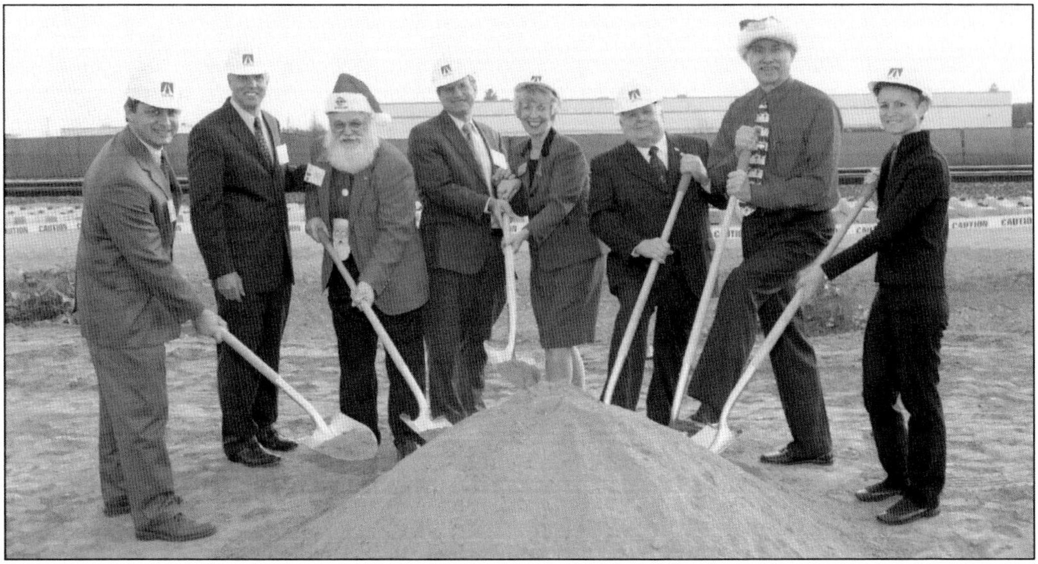

Buena Park had small depots serving the Santa Fe and the SP railroads. Railroad passenger service was planned to return to Buena Park, and the ground-breaking for a new station took place on December 14, 2005. The following leaders were on hand that day (from left to right) Buena Park council member Steve Berry, assembly member Tom Umberg, OCTA director and Buena Park mayor pro tem Art Brown, county supervisor Chris Norby, Mayor Patsy Marshall, Buena Park council members Jim Dow and Don McCay, and assembly member Lynn Daucher. The station opened for Metrolink service on September 4, 2007. (Courtesy of the Orange County Transportation Authority.)

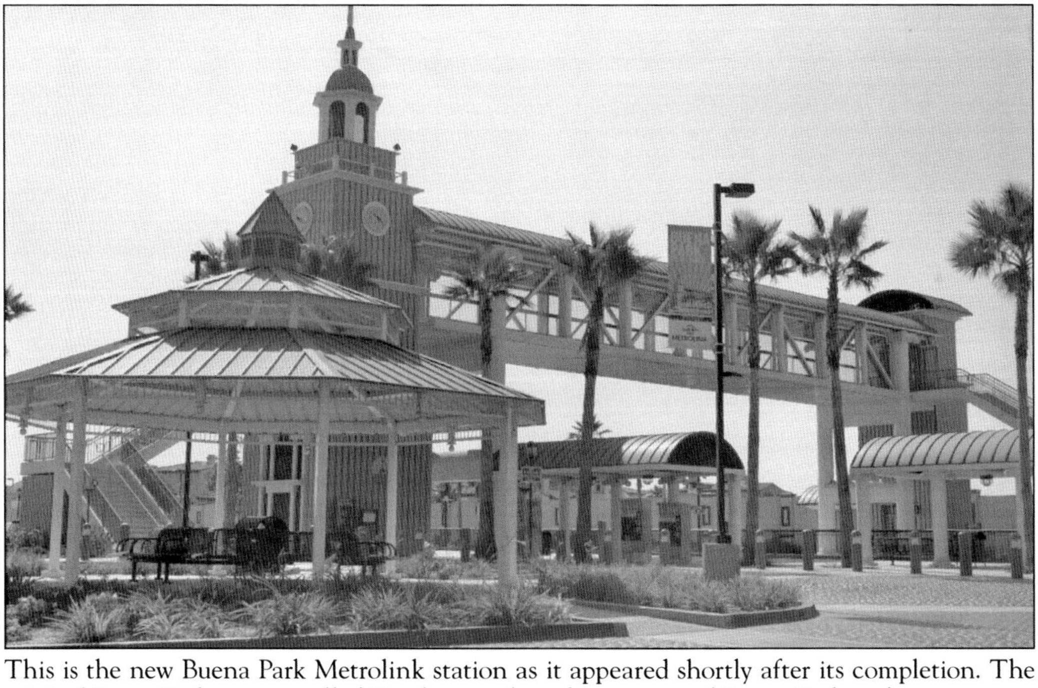

This is the new Buena Park Metrolink station as it appeared shortly after its completion. The original Santa Fe depot was called Northam and was later renamed Buena Park as the town grew. (Courtesy of the Orange County Transportation Authority.)

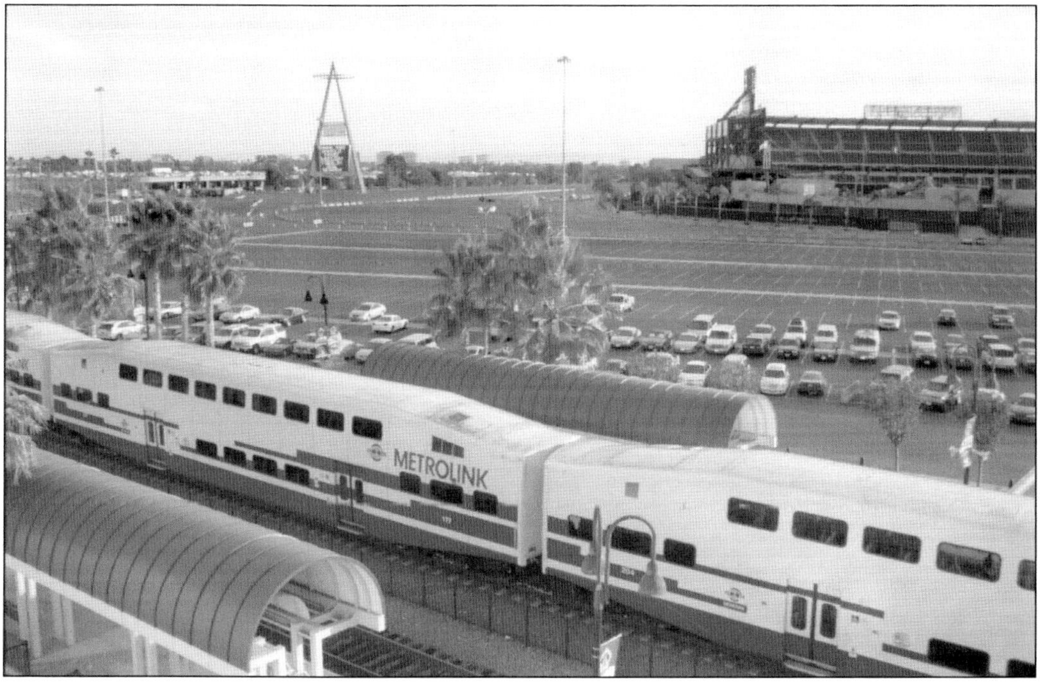

A southbound Metrolink train has reached its station stop at Anaheim Stadium. Amtrak also serves Anaheim from this depot, which was built in 1983. (Courtesy of the Orange County Transportation Authority)

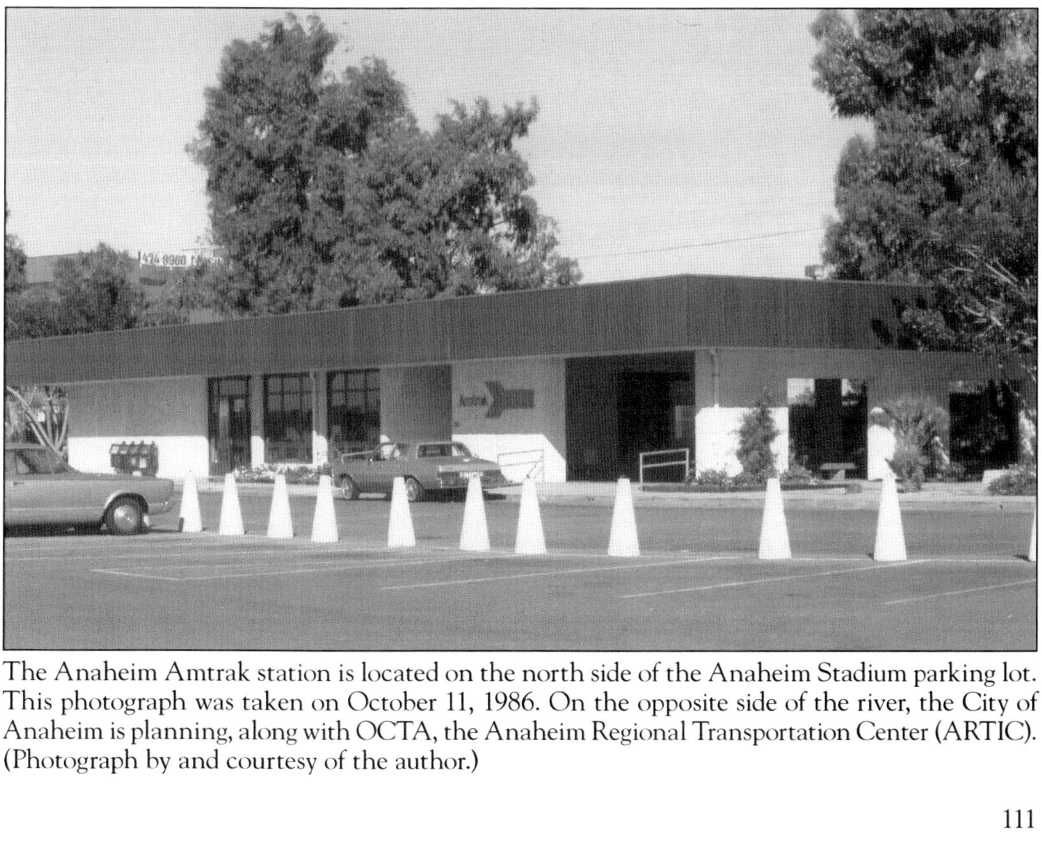

The Anaheim Amtrak station is located on the north side of the Anaheim Stadium parking lot. This photograph was taken on October 11, 1986. On the opposite side of the river, the City of Anaheim is planning, along with OCTA, the Anaheim Regional Transportation Center (ARTIC). (Photograph by and courtesy of the author.)

Metrolink No. 885 is arriving at the Orange depot. For several years after the Santa Fe ended passenger service, no passenger trains stopped in Orange. With the advent of Metrolink, a tradition dating to 1887 has been renewed. (Photograph courtesy of Robbe Gibson.)

Eight

Amusement Park Railroads

Any review of Orange County's railroad story needs to focus on the great amusement park railroads. In the postwar period, the development of Knott's Berry Farm and Disneyland were watershed events for the future of Orange County. People across America now knew of Orange County for reasons beyond citrus, military service, and good weather. In fact, the Orange County farmland was well suited for the development of new housing and provided the space needed for large-scale amusement parks unlike any other in the United States. Early television watchers witnessed Walt Disney open Disneyland with a program narrated by future California governor and U.S. president Ronald Reagan. Both Knott's Berry Farm and Disneyland became major tourist attractions. Flanged wheel operations are major attractions in both parks to this day.

Other miniature trains also operate in Orange County. Two of the newest are at Irvine Regional Park and the Santa Ana Zoo at Prentice Park in Santa Ana. Some of the miniature trains were short-lived, such as the Buffalo Ranch railroad or the small gauge train that ran around a lake at Knott's Berry Farm on the east side of Beach Boulevard. Trains are loved by kids of all ages, and that is why trains evoke such a prominent place in the nation's historic development. As the Amtrak slogan once said, "There's something about a train that's magic."

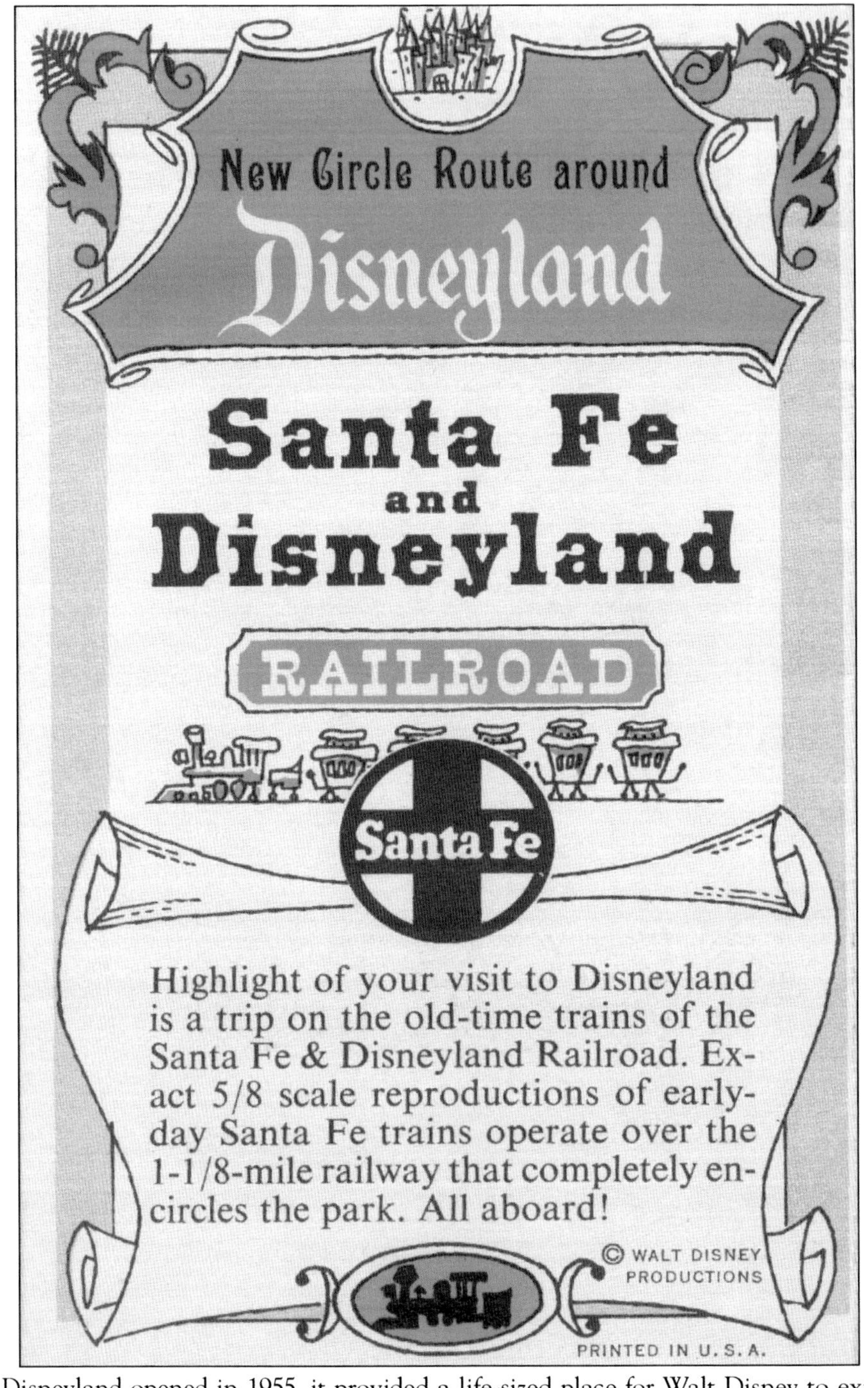

When Disneyland opened in 1955, it provided a life-sized place for Walt Disney to express his great interest in trains and the history of this country. The new railroad ringing Disneyland was sponsored by the Santa Fe and was, in turn, called the Santa Fe and Disneyland Railroad. In the mid-1950s, Santa Fe's named trains such as the *Super Chief* and *El Capitan* were in their heyday running between Chicago and Los Angeles. The marketing savvy of Santa Fe seized a great opportunity to showcase the business in a novel fashion. (Courtesy of the author.)

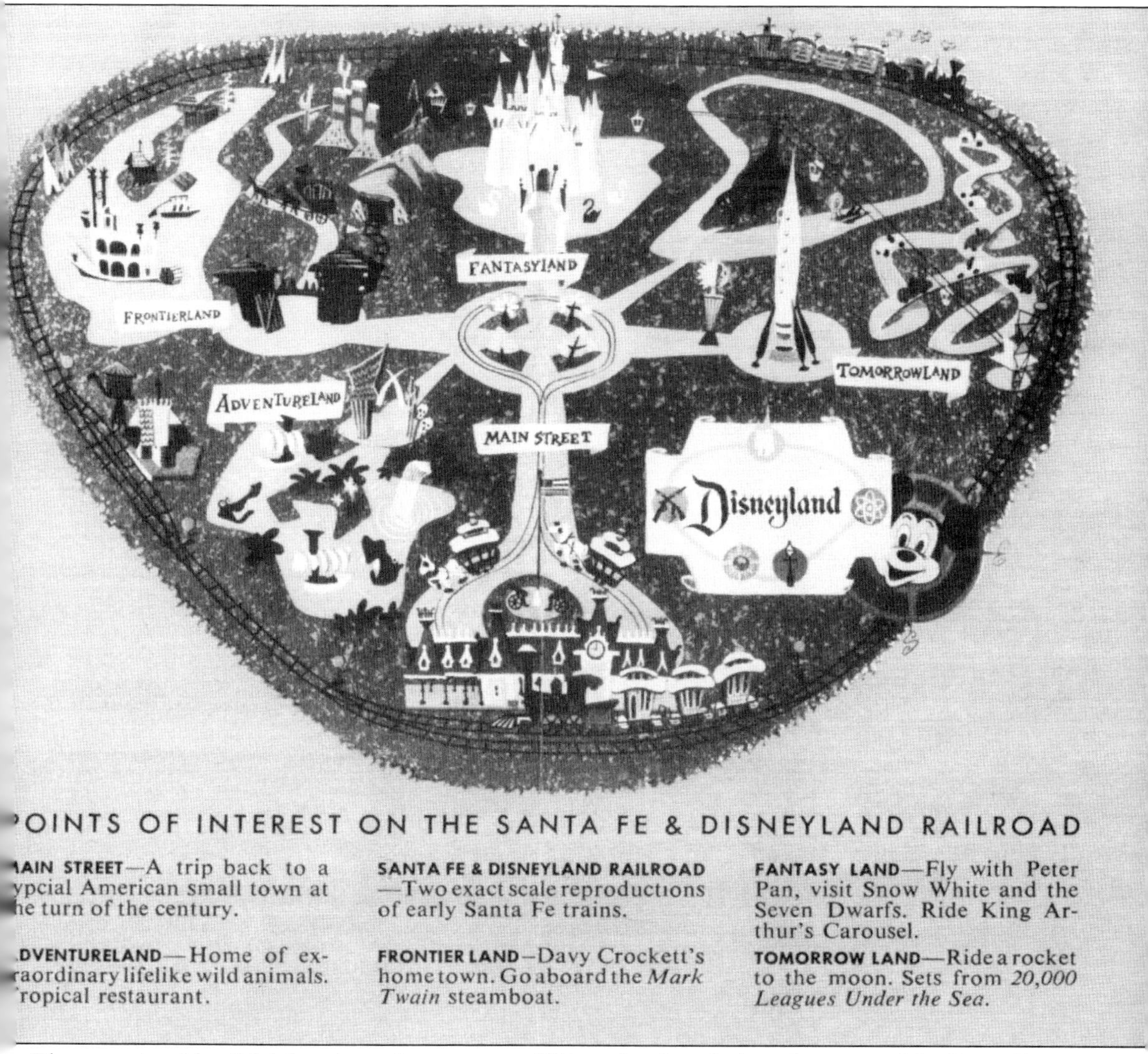

OINTS OF INTEREST ON THE SANTA FE & DISNEYLAND RAILROAD

AIN STREET—A trip back to a ypcial American small town at he turn of the century.

DVENTURELAND—Home of ex-raordinary lifelike wild animals. ropical restaurant.

SANTA FE & DISNEYLAND RAILROAD—Two exact scale reproductions of early Santa Fe trains.

FRONTIER LAND—Davy Crockett's home town. Go aboard the *Mark Twain* steamboat.

FANTASY LAND—Fly with Peter Pan, visit Snow White and the Seven Dwarfs. Ride King Arthur's Carousel.

TOMORROW LAND—Ride a rocket to the moon. Sets from *20,000 Leagues Under the Sea.*

The opposite side of this brochure shows a map of Disneyland, including the route of the Santa Fe and Disneyland Railroad. (Courtesy of the author.)

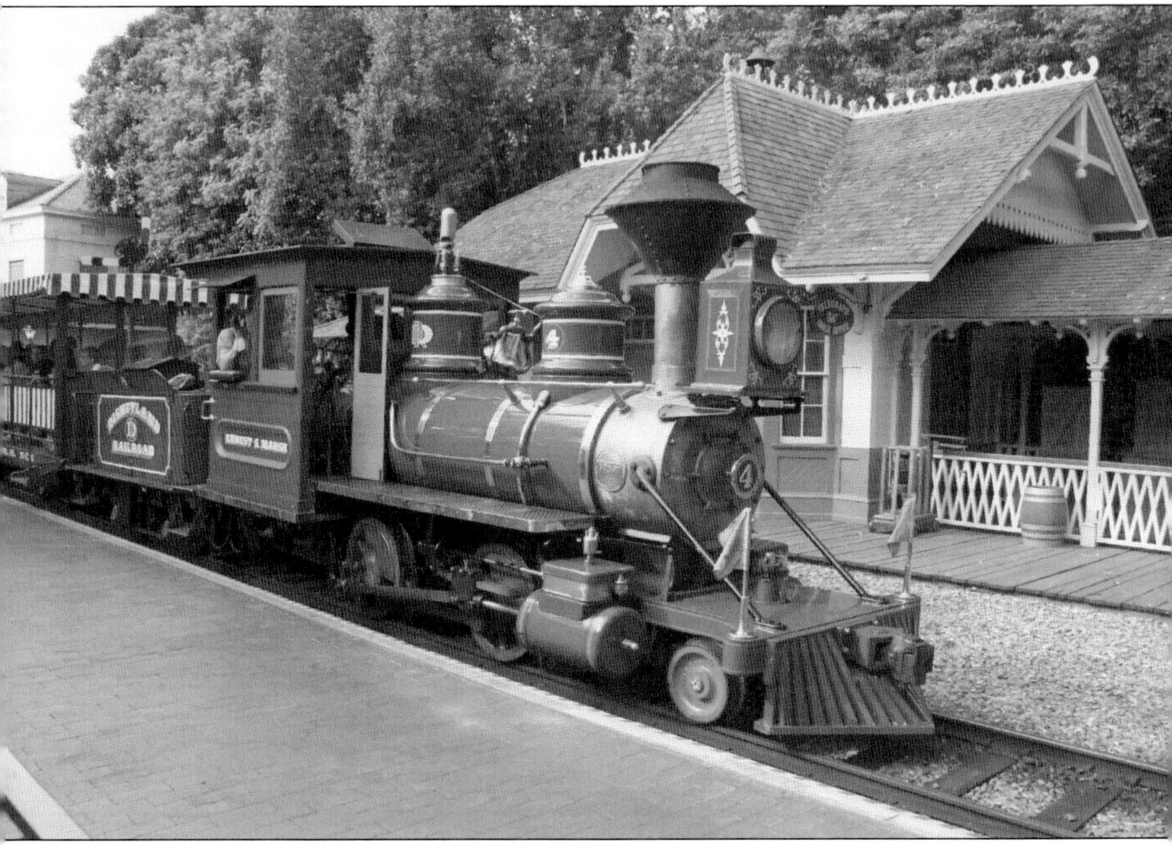

No. 4 is pulling a train to the first stop after Main Street on the Disneyland Railroad. This is the New Orleans Square station. This locomotive ties to the heritage of the original Santa Fe and Disneyland Railroad through the name "Ernest Marsh," emblazoned on the side. Marsh was a president of the Santa Fe, and other locomotives were named for previous Santa Fe presidents, including C. K. Holliday, E. P. Ripley, and Fred Gurley. (Courtesy of Doug Marsh.)

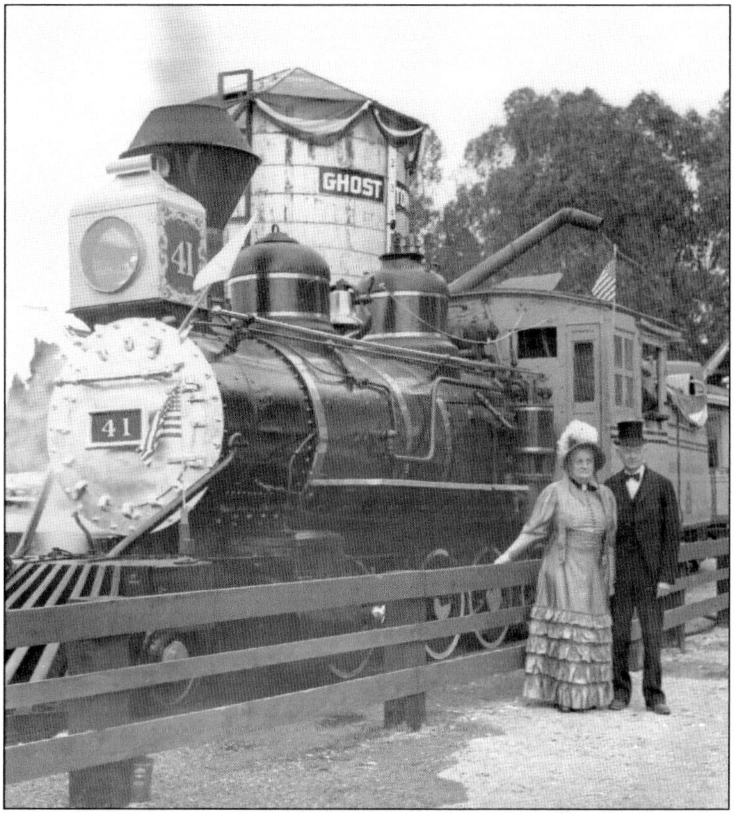

This marked the celebration of the golden spike and the completion of the narrow gauge rail line at Knott's Berry Farm on January 12, 1952. This train is unique because most of the rolling stock had been used in revenue service on the Denver and Rio Grande Western Railroad in Colorado. It is interesting to reflect that while the "real" railroads were converting from steam to diesel, it can be said that steam has operated continuously in Orange County railroading from the very beginning backing 1877. Not too many places can claim this obscure fact. (Courtesy of the Orange County Archives.)

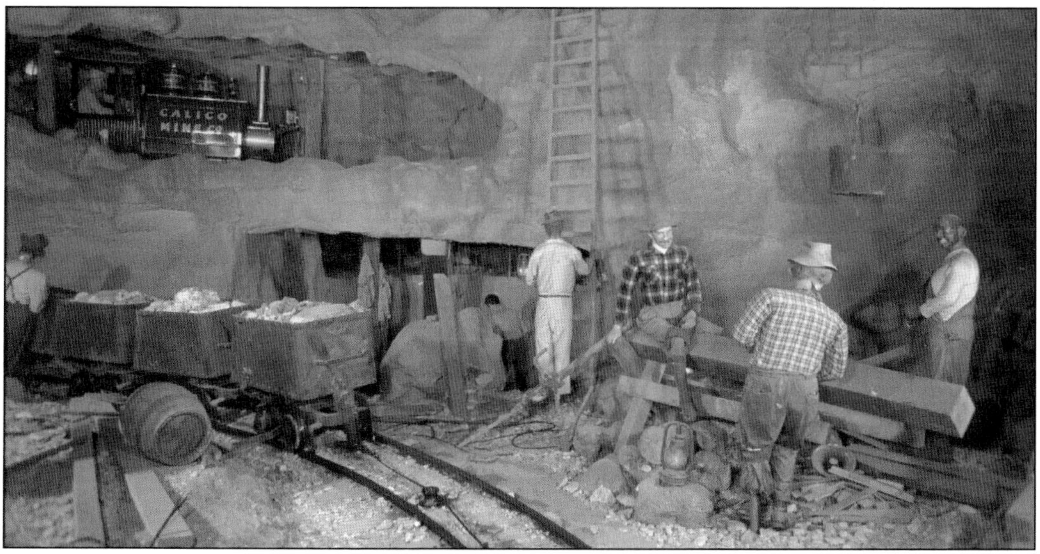

When one thinks of trains in Orange County, the Calico Mine Ride at Knott's Berry Farm might not be the first to come to mind. This train ride remains captivating after more than 40 years of operation. Who can forget the ride on this little mine train featuring all the miners going about their business and the narrow escape as the mine threatens to collapse. As described by Knott's: "Descend into the dark depths of Knott's very own gold mine to the infamous Calico Glory Hole." (Courtesy of the Orange County Archives.)

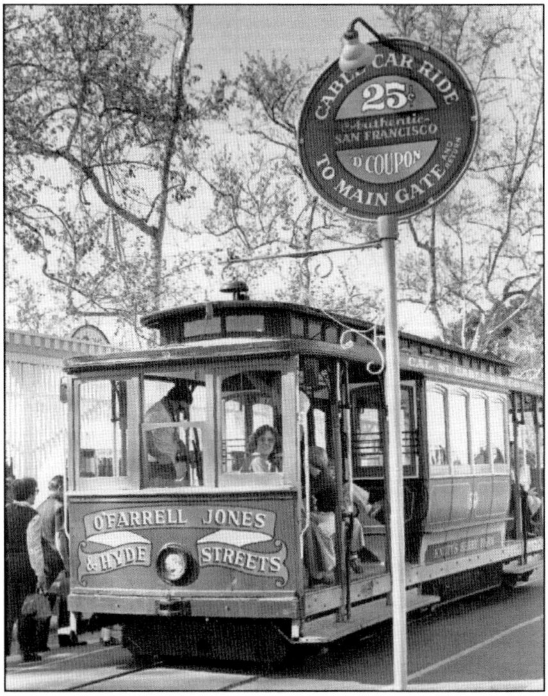

During the late 1950s, a number of San Francisco cable cars were equipped to operate at Knott's Berry Farm. This service was continued into the early 1970s. A resurgence of the famed city's cable cars led to many of the Knott's cars eventually returning to San Francisco. (Courtesy of the Orange County Archives.)

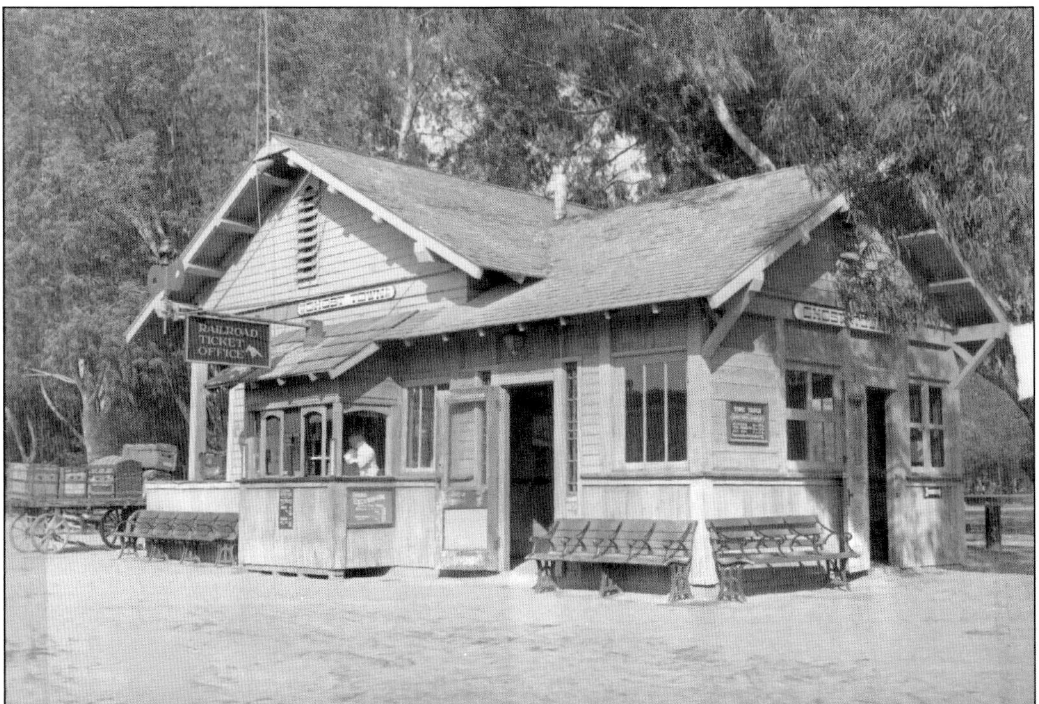

This depot now serves the Knott's Berry Farm narrow-gauge train. The structure originally served as the Hansen depot on the Santa Ana line of the PE. The depot, along with the trains and landscaping, made the Ghost Town at Knott's Berry Farm seem just like the Old West. (Courtesy of the Orange County Archives.)

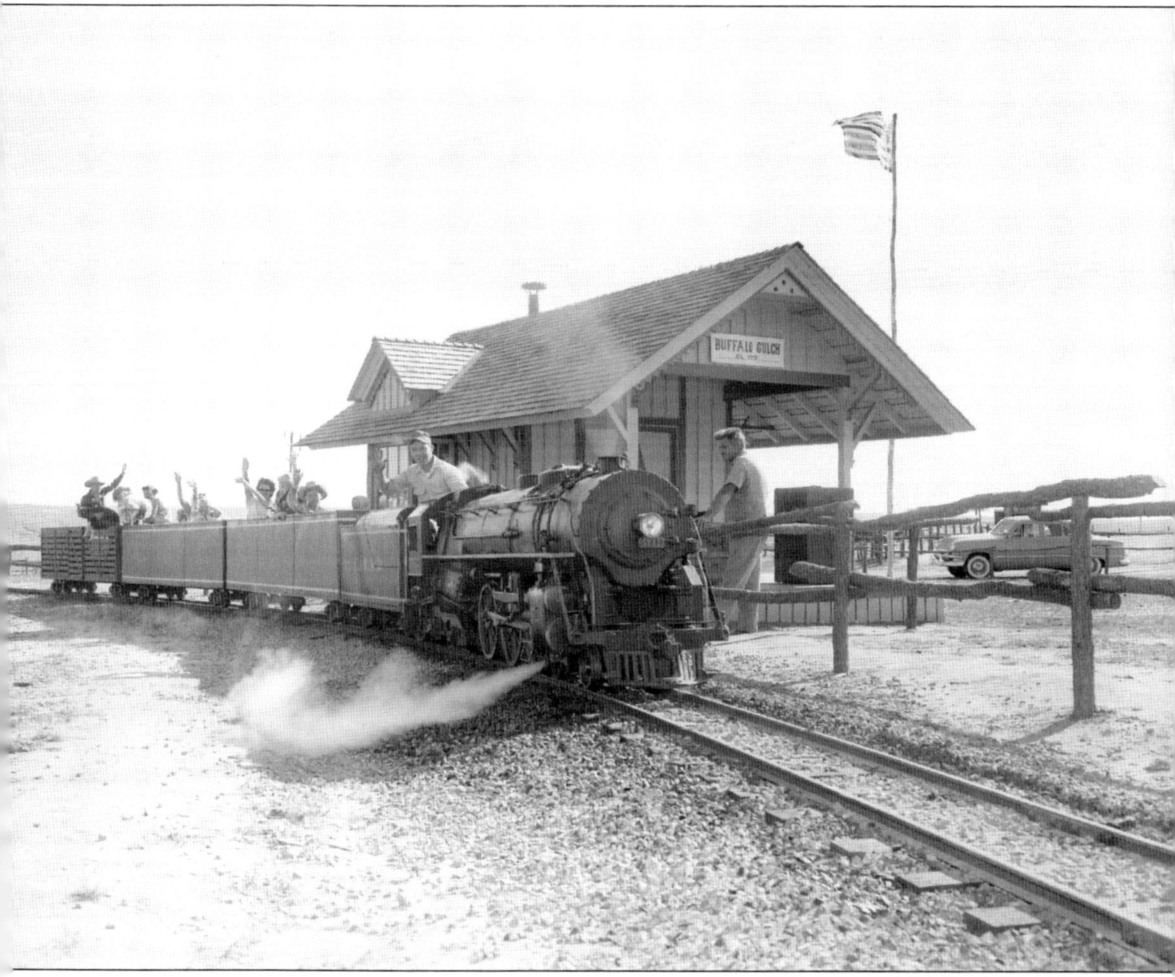

Visitors to Newport Harbor's Buffalo Ranch in 1955 might have enjoyed a ride on the short-lived theme park's miniature train. It appears to be a full-scale live steamer. It looks like the passengers were either having fun, practicing for a hold up, or both! (Courtesy of the Orange County Archives.)

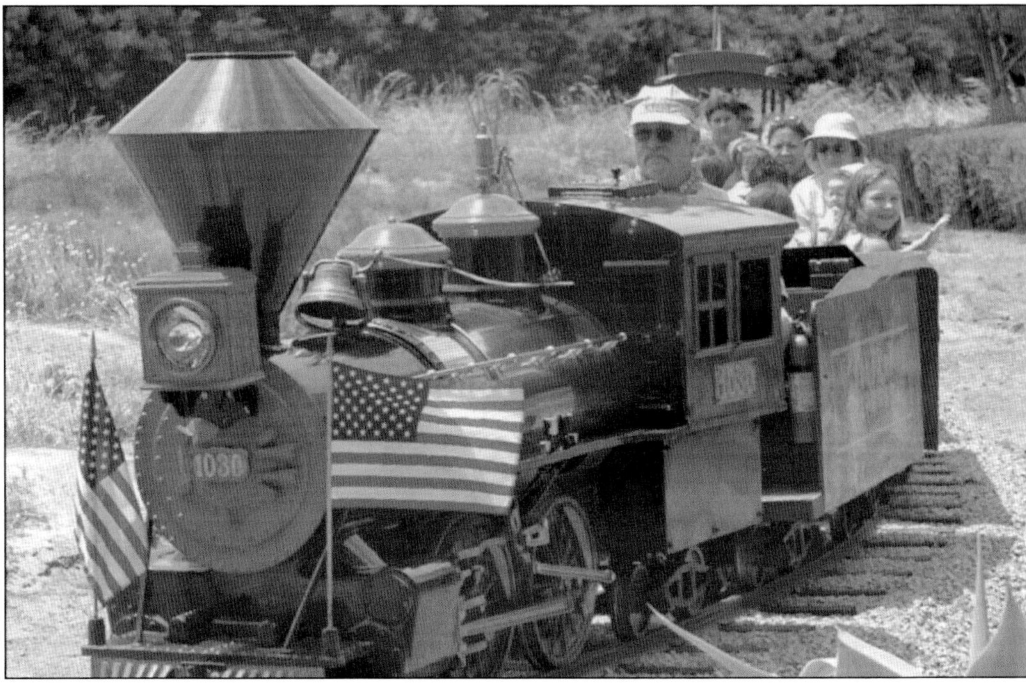

The Santa Ana Zoofari miniature train runs on weekends at the Santa Ana Zoo at Prentice Park. The original train arrived in Santa Ana following the closure of Santa's Village in the Lake Arrowhead area. (Courtesy of the Recreation and Community Services Agency of the City of Santa Ana.)

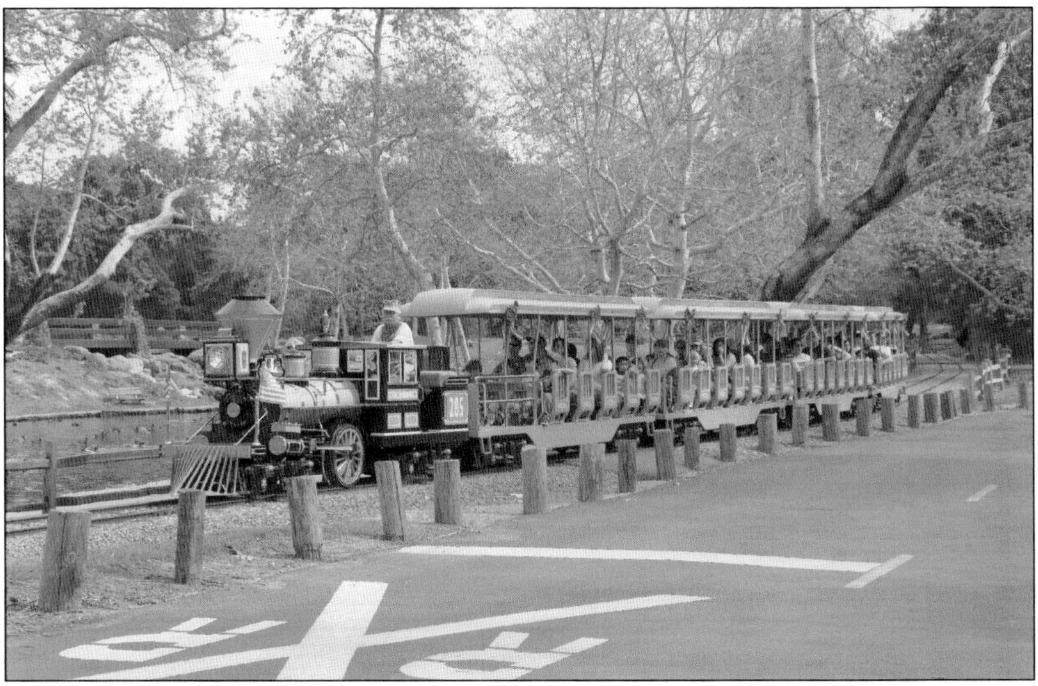

The Irvine Park Railroad operates in the county's Irvine Regional Park. This one-third-scale miniature railroad runs nearly every day. (Courtesy of the Irvine Park Railroad.)

Nine

MISCELLANY

In this final chapter, a few more additional items are presented from Orange County's 120-year railroad history. This book offers the reader a sampling of the key events and key players in Orange County's railroad history. Many of Tom Gildersleeve's photographs are included in this volume. As he reflected, his photographs were taken primarily 45 and 60 years ago. During those years, there has been dramatic change for Orange County and Orange County's railroads. It is hard to believe that the common place then becomes today's history. And so the cycle goes. Here are a few final odds and ends from the ever-changing railroad scene in Orange County.

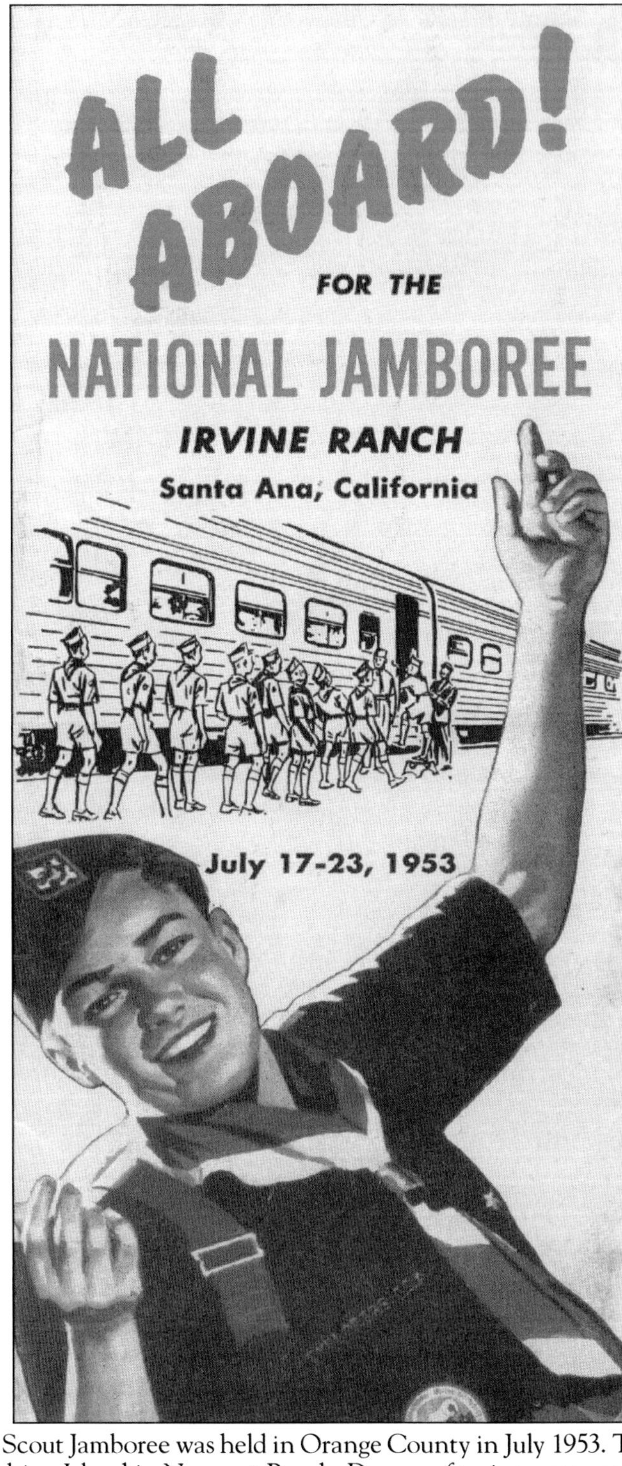

The National Boy Scout Jamboree was held in Orange County in July 1953. The event took place on what is now Fashion Island in Newport Beach. Dozens of trains were used to haul the Scouts to Santa Ana. This photograph shows a brochure promoting the event and boys riding the train to get there. (Courtesy of the author.)

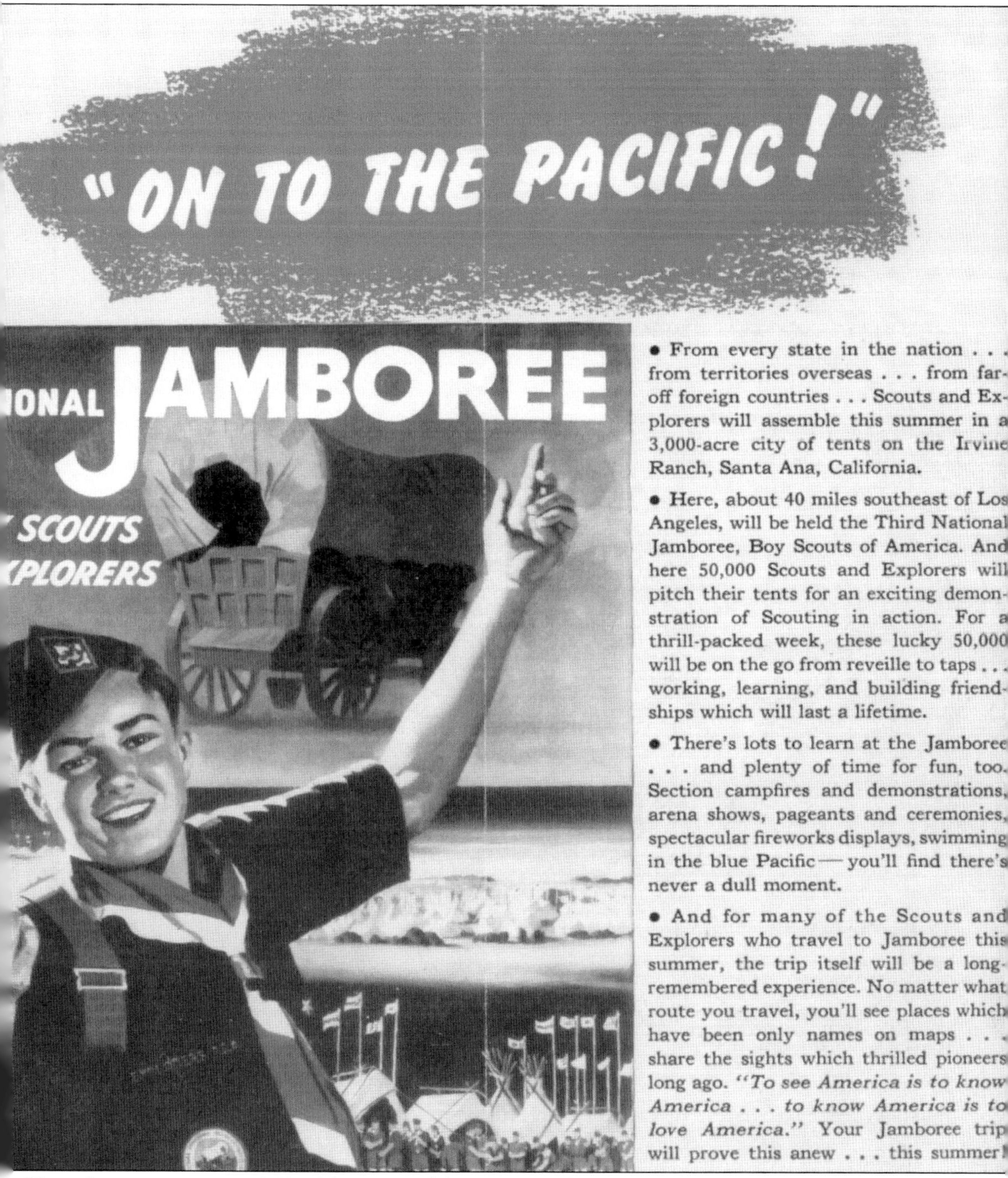

This advertisement touted: "And for many of the Scouts and Explorers who travel to the Jamboree the trip itself will be an experience. . . . 'To see America is to know America . . . to know America is to love America.'" (Courtesy of the author.)

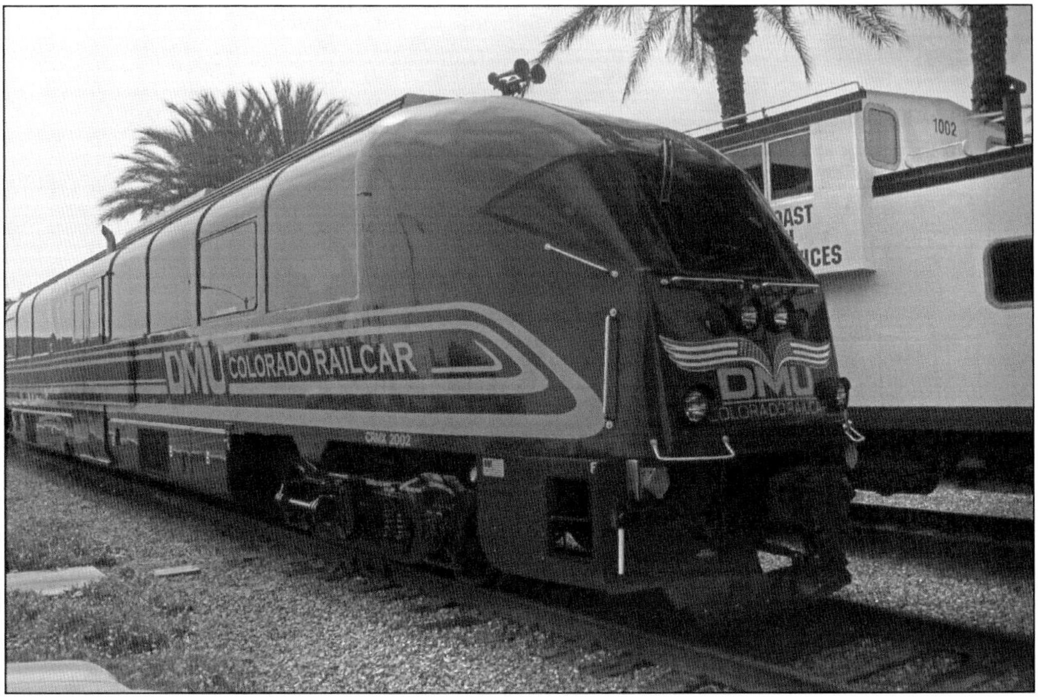

A special Colorado Railcar was on display at the Fullerton train depot in 2003. The company was attempting to find buyers for this self-propelled diesel car in Southern California. (Photograph by and courtesy of the author.)

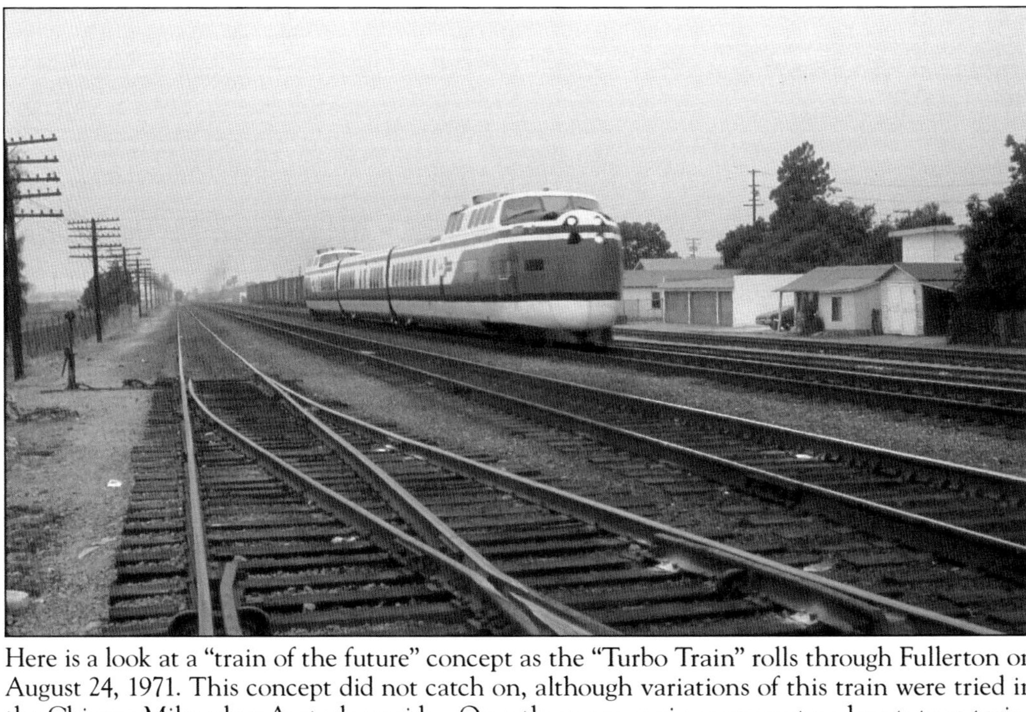

Here is a look at a "train of the future" concept as the "Turbo Train" rolls through Fullerton on August 24, 1971. This concept did not catch on, although variations of this train were tried in the Chicago-Milwaukee Amtrak corridor. Over the years, various concept and prototype trains have operated through Orange County. (Photograph by and courtesy of Cliff Prather.)

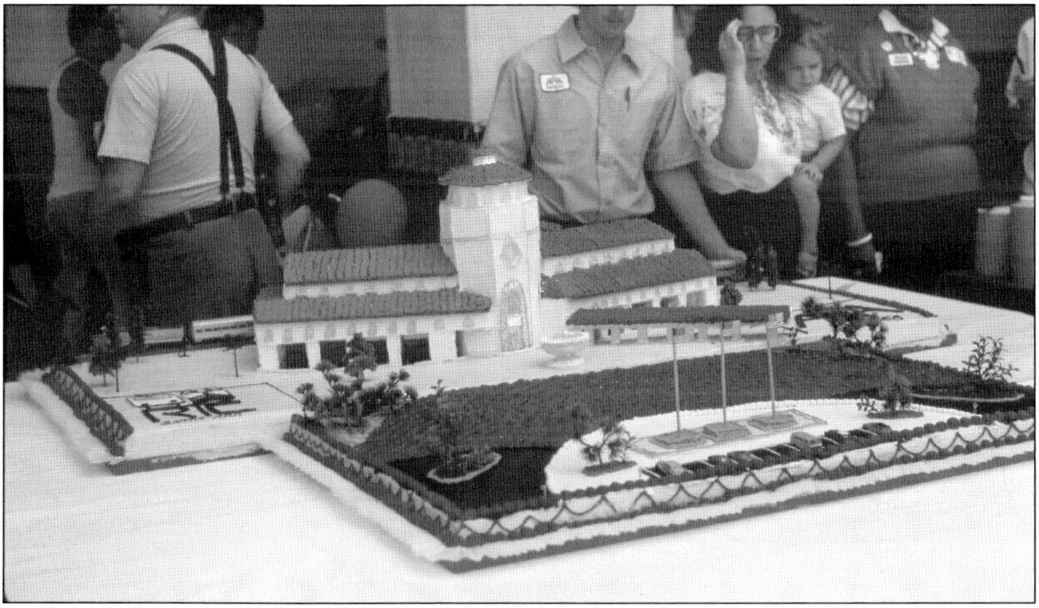

Dedication day for the new Santa Ana RTC featured a replica depot cake on September 7, 1985. Thankfully the station is known today simply as the "Depot." (Photograph by and courtesy of Cliff Prather.)

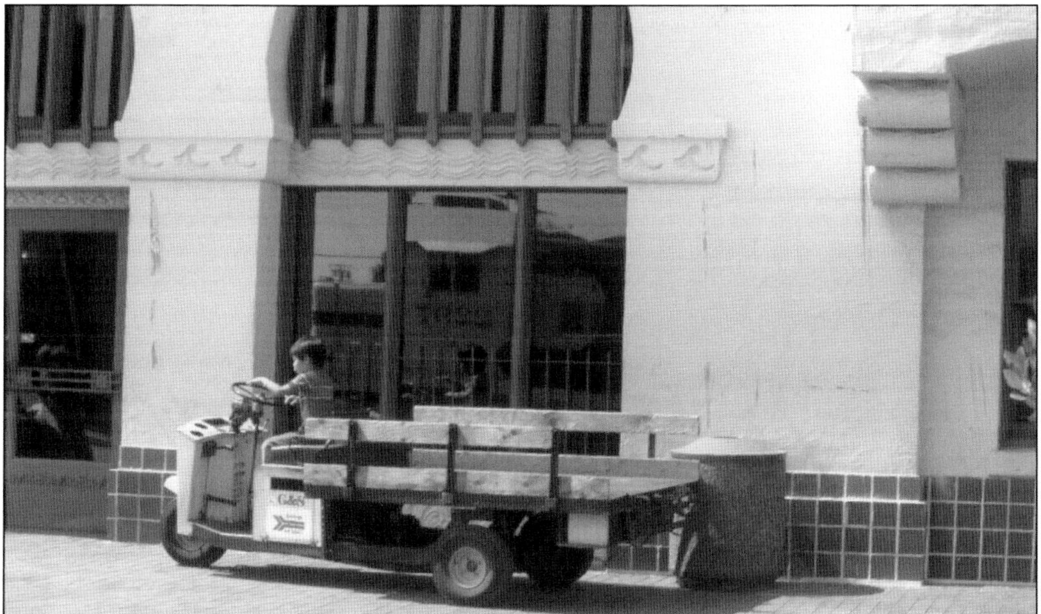

This youngster found something more interesting than a train at the Fullerton train station in 1987. This small cart was used to transport checked luggage to and from passing trains. Note the reflection of a Santa Fe locomotive in the window. Up until this time, Santa Fe locomotives assigned to Fullerton switches were stored on the sidetracks along with cabooses immediately across from the station. Cabooses have gone the same way as steam engines; however, three privately owned cabooses are stored on the house tracks at the Fullerton depot. (Photograph by and courtesy of the author.)

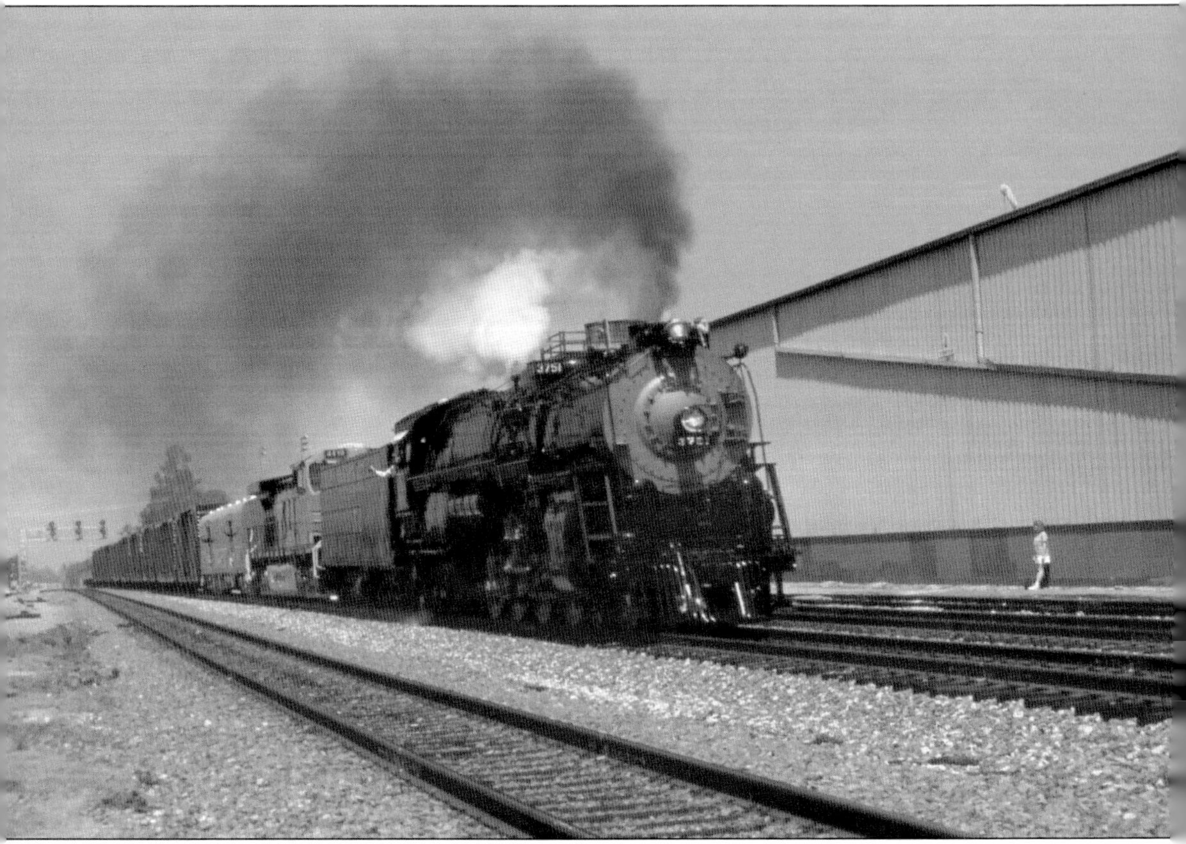

Steam is back in Fullerton. On June 13, 1999, the old Santa Fe No. 3751, a 4-8-4, and BNSF No. 4419 are nearing Fullerton. This locomotive can sure turn out a crowd. The author and Mike Spurgeon of Orange chased this train all the way to the Cajon Pass. Steam engines like the No. 3751 regularly served Orange County before the end of steam service in the early 1950s. See page 44 for a view of No. 3751 in regular service. (Photograph by and courtesy of the author.)

BIBLIOGRAPHY

Donaldson, Steve and Bill Meyers. *Rails through the Orange Groves.* Volumes 1 and 2. Glensdale, CA: Trans-Anglo Books, 1989 and 1990.

Gustafson, Lee and Phil Serpico. *Coast Lines Depots.* Palmdale, CA: Omni Publications, 1992.

Miller, Erick. *The Hayburners of Orange County.* Irvine, CA: Hendricks Printing Company, 1978.

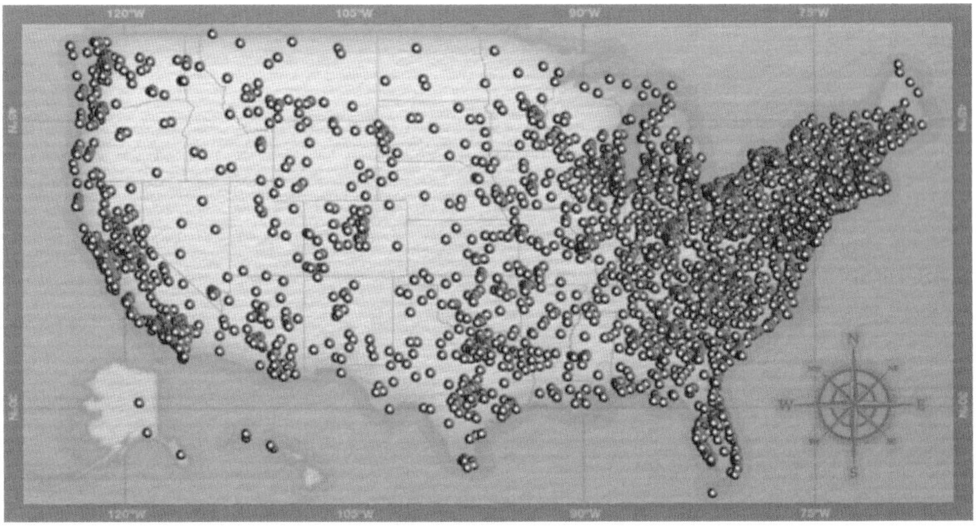